The
Psychology
of
Dictatorship

The Psychology of Dictatorship

FATHALI M. MOGHADDAM

AMERICAN PSYCHOLOGICAL ASSOCIATION
WASHINGTON, DC

Published by
American Psychological Association
750 First Street, NE
Washington, DC 20002
www.apa.org

To order
APA Order Department
P.O. Box 92984
Washington, DC 20090-2984
Tel: (800) 374-2721; Direct: (202) 336-5510
Fax: (202) 336-5502; TDD/TTY: (202) 336-6123
Online: www.apa.org/pubs/books
E-mail: order@apa.org

In the U.K., Europe, Africa, and the Middle East, copies may be ordered from
American Psychological Association
3 Henrietta Street
Covent Garden, London
WC2E 8LU England

Typeset in Goudy by Circle Graphics, Inc., Columbia, MD

Printer: Maple Press, York, PA
Cover Designer: Berg Design, Albany, NY

The opinions and statements published are the responsibility of the authors, and such opinions and statements do not necessarily represent the policies of the American Psychological Association.

Library of Congress Cataloging-in-Publication Data

Moghaddam, Fathali M., author.
  The psychology of dictatorship / Fathali M. Moghaddam.
      pages cm
  Includes bibliographical references and index.
  ISBN-13: 978-1-4338-1298-9
  ISBN-10: 1-4338-1298-3
  1. Dictatorship. 2. Psychology. I. Title.
  JC495.M583 2013
  321.901'9—dc23
                            2012039115

British Library Cataloguing-in-Publication Data
A CIP record is available from the British Library.

Printed in the United States of America
First Edition

http://dx.doi.org/10.1037/14138-000

To the memory of my mother and father, and to the countless other women and men forced to live in dictatorships but who in their hearts keep alive and pass on the torch of freedom.

CONTENTS

ACKNOWLEDGMENTS

First and foremost, I want to acknowledge my deep debt to Rom Harré in his role as friend, colleague, mentor; Chaucer, who knew Rom personally, wrote a timeless description of him as the Clerk of Oxford: "And gladly wolde he lerne, and gladly teche."

Over the years a number of friends and colleagues have, often unwittingly and perhaps even unwillingly, helped me move this project forward by talking to me about, or demonstrating for me, the dangers of dictatorship and the merits of the open society. These helpers include Don Taylor, Bill Bryson, Jim Lamiell, Steve Sabat, Jim Breckenridge, John Lavelle, and Phil Zimbardo.

I am very grateful to a number of people at the American Psychological Association, particularly Maureen Adams for her patient guidance and support throughout the publication process as well as Tyler Aune and Peter Pavilionis, who provided invaluable feedback in the final shaping of this book. A number of anonymous reviewers have also influenced and improved this book from the book proposal stage to the final version, and I hope they get to read this and accept my sincere thanks.

The
Psychology
of
Dictatorship

INTRODUCTION

I wrote this book first because of a profound mismatch I experienced between, on the one hand, life in dictatorships and, on the other hand, academic discussions of dictatorships. In my personal experience, most people living in dictatorships are well aware that the government is ruling without the consent of the people; they know firsthand about the repression and corruption that pervades their societies; and, most important, they know that they will be able to change the government only by collective action deemed illegal by the regime in power. What prevents people living in dictatorships from speaking out and taking collective action to protect their own interests is the loaded guns pointed at their heads. Naked power is what keeps the masses downtrodden in dictatorships. Very few people dare to shout "Death to the dictator!" when they are looking into the barrel of a loaded gun.

But academic discussions of dictatorship ignore the stark reality of brute force and instead focus on *ideologies*; academics would have one believe that the people remain downtrodden because they misperceive the situation and

DOI: 10.1037/14138-001
The Psychology of Dictatorship, by F. M. Moghaddam

directly or indirectly perpetuate their own powerlessness. By implication, ideologies serve to justify the system for the masses and maintain dictatorships. This disproportional focus on ideas arises from the fact that many academics who have written about dictatorships have never lived in a dictatorship, nor have they experienced how people can be painfully aware of suffocating repression while living in a dictatorship but not be able to say or do anything about this terrifying reality—not because they lack the necessary liberating ideas but because they fear torture, imprisonment, and assassination for themselves, their families, and friends. These fears are justified and not just a misperception because dictatorial regimes have shown that they will imprison, torture, and kill any political opposition that threatens their power monopoly.

Academics discussing the role of ideologies (see Moghaddam, 2008b, for a review of some major examples) tend to live in democracies and mistakenly believe that group-based resource inequalities and power disparities exist in dictatorships for the same reasons that they exist in democracies—because the masses fail to recognize and to defend their own collective interests. But the mechanisms of elite control are in foundational ways different in dictatorships and democracies. In dictatorships, the ruling elite do not need to give priority to convincing the masses of the legitimacy of the state because they can rely on sheer force, the power of the gun, and torture. In contrast, it is in democracies that ideologies of justification are needed to legitimize the existing order with its large and increasing group-based inequalities. The shift from torture to imprisonment that Foucault (1995) explored in *Discipline and Punish: The Birth of the Prison* has necessitated a more powerful ideology to maintain control in capitalist democracies. In dictatorships, brute force is the front line to defend power elites; in capitalist democracies, ideology is the front line.

There is a vitally important role for ideology in dictatorships, but one has to look very carefully to identify it. In dictatorships, *false consciousness* and *false ideologies* that justify the existing order are most important for keeping the members of the power elite in line but less so for the masses. Whereas the masses are kept in place by force and only at a secondary level by false ideologies, it is the dictatorial leadership and the power elite who need the crutch of strong legitimizing ideologies justifying their rule in dictatorships within their group and for themselves. Thus, the role of ideology in dictatorships is to enable the ruling elite to achieve a high level of cohesion and unity within their own group so that they feel justified in using brute force to maintain control over the masses. As this book goes to press, President Bashar al-Assad's troops are pummeling civilian demonstrators in Syria who have courageously risen against his regime; these troops are using tanks and heavy weapons to kill thousands of children, women, and men. Again and again in history one finds that the fate of dictatorships depends on the ruling elite sticking together and using force to crush opposition. The disintegration of the elite is what most often initiates and speeds the fall of dictatorships, sometimes enabling and facilitating rebellion by the masses.

A second reason why I wrote this book is because of an obvious gap in the literature: It has been more than 60 years since a book was published under the title of *The Psychology of Dictatorship* (Gilbert, 1950). In the same decade, Barbu (1956) published *Democracy and Dictatorship: Their Psychology and Patterns of Life*. It seems appropriate that these books were published immediately after World War II, a period during which Western democracies faced serious and immediate threats from dictatorships. Yet dictatorships are still prevalent in many parts of the world today.

I also have strong personal reasons for wanting to author this book, being a psychologist who has had the bitter experience of living in a dictatorship as well as living through a historic revolution that overthrew one dictatorship only to be replaced by another, even harsher one.

I was born in Iran and lived my early years in the dictatorship of the last Pahlavi Shah; I was painfully aware of how much my parents longed to raise their children in a freer society. I was sent to a boarding school in London at an early age and went on to complete my university education in England, becoming increasingly conscious of the contrast between the political and cultural freedoms I enjoyed in the West and those denied to me and everyone else within the borders of Iran.

During my student years in England, I travelled overland several times from England to Iran, gaining familiarity along the way with the Communist Eastern Bloc countries. I could feel the light of freedom diminish as I moved eastward, and I saw the light disappear in countries such as Bulgaria. However, wherever I made the extra effort to actually talk with locals and gain some level of genuine friendship, the masks slipped, and it became clear that people understood the corruption and despotism reigning in their countries, just as I myself understood the tragedy of dictatorship in Iran. Indeed, over my past few decades of travel and research around the world and in discussions with people in more politically closed systems (e.g., in China and Russia) and more politically open systems (e.g., in the United States and the United Kingdom), I have found that even people with low levels of education in closed societies often have a political awareness and cunning that surpasses that of many free citizens in democracies, particularly democracies such as the United States, where political participation in even national elections barely reaches 50%. I have met illiterate people on the streets of Tehran whose political acumen would astound (and surpass!) many Westerners: Living in a dictatorship sharpens the political sensitivities of many people perhaps because in dictatorships just about every job from street cleaner to mayor, every bank loan, every educational opening for one's children, every opportunity to rent a house or start a business, and every improvement in one's life depends on political connections and position. In a dictatorship, the garbage collector has to be as politically tuned in as the mayor because everyone is continuously under threat.

My father did not live to see the 1978–1979 revolution in Iran; he did not experience the brief gasp of freedom enjoyed by Iranians after the revolution. However, my mother was alive at that joyous time, and I sped back from England to be back in Iran to join her in the celebration of our freedom. Both of us were hopeful, but our hopes were soon dashed. The rise to power of Khomeini and the reestablishment of dictatorship under a religious guise was a bitter pill to swallow. However, my optimism was not quelled immediately. I remained in Iran for 5 years after the revolution, continuing to believe that Iranians could avoid a return to full dictatorship. My mother died in Iran with the hope for an open and just society unfulfilled. This book is written in the spirit of that hope.

The Psychology of Dictatorship provides a theoretical model of dictatorship grounded on current empirical research. In the 10 chapters in this book, I explore the psychology of dictatorship and present a *springboard model* that serves as a framework for readers to better understand modern dictatorships and also to stimulate further psychological and political science research.

My primary focus is on dictatorship as a political system rather than a dictatorial style of behavior at the level of personality. A number of the greatest scientists and thinkers behaved as *little dictators* when they had the opportunity. For example, Sir Isaac Newton (1642–1727) ranks with Alfred Einstein (1879–1955) and Charles Darwin (1809–1882) as arguably one of the three greatest scientists of all time. Alexander Pope (1688–1744) celebrated Newton in the following famous couplet:

> Nature and nature's laws lay hid in night;
> God said "Let Newton be" and all was light.

But once Newton gained power and influence, his treatment of his scientific rivals, such as John Flamsteed (1646–1719) and Robert Hooke (1635–1703), was despicable and certainly qualifies as despotic. However, Newton and little dictators like him do not fall within the compass of this study because he never had dictatorial power in a large society.

This book is intended for students and scholars as well as lay readers interested in better understanding dictatorship from the perspective of psychological science. The target college courses are political psychology, political science, government, social psychology, community psychology, cultural psychology, conflict resolution, intergroup relations, democracy studies, peace studies, national development, among others.

In this text, I refer to the dictator as *he* rather than *she* because with very few exceptions dictators have been male rather than female: "Except for women who served as interim leaders—Queens Dzeliwe and Ntombi in Swaziland during the early 1980s, Ertha Pascal-Trouillot in Haiti in 1990 and Ruth Perry in Liberia in 1996—dictators are men" (Gandhi & Przeworski, 2006, p. 1, Footnote 1). Some imagine that the rise of women in equal numbers to men at the highest levels of political leadership will have a civilizing and democratizing influence on the world, so that societies will move closer to the end of dictatorship. I believe such an outcome will be possible only through major structural changes in societies, irrespective of how equally women and men are represented in the power elite.

This book goes beyond a descriptive analysis of the psychology of dictatorship by presenting (see Chapter 3) the springboard model of dictatorship and using it as a framework for critical analysis. This model sets out the conditions in which a springboard is created to enable potential dictators to spring to power.

Rather than treating dictatorship and democracy in a categorical manner, I treat them as the extreme poles of a continuum. Societies are located at different places on this continuum, some closer to the pure dictatorship end and others closer to the pure democracy end. However, societies are dynamic and changing, and their position on the dictatorship–democracy continuum can and often does shift over time, sometimes dramatically. These definitional issues are explored in Chapter 1, with a particular focus on the continuing danger of even democratic societies slipping back toward the dictatorship end of the continuum. One of the important messages of this book is that societies are continually moving on the dictatorship–democracy continuum, and movement toward the dictatorship end is possible for all societies, including capitalist democracies such as the United States.

Part I begins with Chapter 2, in which I critically assess the kind of psychological science needed to understand dictatorship. I argue that a useful distinction can be made between behavior that is causally determined and can be validly explained through causal accounts and behavior that is normatively regulated and needs to be explained through normative accounts (Moghaddam, 2002). Unfortunately, in traditional psychology the causal account has been used for explaining all behavior, resulting in incorrect analysis. Most of the behaviors central to dictatorship, such as conformity, obedience, and dictatorial leadership, are normatively regulated rather than causally determined. Fortunately, there is an effective psychology that stands in contrast to traditional psychology and is appropriate for my assessment (Harré & Moghaddam, 2012), and this is explored in Chapter 2.

The springboard model, discussed in Chapter 3, incorporates three broad categories of processes. The first two sets of processes serve as the springboard for the launching of the dictator. These are as follows: (a) factors associated with perceived threat that create the context for people to support dictatorship and (b) situational factors that lead to support for dictatorship as the solution to current problems faced by society. These processes lead to (c) the launch, the presence of an opportunistic leader who both helps to create and uses the springboard to launch himself as dictator.

Dictatorship can come about only when there is available a potential dictator, a person motivated and able to monopolize power and rule against the consent of most people. Soviet dictatorship required a Stalin; Nazi Germany required a Hitler. At the same time, Stalin could become dictator only in the Soviet system, and Hitler only in Nazi Germany. The relationship between the context for dictatorship and the dictator is reciprocal and interdependent. The conditions can come about for the creation of a dictatorship, but without a potential dictator to take advantage of the opportunity, the dictatorship would not come into existence (although research psychologists have given little attention to dictatorship as a phenomenon, the role of both individual-level factors and situational factors is strongly suggested by research on leadership; see the readings in the special issue of *American Psychologist* titled "Leadership" 2007; see also the readings on power in Guinote, Weick, & Cai, 2012).

In Part II, I explore, in historical context, the role of a number of psychological processes central to creating and sustaining dictatorships.

The main question taken up in Chapter 4 is the puzzle of continuity in dictatorships and why it is so difficult to instigate foundational change in political systems. I explore varieties of change and the role of narratives and cultural carriers in bringing about continuity. Even after major revolutions in which the previous power elites were toppled and pushed aside, often there is a return to dictatorship under a new power elite—a classic example being the continuation of dictatorship in Iran after the fall of the Shah's dictatorship in 1979. Continuity in dictatorship is made possible through a number of psychological mechanisms, with displacement as a major example.

In Chapter 5, I focus on the example of dictatorship in Iran to explore displacement of aggression and the tactic of constructing and exaggerating external threats and displacing aggression onto outgroup targets. This tactic is associated with a strengthening of nationalism and militarism as well as ingroup cohesion more broadly. In an atmosphere of hypernationalism and militarism, when people are constantly reminded of "the enemy at our door," conformity and obedience can be maximized, and individuals can be forced to abide by what the masses seem to want (of course, what the masses seem to want is often purposefully misrepresented by the dictator). The dictator and his regime manufacture external and internal enemies as a strategy to displace aggression onto targets categorized as "the other" as well as to force people to fall in line with the requirements of the regime.

Central to all dictatorships is extreme *obedience*, changes in behavior that arise when people follow the instructions of persons in authority, and *conformity*, changes in behavior that arise from real or imagined group pressure. The rich psychological literature on obedience and conformity is discussed in Chapter 6. This literature clearly suggests that in certain conditions, when the social pressure is strong enough, many people with normal psychological profiles will tend to obey and conform—even when such behavior results in grave harm and even death to others. Unfortunately, there are many, many historical examples of this trend. However, the good news is that not everyone obeys and conforms; there are always some individuals who refuse to buckle under pressure; these individuals do the right thing and show the way forward to a better world.

But everyday life in dictatorships demonstrates obedience and conformity to be the norms for most people. In Chapter 7, I discuss how this experience of "pressure cooker compliance" can result in coerced participation, with people feeling that they have no control over their lives. Terror and torture are used by dictatorships to heighten this collective feeling of helplessness. By involving people (particularly the young) in activities such as coerced elections and forcing participation in "good citizen" activities, dictatorships can lead people to experience cognitive dissonance and at least public displays of attitude change. However, the cognitive dissonance in question here has to do with societal processes and collectively shared social constructions rather than the private thoughts of isolated individuals. This focus on collective processes continues in Chapter 8, which is concerned with leadership in dictatorships.

The traditional approach to understanding dictatorship has been to focus on the personality of the dictator and the leadership he provides. In Chapter 8, I examine leadership in dictatorships, and I consider both traditional and alternative approaches to understanding leader–follower relations. Of particular interest is *transformational leadership* through which the dictator uses force to try to remold human beings to conform to the ideal citizen he has in mind. I argue that to understand leadership, particularly in the context of dictatorship, it is necessary to move beyond the traditional focus on traits and, instead, consider both the power of the context and the role of the shared social ways of thinking that become normative in dictatorships. Certain cognitive styles of leaders and followers support the continuation of dictatorships, a topic that links to Chapter 9.

In Chapter 9, I examine styles of cognition and action that serve to support dictatorship. Research suggests that personality development, integral to which is identity development, is of critical importance in relation to support for dictatorship. Extensive psychological research demonstrates an important role for authoritarianism: Highly authoritarian individuals tend to support strong, aggressive leaders as well as group-based inequalities. Research on ethnocentrism suggests that these individuals are strongly biased against outgroups and threatened by outsiders who hold dissimilar beliefs. From the classic studies of authoritarianism after World War II to current research, a major theme in research on *closed societies* has been *closedmindedness* in the shape of a need for psychological closure—to prefer specific answers to questions rather than to have questions unanswered or left with multiple possible answers. Psychological characteristics such as need for psychological closure are socialized in families, which serve as the important link between collective processes and individual processes.

In Chapter 10, I examine the future of dictatorship and democracy. Received wisdom says that globalization brings openness and the spread of democracy. This is in line with the assumption that there is an inevitable global march toward democratic capitalism. However, these are naive assumptions. First, there is no inevitability to the direction of change in history. Second, globalization has also resulted in threatened collective identities, particularly among traditionalists and fundamentalists (Moghaddam, 2006), in the shape of violent Islamic extremists fighting secular Western culture or violent Western extremists fighting "an Islamic invasion," among many other forms. I argue that globalization is both additive and subtractive with respect to democracy, and increased globalization does not necessarily result in increased democratization. Thus, the consequences of globalization are mixed, complex, and in some ways associated with increased threat and insecurity (Moghaddam, 2010) rather than cohesion and democracy.

The springboard model suggests a number of strategies for ending dictatorships. The springboard model suggests that the power elite and the nonelite masses in dictatorships have to be treated very differently: The power elite succeed and fail on the basis of their cohesion and unity, founded on a common ideology. Thus, every effort must be made to peel away segments of the power elite, to help create a counterelite, and to challenge the ideological cohesion of the power elite. The nonelite masses, on the other hand, are dissatisfied and disaffected but lack organization and leadership to mobilize collectively.

In the second part of Chapter 10, I focus on challenges confronting democracies and the danger of movement from democracy to dictatorship. History shows that this is a real and ever-present danger, one that is magnified in times of economic stress and political gridlock. I end by considering an ideal model of the open society, one inspired by a democracy of ideas in academic research.

1

PSYCHOLOGY AND DICTATORSHIP: THE HISTORIC AND CONTEMPORARY CHALLENGE

For sweetest things turn sourest by their deeds;
Lilies that fester smell far worse than weeds.
—Shakespeare, "Sonnet 94"

They were both returning to public life in their native lands after many years of forced isolation: Ruhollah Khomeini (1902–1989) after 14 years of exile outside Iran and Nelson Mandela (b. 1918) after 27 years of imprisonment in South Africa. Their returns to center stage—Khomeini on February 1, 1979, and Mandela on February 11, 1990—were followed with equally frenzied interest on the part of the international media and cheered on by tens of millions of fiercely loyal supporters in their homelands. Both leaders were old men by the time they came to power, Khomeini was 77 and Mandela was 72, and both were very well positioned to spearhead revolutionary changes toward justice and peace, fueled by the raw energy of tens of millions of young followers at home as well as hundreds of millions of international sympathizers.

Lionized, almost worshiped, there seemed to be no limits to the peace, prosperity, and progress that Khomeini and Mandela could inspire and help bring about in their respective native countries. Both of these aged leaders

DOI: 10.1037/14138-002
The Psychology of Dictatorship, by F. M. Moghaddam

had historic opportunities to heal the deep rifts and quell the violence that had erupted in their homelands, to guide their young populations to peaceful paths, and to move their societies away from dictatorship, a form of government in which a sole leader or a ruling clique has absolute power and rules against the wishes of the people; put simply, "dictators are dictators because they cannot win elections, because their preferences diverge from those of the majority of the population" (Gandhi & Przeworski, 2006). But the similarities between Khomeini and Mandela ended abruptly, just as soon as they grasped the reins of power firmly in their hands.

Mandela, enabled by the inspired leadership of President de Klerk, chose a path of peace and reconciliation. The cruel South African apartheid regime had collapsed, and miraculously, Mandela now had power over the former government officials who had kept him locked away in jail for 27 years. Hotheads and extremists urged him to take revenge; many ordinary Blacks and Asians, and also some Whites who had suffered the injustices of apartheid, would have understood, even been pleased, if Mandela had sought retribution, an eye for an eye. But that was not his way.

Mandela chose the path of peace and reconciliation and used his moral authority to inspire others to follow. The example he set helped to nurture new procedures through which communities and individuals learned to better heal their wounds (South Africa Truth and Reconciliation Commission, 1999). After serving as the first president of postapartheid South Africa, Mandela stepped aside, released the reins of power, and let others take their turn to lead the reborn country. Like George Washington (1732–1799), the first president of the United States, Mandela proved to be one of those rare leaders who insisted on stepping down after having his turn to serve in the highest office in the land, even when his followers implored him not to relinquish power and there was as yet no tradition established in the formal law of the land demanding that he step down. Absolute power did not corrupt him.

Khomeini, on the other hand, clutched and clung to absolute power until his dying breath (of course, like the Libyan leader Muammar al-Qaddafi, Khomeini could claim that he did not hold an official government position and therefore could not resign). He continued dictatorial rule in the same way as he started, by muzzling, imprisoning, and killing anyone who opposed his commands.

The anti-Shah revolution of 1978–1979 had been brought about by a wide spectrum of Iranian people representing different social classes, political factions, ethnic groups, and religious orientations, ranging from the secular to the fanatically religious, from the political left to the right. But rather than adopting inclusive policies and positioning himself to serve as the representative of all the people, Khomeini mobilized and maneuvered a band of fanatical followers to use brute force to achieve a complete power mono-poly throughout the country and to become the absolute ruler, the so-called Supreme Leader.

I was in Iran during this traumatic period and witnessed the horrific suf-focation of democratic voices by Khomeini and his followers. Very quickly, the prisons that had been miraculously liberated by the people and joy-fully emptied during the revolution were once again brimming over with political prisoners and their torturers, hired to keep society moving along Khomeini's path. Most of the worst elements of the Shah's secret police and torturers found themselves in demand and amply rewarded again to safeguard Khomeini's brand of revolution.

Not satisfied with crushing all opposition in Iran, Khomeini strove to export his brand of dictatorship to other countries. Of course, this upset the neighboring dictators, and in 1980 the Iraqi despot Saddam Hussein (1937–2006), who was also eager to expand his dictatorship, invaded Iran, resulting in 8 years of bloody warfare that proved devastating for both Iran and Iraq. By the time Khomeini died in 1989, the new revolutionary Iran had taken shape as a war-ravaged, corrupt, dark society ruled by national and local des-pots. The oil money that should have been used to develop the country and improve the lot of the masses was further invested in the apparatus for war and oppression or siphoned off to secret bank accounts set up by the regime's stooges abroad. The Shah's corrupt police state had been put on steroids by the ruling mullahs.

The profoundly different leadership styles of Khomeini and Mandela, the founding fathers of new regimes in Iran and South Africa, respectively, seem to endorse traditional leadership-based explanations of dictatorship. Such traditional explanations see the roots of dictatorship in the personality traits of leaders, and along these lines there has emerged an enormous litera-ture on the *dictator personality*. A classic example of this is the report prepared by Walter Langer for the Office of Strategic Services during World War II but published in 1972 on *The Mind of Adolf Hitler* in which Langer used psychoanalytic techniques to famously predict that Hitler would probably commit suicide and there would be attempts by German officers to assassinate Hitler—both predictions proving to be correct.

From this perspective, the personality of the leader shapes the larger society. Khomeini was an absolute dictator, and Iran continues to be a closed, dark, and largely isolated dictatorship characterized by fraudulent elections, state-sponsored killings, mass political arrests and torture, corruption, and repression. Mandela, on the other hand, encouraged openness, and this would seem to explain why South Africa has become the most important democracy in Africa, with an expanding economy and active intellectual and artistic communities. Of course, group-based inequalities have not ended in South

Africa, and there is a high level of crime, but South Africans do now enjoy a relatively open and free society with open elections that meet international standards.

BEYOND EXPLANATIONS OF DICTATORSHIP THAT FOCUS ON THE DICTATOR PERSONALITY

To be sure, Khomeini and Mandela did have a profound impact on the development of their respective societies, the first toward and the second away from dictatorship. Certainly, leadership does matter in dictatorships; anyone who reads accounts of Stalin's last days and how he was feared even while he was in a coma ("Stalin's heirs still harboured almost superstitious fear of the paralyzed dictator"; Ra'anan, 2006, p. 18) recognizes the terrifying power of the dictator. However, it would be a gross oversimplification and a fundamental mistake to explain the political situation in Iran and South Africa by reference only or mainly to leadership. A myriad of social, economic, cultural, geographic, and other factors are important in shaping dictatorship (Acemoglu & Robinson, 2006; Arendt, 2004; Moore, 1966). A second point is that among all the factors that influence the coming into being and continuation of dictatorship, psychological factors are centrally important and at the same time grossly neglected.

However, by *psychological* I do not refer only to intrapersonal (dispositional) characteristics and the traditional trait-based approach to understanding behavior (Moghaddam, 2005). There are a number of important reasons why the traditional psychological approach is inadequate and inappropriate for understanding dictatorships (I expand on this point in Chapter 2, this volume). First, the traditional approach is reductionist in that it attempts to explain societal processes and what is social and collective by reference to dispositional factors such as narcissism as a personality trait of the dictator. The fact is that many individuals score high on narcissism—and some probably score even higher than known dictators—but never get the opportunity to spring to power and serve as dictators. It is important to look more closely at the contextual factors that enable potential dictators, of which there are some in every society, to come to power.

A second reason why the traditional approach in psychological research is inadequate for understanding dictatorship is that it adopts a mechanistic causal model of behavior (Harré & Moghaddam, 2012). Some types of behavior are effectively explained using a causal model (Moghaddam, 2002), but complex social, political, and cultural systems such as dictatorships do not fit this category. The traditional causal experimental design in psychology (and, increasingly, in political science and other social sciences) involves manipulation of independent variables to test their effect on dependent variables. This is *efficient causality*, as Aristotle discussed it, in which the cause precedes the effect it produces. Unfortunately, researchers interested in political behavior from diverse backgrounds including psychology, political science, sociology, and anthropology have increasingly adopted this mechanistic model of causation on the false assumption that the move will bring them closer to the natural sciences and acceptance as "real" sciences. But a far more appropriate model of causality for research on topics such as dictatorship is what Aristotle termed *formal causality*, concerned with the form or structure of a process, and *final causality*, concerned with purpose or meaning of a process. What emerges from this alternative approach is a psychological science far richer, a great deal more sophisticated and complex, and far more capable of explaining social behavior (Harré & Moghaddam, 2012).

The third reason for adopting what I have termed a *normative* rather than a mechanistic causal model of behavior (Moghaddam, 2002, 2005) has to do with intentionality and assigning responsibility for behavior in dictatorships. Over the past few decades there has been a constant and growing attack on the idea of free will and human conscious decision-making (e.g., see Wegner, 2002). If one really accepts the idea that every behavior has a cause in the sense of efficient causation, one reaches the absurd situation of not being able to assign responsibility to persons (including dictators) for their actions. Of course, in the real world people insist on assigning responsibility to individuals for their actions, as is clear from the workings of the justice system. Intentionality and free will are assumed in a normative model of behavior, and I discuss the nature of the psychological science needed in greater detail in Chapter 2.

My approach is to focus on the collectively constructed and collaboratively upheld social world with its normative systems consisting of values, norms, rules, and so on. Social behavior is regulated by local normative systems in the sense that most individuals most of the time tend to follow local norms and rules for "correct" behavior. The best psychological explanation of the behavior of people in dictatorships is based on a normative rather than a causal account of behavior.

WHAT IS DICTATORSHIP?

In this era of moral relativism when representatives from countries ruled by tyrants sit on United Nations human rights committees, can people agree on criteria by which to define dictatorship and separate this form of government from democracy? I believe it can be done by first carefully examining the roots and meaning of the term *dictatorship*.

Historic Roots of the Term Dictatorship

> As Caesar loved me, I weep for him; as he was fortunate, I rejoice at it; as
> he was valiant, I honour him: but, as he was ambitious, I slew him: there
> is tears for his love; joy for his fortune; honour for his valour; and death
> for his ambition.

> —Shakespeare, *Julius Caesar*

The term *dictatorship* has its roots in the constitution of the ancient
Roman Republic, whereby a single leader is temporarily given extraordinary
powers to lead Rome through an emergency (Lintott, 1999). In contemporary
terms, this is equivalent to the powers given to governments in democracies
during times of extreme emergency, such as when a nation faces grave terrorist threats (McCormick, 1997). But in ancient Rome, as throughout history, there was always the danger that ambitious leaders would misuse power
and try to establish and perpetuate dictatorship. Thus, there has always been
a tension between the need to trust leadership with power and the need to
keep in check ambitious leaders. In Shakespeare's play of the same name,
Julius Caesar is assassinated because it is feared that his personal ambition
for power will end the republic. As Freeman's (2003) case studies of modern
Uruguay, Canada, Peru, and Britain demonstrate, the fear that governments,
even democratic ones, sometimes misuse emergency powers is well founded.
The most notorious recent example of this is Hitler's manipulation of emergency powers to move Germany from democracy to dictatorship in the 1930s.

But modern dictatorships are profoundly different from the temporary
dictatorships in the tradition of ancient Rome and the temporary concentration of power that comes about through emergency power acts in democracies such as Canada and Britain. Whereas temporary dictatorships in ancient
Rome and emergency powers in modern democracies are designed to safeguard openness (and in this sense are prodemocracy), modern dictatorships
are antidemocracy. I further clarify this point in the following section.

Distinguishing Dictatorship and Democracy:
Inadequacy of the Formalist Rule of Law as a Criterion

Dictatorship and democracy are systems of government that can be
distinguished through tests of openness: Put simply, dictatorships are relatively closed, and democracies are relatively open. Dictatorships do not and
democracies do allow citizens to regularly criticize and change political leaders. Following contemporary fashions, one could focus on rule of law and
claim that dictatorships do not and democracies do adhere to rule of law.
From this perspective, irrespective of the characteristics of the laws in place,

democracy is strengthened when all citizens are treated equally before the law; a problem in dictatorships is that the law applies to some people but not others.

However, this *formalistic* interpretation of rule of law is necessary but not sufficient to guarantee that a society will be a democracy rather than a dictatorship because the laws might well be supportive of dictatorship rather than democracy (see Kritz, in press). For example, in 2011 Vladimir Putin announced that he would once again be a candidate for the presidency in Russia, having already served 8 years as president (2000–2008). This is perfectly legitimate according to the Russian constitution, and he could well serve another two consecutive 6-year terms to extend his presidency to the year 2024—giving him a quarter of century at the top since 2000 (on March 6, 2012, Putin won the first of these 6-year terms, in a presidential election in which he had no real competitors). Of course, all these perfectly legal maneuvers support the continuation of dictatorship rather than a switch to democracy in Russia. Despite critical assessments of Putin in the wider world as a KGB (Russian state security committee) thug and antidemocratic (e.g., Gessen, 2012), his control of the Russian media ensures that within Russia he presents himself as a heroic champion of the people (see his "frank" autobiography; Putin, 2000).

To take another contemporary example, the constitution of the Islamic Republic of Iran stipulates that according to the principle of governance by a qualified religious leader (*velayat-e-faghih*), this single leader can overrule all other authorities, including the *Majlis* (parliament), president, and other "elected" bodies. Thus, even if fair and open elections did take place in the Islamic Republic of Iran (which has not happened), according to the Iranian constitution one man (and of course the supreme spiritual leader has to be a man) is the ultimate decider on absolutely everything. This is formalist rule of law.

It is clear from the previous examples that rule of law as interpreted according to formalism is by no means a sufficient criterion for distinguishing between democracy and dictatorship. If the law of the land supports dictatorship, as it does in places like Iran and Russia, then rule of law simply reinforces dictatorship. One must move to a *substantivist* interpretation of rule of law, which argues that in addition to fair process and procedure, rule of law must involve the protection of rights that are fundamental to being human as espoused in the United Nations' (1948) *Universal Declaration of Human Rights*, I would contend.

The influential definitions of dictatorship (e.g., Friedrich & Brzezinski, 1956; Huntington, 1991) have focused on rule by a single leader or a group, with ill-defined or minimal political limits to the power of the leader(s), weak or nonexisting mass political participation, very limited political pluralism, and nonexisting or ineffective political parties (for further discussions, see Brooker, 2000; and Ezrow & Frantz, 2011). With the various definitions offered in mind, I next provide a specific definition of dictatorship in the context of the dictatorship–democracy continuum.

Defining Dictatorship

One can conceptualize a continuum with pure dictatorship at one end and pure democracy at the other. Most societies fall somewhere in between these two poles with some societies falling closer to the pure dictatorship end and other societies positioned closer to the pure democracy end. But even extreme cases that fall closer to one pole or the other must be seen as changeable because dictatorships can, under certain conditions, move toward the democracy end, and democracies can shift back toward the dictatorship end (this is in line with Tilly's, 2007, analysis of democratization and de-democratization).

What are the characteristics of societies that are closer to the dictatorship end of the continuum? *Dictatorship* is rule by a single person or a clique that is not elected through free and fair elections by the subject population and not removable through popular election, with direct control of a security apparatus that represses political opposition; without any independent legislative and judicial checks; with policies that reflect the wishes and whims of the dictator individual or clique rather than popular will; and with a high degree of control over the education system, the mass media, the communication and information systems, as well as the movement of citizens toward the goal of continuing monopoly rule by the regime.

A first point is that the preceding definition conceptualizes dictatorship as rule by a single leader or a clique, and thus it encompasses leadership as found in dictatorships as apparently different as China (ruled by an unelected clique) and Iran (ruled by an unelected Supreme Leader).

A second point is that a foundational theme linking the different elements of this definition of dictatorship is *lack of voice*. In dictatorships, the vast majority of people have no voice and feel less attached to the group (see Tyler's, 2012, research regarding the role of voice in justice generally). Thus, the mechanism of control in dictatorships becomes brute force rather than identity and emotional attachment.

On the surface, parts of this definition could be used to argue that countries such as Russia and Iran are not dictatorships because, for example, they have "popular elections," which in theory could remove the leadership. Although such a case could be made, I would argue against it because, as I explained in the preceding discussion of formalist versus substantivist rule of law, elections that are not free and fair can be and have been used by some regimes to justify and to continue dictatorial rule. Besides, it is important to apply this definition as a package and not to isolate bits.

At the same time, it is important to keep in mind the need to view societies at different points on the dictatorship–democracy continuum. Not all the societies I label dictatorships are on the same point on this continuum; Stalin's dictatorship is closer to the pure dictatorship pole than is Putin's dictatorship. Similarly, Mao's dictatorship is closer to the pure dictatorship pole than is the unelected clique's dictatorship in contemporary China. Thus, a number of major dictatorships have moved away from the pure dictatorship pole and a little toward democracy. On the other hand, the mullahs' dictatorship in Iran is now closer to the pure dictatorship pole than was the Shah's dictatorship before the 1978–1979 revolution, so movement of all societies is not in the same direction on the dictatorship–democracy continuum.

But irrespective of the exact distance that countries such as China, Russia, Iran, and North Korea are from the pure dictatorship pole of the dictatorship–democracy continuum, my focus in this book is on the common social and psychological processes underlying such repressive regimes. Such social and psychological processes are to some degree also evident in societies located closer to the pure democracy end of the dictatorship–democracy continuum, and this reflects the dynamic and fluid nature of societies and the tendency for all societies to move over time along the dictatorship–democracy continuum, sometimes toward the pure democracy end and at other times toward the pure dictatorship end. It would be a grave error to assume that any society is immune from sliding toward the pure dictatorship end.

Minimal Conditions for a Democracy

I have argued that dictatorship and democracy should be considered not in categorical terms but as the end poles of a continuum. Having defined dictatorship, I next set out the minimal conditions for a democratic state. I propose four criteria by which to assess whether a state has met the minimal conditions required to qualify as a democracy. Of course, I am not proposing that all societies that are not democracies are necessarily dictatorships. Rather, my concern is with the dictatorship–democracy continuum, and in the sections that follow, my focus turns to the democracies that are closer to the pure democracy pole of the continuum.

Town Square Test

The first condition is the *town square test:* Can a person go to the local town square and speak out freely without fear of arrest, imprisonment, and physical harm (Sharansky & Dermer, 2004)? Clearly, some countries fail the town square test and some pass; I can say from bitter personal experience that Iran fails and the United States passes this particular test. It is possible to speak out freely in local town squares in America, to call in and express opinions on local radio shows, to publish contrary opinions in local newspapers, and so on. Americans think nothing of publicly criticizing the president, the highest authority in the land, in the severest of terms. In Iran, anyone who criticizes the so-called Supreme Leader in the local town square or the equivalent would find him- or herself in jail or worse. A similar situation exists in North Korea, Saudi Arabia, and other 21st-century dictatorships.

Encompassed in this town square test are a wider variety of rights protections, such as protections for whistle-blowers in the work context: Employees must be protected from retribution if they serve as whistle-blowers to remedy mismanagement at work. This is a protection that still needs to be more fully developed even in advanced democracies and particularly in the United States, where the power of private capital in politics is considerable and legislation has not been able to provide the necessary protection needed to ensure full protection for whistle-blowers (Earle & Madek, 2007). If democracy means also being able to go to the local water cooler and speak out against what is wrong at work, then in many work settings democracy is still weak in America.

Vote-Them-Out Test

The second way in which to test whether a society meets the minimal conditions required to qualify as a democracy is the *vote-them-out test*: Can citizens vote out their most powerful leaders through free, fair, and regular elections in which truly alternative candidates compete? The elections must be regular in two senses. First, elections must take place every few years, and there must be term limits for the highest offices. Second, elections must meet international standards of fairness. Also, truly alternative candidates must compete in the elections, meaning that the ruling group must not screen the candidates using ideological or other litmus tests. For example, even in the 21st century, the elections for the highest political offices in Russia do not qualify as democratic in part because the candidates have been screened to meet criteria set by Putin and his associates. Thus, in Russia, China, Iran, and a number of other societies, power transfer is closed rather than open despite the various types of voting that take place either directly by the people or by the so-called representatives of the people.

Minority Rights Test

One can imagine a society that passes the town square test and in which citizens can vote out political leaders through regular and fair elections, but the majority of the population vote to discriminate against minorities. Does such a society governed by majority rule qualify as a democracy? My answer is a categorical no because such a society fails the *minority rights test*.

The third essential criterion for democracy is the protection of minority rights. Thus, for example, even if during the era of slavery in the United States, the majority of voting citizens endorsed slavery as legitimate, that society would not qualify as a democracy because slavery violates minority rights.

Independent Judiciary

The town square test, vote-them-out test, and minority rights test can only really be implemented if there is an independent judiciary. Even in the more mature democracies of North America and Western Europe, the judiciary as a whole comes under scrutiny and under pressure when the courts make decisions that are unpopular with the larger public and/or the political establishment (see the readings and particularly the concluding chapter in Russell & O'Brien, 2001).

Criteria Must Not Be Applied Categorically

The criteria for defining a dictatorship must not be applied in a categorical, all-or-nothing manner; rather, they are viewed as a matter of degrees. As a number of authors have discussed (e.g., Diamond, 2002; Geddes, 1999; Hadenius & Teorell, 2007; Svolik, 2009), dictatorships vary in how closed they are and the mechanisms they use to maintain power. All societies are to some degree open and to some degree closed, to some degree democratic and to some degree dictatorial. The question is, does a society come closer to the open and democratic end of the continuum or the closed and dictatorial end? Conceptualizing this as a continuum rather than a categorical determination also allows one to recognize that societies can move from one part of the continuum to other parts; a society that is dictatorial today can become democratic, and one that is democratic today can slip back into dictatorship.

Indeed, a number of critics, including legal scholars (e.g., Turley, 2012), have argued that the United States has had serious setbacks in maintaining its democratic traditions since the 9/11 terrorist attacks. This is, on the one hand, associated with restrictions on civil liberties that were supposedly necessary to safeguard security. On the other hand, some would contend that the greater intrusion of money into the election process and the widening wealth gap in America between the richest group and the rest of the population have weakened democracy in America. I discuss this issue further in Chapter 10.

The Dictatorial Roots of Contemporary Societies

All contemporary societies began as dictatorships and have within them elements that either keep them as dictatorships or have the potential to move them back from democracy to dictatorship. The prime examples of such elements are the church and the military, which play a central role in contemporary dictatorships. It is through the military and security apparatus that dictatorships such as Syria, Burma, and North Korea maintain control, and of course it is through a combination of religion and security apparatus that some other contemporary dictatorships, such as Iran and Saudi Arabia, continue to survive. Within communist dictatorships such as China and North Korea, the state ideology (of communism) plays the same role as religion does in dictatorships such as Iran and Saudi Arabia.

The danger in democracies such as the United States is that the church and the military will play a larger role in political life and eventually force a move back to dictatorship (of course, there are some instances in history in which the church and the military play an antidictatorship role, but such instances are uncommon and against their historical inclinations, as discussed in Chapter 3, this volume). This is more likely during periods when an external enemy is clearly identified and seen as a serious threat, such as during the cold war years when Senator Joseph McCarthy (1908–1957) used communism as the threat or more recently when the apparent threat of Islamic fascism has been used to limit internal liberties in America (Turley, 2012). Thus, within democracies such as the United States, there are still elements that continue from the earlier closed periods and that can serve as a platform for forces motivated to move society back to dictatorship.

Although the United States meets the minimal criteria for democracy, this does not mean that the policies of the United States are in support of openness and democracy on the global stage. The United States is an example of a *strategically open democracy*, societies that as a rule tend to support openness at home but only selectively support openness internationally. For example, despite the many freedoms American citizens enjoy at home, the United States government supports dictatorships such as Saudi Arabia through its military and financial resources abroad. Strategically open societies demonstrate that openness at home does not guarantee support for open societies abroad or support for basic policies in line with the United Nations' (1948) *Universal Declaration of Human Rights*. This schism between democratic ideology and actual practice reflects a deeper issue: the tendency for the role of ideology in dictatorships and democracies to be different.

THE FUNDAMENTAL ACADEMIC FALLACY

Academics live and breathe ideas, and it is natural that they should give highest priority to the power of ideas. This is not just the tendency of 21st-century academics but the trend among intellectuals in general, including revolutionaries. At the heart of Marxist theory is the idea that through continued and repeated clashes between the capitalist and proletariat classes, the proletariat will eventually attain class consciousness: There will arise among the proletariat the ability to recognize themselves as forming a distinct social class with interests that contradict those of the capitalist class. The revolutionary solution, then, from a Marxist perspective is for the proletariat to overcome false consciousness and the misleading ideologies propagated by the capitalist class, including social divisions on the basis of race, ethnicity, gender, language, and the like. It is through a "liberation" in thinking, a breakthrough in the realm of ideas and consciousness, that the Marxist revolution comes about.

The same emphasis on the power of ideas to shape history is central to the work of right-wing thinkers (Lincoln, 1984). The popularization of ideas such as the American dream, self-help, individual responsibility, and the like reflects the influence of right-wing thinkers among the masses. In recent years, the novels of Ayn Rand have been instrumental in spreading right-wing ideas, as espoused in *The Fountainhead*:

> Now observe the results of a society built on the principle of individualism. This, our country. The noblest country in the history of men. The country of greatest achievement, greatest prosperity, greatest freedom. This country was not based on selfless service, sacrifice, renunciation of any precept of altruism. It was based on a man's right to the pursuit of happiness. His own happiness. Not anyone else's. (Rand, 1943/1971, p. 684)

Obviously, the "greatest country" referred to is the United States, and the key to this greatness is depicted as the idea of the individual pursuit of happiness.

The assumption has been that it is by influencing ideas that political groups manage to attain power. This reflects the views of both left-wing and right-wing thinkers working in Western societies. Thus, for example, in Thomas Frank's (2005) popular book *What's the Matter With Kansas? How Conservatives Won the Heart of America*, the basic thesis is that although objectively the material interests of the majority of people in Kansas are best served by the Democratic Party, the majority vote has been in support of Republicans such as George W. Bush because the Republicans did a better job of communicating their ideas and getting people in Kansas to think their way. From this perspective, in capitalist democracies elites can use ideas to persuade the majority of people to support existing group-based inequalities even when it is against the interests of the majority to do so.

But is the role of ideology with respect to the ruling elite and the masses the same in dictatorships as it is in democracies? In discussions of political transitions, the main threat to the power of a dictator is seen to be mass uprising (Acemoglu & Robinson, 2001). First, this is an assumption that needs to be tested. Second, even if mass uprising is a threat to dictatorships, what prevents the masses from revolting? Is it ideology? I argue that mass revolt is not the most important threat to dictatorship despite the popular interpretations of the Arab Spring of 2011–2012. Second, I propose that what prevents the masses from rising up and overturning the dictator is the guns pointing at them. Brute force keeps the masses downtrodden in dictatorships. Ideology does have a role; the role of ideology is as important in dictatorships as it is in democracies but for a different reason.

In capitalist democracies, group-based inequalities are maintained mainly through ideology. There is competition between different elites for power, but the ruling elites agree on the basic characteristics of group-based inequalities in society. For example, there is not a great deal of difference between the views of the Republicans and Democrats in the United States or the Conservative and Labour parties in the United Kingdom about the legitimacy of group-based inequalities as they exist in their respective countries. The differences in opinion are about the degree of inequality that is justified, not about the legitimacy of the sociopolitical system. The challenge for the elite is to keep the masses, the 99%, wedded to the same beliefs, and in capitalist democracies this is achieved mainly through ideology disseminated through a variety of channels, including the mass media, the formal education system, and religious institutions.

Whereas some disagreement among the power elite is tolerated in democracies, in dictatorships such disagreement is not tolerated. The ruling elite must display utter loyalty to the dictator (or the dictatorship clique) and to his vision. This is achieved through absolute adherence to a shared ideology. The power elite controls its members through strict ideological conformity. But control of the masses, the 99%, and their acceptance of group-based inequalities is maintained mainly through the exercise of brute force made possible by ideological cohesion in the elite ruling group.

Rethinking Mass Revolt

There are two lines of argument against the idea that the greatest danger faced by dictators is mass revolt. The first is perhaps the simplest and most direct because it is based on empirical evidence. Historical evidence shows that despite the initial interpretations of the Arab Spring, dictators are not in general toppled by mass revolt. Svolik (2009) identified all 316 authoritarian leaders who held office and lost power by nonconstitutional means in the period 1945–2002. Only 32 out of 316 (i.e., about 10%) were removed from power by popular uprising. The vast majority, 205 (i.e., 68%), of these dictators were removed from power through a coup d'état; that is, they lost power through the opposition of elite insiders. In his analysis of major types of dictatorships, Geddes (1999) also concluded that the main threat to the dictator comes from other members of the power elite rather than from the masses.

A second line of argument against the idea that the greatest danger faced by dictators is directly from mass revolt is theoretical and based on Pareto's (1935) elite model, on the Marxist–Leninist tradition of revolution led by a vanguard, as well as on more recent theorizing discussed in the paragraphs that follow. Pareto argued that all societies are ruled by an elite, but to retain power the ruling elite must allow some level of circulation and social mobility so that talented individuals born to nonelite parents can rise up through the ranks and join the elite and nontalented individuals born to elite parents can move down the social hierarchy and join the nonelite. If circulation is not permitted, then talented individuals born to nonelite parents will mobilize and form a counterelite to lead a mass revolt. If the mass revolt is successful, however, the counterelite will simply take over the role of the former elite and perpetuate group-based inequalities. Thus, according to Pareto, even when a revolution is successful, an elite will continue to rule, and group-based inequalities will continue to exist. The greatest danger facing a ruling elite is a counterelite; the masses are simply used as tools by a counterelite to overthrow and replace a ruling elite (for a more detailed discussion of Pareto's elite theory model, see Taylor & Moghaddam, 1987; for a modern social psychological model that also places emphasis on circulation and vanguard-led revolt, see Taylor & McKirnan, 1984).

The Marxist version of revolution also gives a vitally important role to the vanguard of the revolution, as discussed, for example, by Lenin (1902/1989) in his famous work *What Is to Be Done?* Lenin's vanguard is the equivalent of Pareto's counterelite in the sense that it is the leadership of this small, talented group (vanguard or counterelite) that channels the energies of the masses and mobilizes and directs the masses to successfully overthrow the ruling group. Thus, to maintain their control and stay in power, the ruling group must ensure that a vanguard (counterelite) does not form. Without the intellectual and other resources of the vanguard (counterelite), the masses would remain unfulfilled in their revolutionary potential.

The idea that the main danger confronting the ruling power lies within the elite groups themselves is also entailed in resource mobilization theory (McCarthy & Zald, 1977) and the focus on resource mobilization in the applied domain of social movements (Lofland, 1996), including in areas such as health care (Johansson, Eriksson, Sadigh, Rehnberg, & Tillgren, 2009). Resource mobilization theory depicts resources (defined broadly to include knowledge and skills as well as material wealth) as the most important factor in social movements. Those who control resources, it is argued, are able to instigate and shape social movements. From this perspective, class consciousness and feelings of relative deprivation and dissatisfaction among the masses can be influenced through resources. Just as advertising campaigns can make a new perfume fashionable around the world and create a "need" for deodorant in a third-world country, through resources it is possible to influence in important ways the popularity of a government and even bring down a government. In short, the people with resources are critically important because they can shape the emotions, thoughts, consciousness, and actions of the masses.

In conclusion, then, one can see that in Pareto's (1935) elite theory, and to some degree in classic Marxist theory, the key factor to the survival of the ruling elite is their cohesion. Ideology is needed to keep the elite united and to prevent a vanguard or counterelite from forming to challenge the existing social order. In line with this, resource mobilization theory proposes that without the leadership of a counterrevolutionary group with intellectual and other resources, the revolutionary energy of the masses will remain dormant. In dictatorships, such well-resourced counterrevolutionary leadership is typically a splinter group emerging from the ruling dictatorship.

Cohesion of the Ruling Elite in Dictatorships

Even when mass revolt takes place, as in the case of mass revolts that toppled regimes in Tunisia, Egypt, and then Libya in 2011, the key factor in regime continuation is the cohesion of the ruling elite. What ultimately brought down Bin Ali in Tunisia, Mubarak in Egypt, and Qaddafi in Libya was the desertion of key segments of the ruling elite, such as the abandonment of Mubarak by the military elite in Egypt. This was very similar to the abandonment of the Shah by the military elite in Iran in 1978. Both Mubarak and the Shah would have been far more likely to survive if the military elite in their respective countries had not deserted them.

Unity among the ruling elite is especially important for the survival of the dictatorial regime for a number of reasons. Perhaps the most important reason is to ensure that the security services and other government agencies remain obedient. Experimental research has provided robust support for this view. For example, in Milgram's (1974) seminal experimental studies of obedience to authority (discussed in more detail in Chapter 6, this volume), participants were assigned the role of student, and another participant (actually a confederate of the experimenter) was assigned the role of teacher.

The teacher's task was to teach the student word associations. Each time the student made a mistake, the teacher was instructed by a scientist in a white lab coat, who served in the role of authority figure, to punish the student by administering an electric shock to him.

In one condition there were not one but two authority figures. When the two scientists in white lab coats seemed to disagree on what the student should do, then the level of obedience by the student dropped significantly. Milgram's (1974) findings are directly relevant to the situation in dictatorships because like the student in Milgram's studies, the security forces and some other government employees are ordered to inflict harm on ordinary civilians who have "done wrong." When there is disagreement at the top as to how to proceed, then ordinary people are less likely to obey orders to harm others.

To sum up, in dictatorships, ideology is of paramount importance for keeping the ruling elite cohesive so that they can use force (e.g., assassinations, kidnapping, prisons, torture) to control the masses. The key to dictatorship continuation is elite cohesion. As one expert put it in reference to the transition of power from one dictator to another in North Korea in December 2011:

> Kim Jong Eun has been accepted almost immediately by the leadership. It's clear why. It's not because he is special. It's because the North Korean elite understands—to use an old phrase—that either they hang together or they will be hanged separately. (Andrei Lankov, a North Korean scholar, quoted in Harlan, 2011)

ADDITIVE AND SUBTRACTIVE GLOBALIZATION AND THE QUESTION OF WHY ONE SHOULD STUDY DICTATORSHIP NOW

From a historical perspective, dictatorship rather than democracy is the norm for human societies. Over the last 12,000 years or so of human history since people first established settlements, began crop farming, and domesticated animals, apart from a brief period in tiny Athens around 2,500 years ago and during the past 250 years or so mainly in Western societies, dictatorship rather than democracy has flourished. The promise of democracy is great, with India, Brazil, Indonesia, and some other major non-Western countries adopting (albeit weaker forms of) democracy recently. But since the 1990s, a number of revolutions that would have seemed to signal transitions from dictatorship to democracy have had disappointing outcomes in countries such as Russia, Ukraine, and Hungary. Indeed, it is now becoming routine for elections and facades of other democratic procedures to be used to justify dictatorship and to continue the same old system in the mold of *democratic dictatorship*, a dictatorship that uses the language and rituals of democracy, including elections, to both divert attention away from and to justify absolute rule by a dictator (see the related discussion on *totalitarian democracy*, Talmon, 1952). The threat of dictatorship looms large internationally, and it would be foolish to assume that democracy will inevitably become the norm at the global level.

But a widespread assumption has been that globalization will inevitably bring further democratization, and in this sense globalization has been seen as playing an inevitably additive (i.e., strengthening) role vis-à-vis democratization. In particular, the greater interconnectedness and increased trade and information flow associated with globalization have been seen as inevitably additive. But this is a lazy and overly simplistic assumption because in practice globalization has also in some respects had a subtractive impact on democratization, moving societies more toward the pure dictatorship end of the dictatorship–democracy continuum. Thus, globalization has proved to be a double-edged sword, sometimes helping but at other times hindering democratization. Perhaps more than any other factor, electronic technology reflects the nature of this double-edged sword.

The Promises and Perils of Technology

Rapid transformations in technology, particularly those associated with the computer revolution and the Internet, hold the promise of a more open world. Blogs, e-mail, Facebook, desktop publishing, and many other innovations in communications technology have in some ways shifted the focus to the power of ordinary citizens and grassroots organizations (Gillmor, 2006). New technologies have given rise to a multiplicity of voices and news sources and an increase in the power of ordinary citizens. In addition, Western media giants are now being challenged by Al Jazeera, Al Arabiya, and multiple other non-Western media news organizations (Seib, 2008). This would all seem to strengthen the case that technological changes are creating a more open, democratic world.

But there is an opposite trend, as argued forcefully by Morozov (2011). With every passing day, dictatorial regimes make greater investments in technologies to suppress their populations and continue dictatorial rule. This trend is routinely reported in the Western mass media. My local newspaper, *The Washington Post*, reported recently on its front page that there is a "booming business" of surveillance technology using the latest computer innovations. These technologies allow users to

> track hundreds of cellphones at once, read emails by the tens of thousands, even get a computer to snap a picture of its owner and send the

image to police—or anyone else who buys the software. One product uses phony updates for iTunes and other popular programs to infiltrate personal computers. (Horwitz, Asokan, & Tate, 2011, p. A6)

Thus, although advances in electronic communications and other technologies have for the most part been developed in Western democracies and supported greater information dissemination and openness, the same innovations have "ended up in the hands of repressive governments such as those of Syria, Iran and China" (Horwitz et al., 2011, p. A1). In another report, a young Iranian laments he bade farewell to the Internet because government censorship is so effective that "all I can read is official Iranian news Web sites" (Erdbrink, 2012, p. A10). A human rights supporter is quoted as saying that sophisticated technology is "facilitating detention, torture, and execution" (Horwitz et al., 2011, p. A6).

Consequently, it is not the case that globalization and the spread of advanced electronic communications systems will inevitably create more open societies. Indeed, some dictatorships are proving adept at using these new technologies to strengthen ideological orthodoxy. But this threat is not limited to dictatorships.

In democracies also, 21st-century surveillance technologies are being seen as a potential threat to civil liberties (Haggerty & Samatas, 2010). The same technologies that enable private corporations to monitor consumer behavior as a means of increasing efficiency in the marketplace are enabling governments in capitalist democracies to monitor citizen behavior as a means of maintaining stability and preventing terrorism. The so-called war on terror—which has not ended because there is no official body with which to negotiate and sign a treaty—has been used repeatedly since 9/11 to justify government secrecy and the surveillance of ordinary citizens (Turley, 2012). These trends limit openness and raise serious questions about the extent to which democratic ways of life have suffered as a result of the seemingly endless war on terror.

Besides, in influential books such as *Republic.com* (Sunstein, 2009) and *The Myth of Digital Democracy* (Hindman, 2008), the argument has been made that the World Wide Web has not really expanded the voice of ordinary people and has actually accentuated the insular news gathering practices of most people. That is, people tend to live in "echo chambers," using the new electronic communications systems to selectively read, write, speak, and listen in ways that reinforce their own views of the world. Hindman's (2008) study is probably the most thorough undertaken so far on the relationship between the Internet and democracy, and he concluded that "blogging may be the most widely read form of political commentary, but . . . the bloggers in our census are grossly unrepresentative of the broader public" (p. 135), and "in a fractally organized Web, the winner-take-all patterns of the parts are mirrored in the winner-take-all pattern of the whole" (p. 136). Although Hindman did present empirical evidence in support of this pessimistic perspective on the influence of the Internet on democracy, a few empirical studies suggest a more mixed picture. For example, Garrett (2009) showed that once a person has committed to reading a news source, coming across information with which he or she disagrees does not lead that person to abandon the story. Of course, this finding does not necessarily contradict the echo chamber idea, which is that people seldom take the first step of reading news sources that contradict their own views. Also, the trickle-up theory of the web, that the voice of the majority is expanded and can shape decisions at the top, is not reflected in the pattern found by Hindman.

Finally, one must be careful not to assume that just because globalization is associated with a greater number of news outlets, it means that there is greater freedom in the media. In some respects, monopoly of the media is increasing (Warf, 2007), and new outlets are often owned by those whose sympathies lie with dictatorship rather than democracy. For example, Al Arabiya is owned by the Saudis, who are staunchly prodictatorship, and Al Jazeera is owned by the ruling Sheikhs of Qatar, who are more liberated but ultimately not rushing toward democracy.

Illusions of Permanence and the United States

Looking at the international situation from a historical perspective, it is not at all certain that in the long-term democracy will win out over dictatorship as the dominant form of government in the world. The military and economic supremacy of the United States and other Western powers might lead us to conclude that democracy has won out. Indeed, some thinkers (e.g., Fukuyama, 1992) have declared "the end of history" and the triumph of capitalist democracy. But just as Marx was wrong to predict the inevitable march of history toward the "classless society," some supporters of capitalist democracy have made wrong assumptions about an inevitable path to a liberal capitalist end to history. These enthusiastic supporters of communist and capitalist empires all suffer the grand illusion that their government is the final form. It is important to go beyond the limitations of the times and adopt a historical perspective to avoid such illusions.

The Chinese, the Egyptians, the Greeks, the Romans, and all the other ancient empires eventually ended. In more recent times, the British Empire reigned supreme for only about a century, and there is no telling how long the American supremacy will last—another few decades, half a century longer? a century? Sooner or later, there will be an American decline. It is already predicted that the Chinese economy will be the largest in the world before 2030.

Although the passing away of an empire does not necessarily mean the end of a particular form of government, it is possible that the United States will be replaced by a new superpower with a different form of government. What will Chinese global supremacy mean for the future of democracy and dictatorship internationally? Will a resurgent Russia help democracy or dictatorship around the globe? What does the eventual decline of the United States and Western Europe imply for democracy and dictatorship? These questions about the future of democracy and dictatorship at the global level are timely and highly relevant, and they highlight the need to attend more closely to the dangers posed by dictatorship for those who support open societies.

Elections in Democratic Dictatorships

The surface facades of democracy are increasingly adopted in 21st-century dictatorships. Important political offices are now filled through elections even in Russia and Iran. Elections take place in Iraq, Afghanistan, and many other former dictatorships now influenced by Western powers. However, there is extensive evidence to show that, first, in many cases fraud elections are used to prop up democratic dictatorships that are in practice camouflaged dictatorships (Lehoucq, 2003; Schaffer, 2007; Schedler, 2006). Second, although there is in some cases resistance to electoral fraud through citizen action (J. Tucker, 2007), there is also the strong possibility that in some countries where "coerced democracy" is being used to cover a backsliding to dictatorship, democracy might well lose to dictatorship in the longer term. For example, the future of even a weak form of democracy is not at all clear in Russia and Iran. Third, dictatorships continue with little change toward democratic reform in many countries (e.g., Saudi Arabia, China). Thus, the so-called spreading of democracy should not lead us to neglect the continued dangers posed by dictatorship.

The continued danger posed by dictatorship was evident during the spring of revolution in Iran in 1979. For several months immediately after the revolution, Iranian women and men both enjoyed considerable freedom, including free speech; freedom of the press; and freedom to assemble, to organize politically, and to experiment in the arts. Not just on university campuses but all around Iran people witnessed promising signs of the initial growth of civil society and public participation in decision making. Democracy seemed to be on the march in Iran for a fleeting period. Unfortunately, within another year the country was hurled into an 8-year war with Iraq, and crisis after crisis was manufactured and used to justify the ending of freedoms and the reestablishment of dictatorship (this experience is discussed in greater detail in Chapter 5, this volume).

This brief experience with democracy in Iran is a reminder of how difficult it has been to move away from dictatorship in some parts of the world, even through major revolutions. The struggles that have taken place since the start of the Arab Spring are a persuasive testimony to this. It is also a reminder that in past human history, there are numerous examples of societies, from ancient Athens to modern Germany, returning to the spell of dictatorship.

Consequently, it would be foolhardy to assume that dictatorships will disappear and democracy will necessarily triumph in the long-term. It is important to more effectively combat dictatorship by better understanding its psychological foundations. In this book, research from psychological science as well as historical and contemporary examples is used to explore the psychology of dictatorship and the psychological reasons for the continuation of dictatorships.

The Rise of Transformational Dictatorship

An important reason why researchers must study dictatorships now is the rise of *transformational dictatorships,* regimes intending to continue in power through forcing change in the psychological characteristics of their citizens (this topic is further examined in Chapter 8, this volume). Transformational dictatorships have particular social orders in mind, with ideal citizens who would fit in with and uphold the intended social order, and they aim to change people to rigidly conform to an ideal mold. Such regimes use overbearing military force and enormous security systems to implement major political, economic, and cultural programs to try to transform individuals into what they consider to be ideal human types. The continuity of the regime is seen to be dependent on reaching this goal of achieving ideal types. Mao stated this goal very clearly in a 1957 speech: "The need for remolding must be recognized. Rightists just don't admit that they are in need of being remolded" (Leung & Kau, 1992, p. 736). Thus, Mao and Stalin sought to create the ideal communist citizen according to their different interpretations, Hitler sought to create the ideal Nazi citizen, and Khomeini sought to create the ideal Muslim citizen.

Of course, all societies have in mind ideal citizens and attempt to socialize the young toward their envisaged ideal. This includes the capitalist democracies of North America and Western Europe. The educational and cultural systems of capitalist democracies are geared toward teaching young people how to think and act according to specific criteria of good citizenship. This becomes particularly clear during political campaigns when candidates competing for votes accuse each other of deviating from the ideal accepted in their society. For example, in the campaign leading to the 2012 U.S. presidential elections, Republicans are accusing President Obama of steering the United States toward socialism through programs such as government-mandated health care. According to Republican political advertisements, President Obama is against the traditional American ideology of self-help, personal responsibility, and individual effort leading to individual reward. Of course, President Obama and the Democratic Party contend that it is the Republicans who have abandoned the traditional American ideals based on equality of opportunity, fairness, and moderation. Thus, in Western capitalist democracies also, as in all societies, there are conscious efforts to put into practice government programs that socialize citizens toward particular ideals.

But in Western capitalist democracies there is some level of openness to critically discuss societal ideals and to put forward somewhat different versions of ideals and how to achieve them. Second, there is genuine political participation by many of the people (sometimes the majority) in selecting leaders who put forward somewhat different versions (granted, they are not radically different versions) of the ideal as well as different policies for achieving the ideal. These choices are not available in dictatorships: Elections with mass participation are either not held (as in China and North Korea), or when they are held, they are sham elections in which the outcome is determined by the dictators, as happened in the presidential election in Iran in 2009 and in parliamentary elections in Russia in 2011.

In modern transformational dictatorships, the ideal is determined by a dictator and his inner circle and is never put to the people for genuine critical debate and vote. Thus, the Nazi ideal was determined by Hitler and his inner circle in Germany, just as the communist ideal was determined by Stalin, Mao, and Castro in the USSR, China, and Cuba, respectively, and the Islamic ideal was determined by Khomeini in Iran and by the Saudi royal family in Saudi Arabia. The military and security apparatus in each country was used to ensure that the leader's interpretation of the ideal was not threatened, and if it was threatened, that the deviant group was quickly exterminated.

The main challenge in transformational dictatorships has been to keep the ruling elite cohesive and in agreement about the societal ideal and the policies needed to transform people into ideal citizens. The most bitter and lethal fights in transformational dictatorships are at the top, where the dictator fights tooth and nail to ensure that none of the ruling elite deviate from the true path of what the ideal is and how it should be achieved. In this light, one can better understand "revolutions eating their own children" and dictators hunting down their deviant rivals, as Stalin's agents hunted down Trotsky and, after repeated attempts, finally killed him in Mexico in 1933 with an icepick while he was at his desk writing Stalin's biography (it is safe to assume that Stalin was choosy about who wrote his biography!).

CONCLUDING COMMENT

"They hate you, Ralph. They're going to do you."
"They're going to hunt you tomorrow."
"But why?"
"I dunno."
(Golding, 1997/1954, p. 219)

In William Golding's (1997/1954) brilliant novel *Lord of the Flies*, a group of young British boys get stranded on a deserted island during World War II. The paradise island could have been a wonderful escape from the war for the boys. A form of democracy emerges as the boys initially elect Ralph as the leader. A wise boy nicknamed Piggy tries to help Ralph make good decisions to the benefit of all the boys, but another group of boys become hunters under the leadership of the potential (and, later, actual) dictator, Jack, supported by his vicious sidekick, Roger. Soon the hunters overturn democracy and kill the strongest supporters of democracy until only Ralph is left alive to resist. When Ralph asks why he is being hunted (in the dialogue quoted at the beginning of this section), two of the hunters simply say "dunno." This is the same response many of the supporters of dictatorship might provide. The explanation for why dictatorship comes into place, why ordinary people end up doing terrible things (just as his former friends end up hunting Ralph like a wild pig), is highly complex. In this book, I unpack this complexity by exploring the factors that help create the springboard to dictatorship and enable the potential dictator to spring to power.

I

PSYCHOLOGY AND THE SPRINGBOARD MODEL OF DICTATORSHIP

I strongly believe in the dictum "There is nothing so practical as a good theory," and in this spirit, in the two chapters in Part I, I clarify the main theoretical approach adopted in this book. I begin in Chapter 2 by critically discussing why the mechanistic causal, reductionist model central to traditional psychology is inadequate for explaining dictatorship. This traditional model focuses on what is inside individuals, from traits in personality psychology to bits of the brain in contemporary neuroscience, and neglects the socially constructed world "out there." The adoption of this traditional model has resulted in causal accounts of behavior that deny intentionality and conscious will. I have no doubt that future generations will shake their heads in wonderment and disbelief at the wrong turns taken by psychology in this era in the same way psychologists now look back at radical behaviorism as it thrived particularly in the 1930s and 1940s, wondering how so many intelligent individuals could have gone so far wrong.

Of course, there is always a kernel of truth in all of these radical research movements, including radical behaviorism and radical neuroscience. The problem arises when researchers become narrower and narrower in their viewpoints and come to believe that stimulus–response associations (radical behaviorism) or activities in bits of the brain (radical neuroscience) explain the behavior of persons in the larger world.

The hegemony of neuroscience is arising out of economic, political, and social factors divorced from the actual scientific merit of this approach. A first factor is that university administrators are viewing neuroscience research as a promising new revenue source given that research involving brain imaging technology generally involves larger grants. A second is that psychologists concerned with the image of their discipline as not really a science view neuroscience as gaining scientific respectability for them because, after all, neuroscience research typically involves complex machinery in "hard science" or medical school settings. But just as the hegemony of behaviorism led down the wrong path, the hegemony of neuroscience will prove counterproductive despite the contemporary fascination with "the question of what neural events mediate between stimulus and response" (Prentice & Eberhardt, 2008, p. 139).

After clarifying the kind of psychology that is actually useful in understanding dictatorship (see Chapter 2), I present the springboard model of dictatorship (see Chapter 3). The springboard model moves away from the traditional focus on dispositional factors and mechanistic, reductionist causation and gives central place to situational factors in the coming to place and continuation of dictatorship. Of course, the characteristics of the individual dictator also play a role but within the constraints set by the situation. Thus, my contention is that to understand dictatorship, psychologists need a psychology that focuses on the normative system that enables the ideological cohesion of the power elite and its use of brute force to control the masses.

2

EXPLAINING DICTATORSHIP: WHAT KIND OF PSYCHOLOGICAL SCIENCE IS NEEDED?

As opposition activists were rounded up in their homes and "disappeared" into clandestine detention centers to be tortured and later assassinated, whatever was found in their homes was declared "war booty" and ransacked. This included infants and young children of the victims.
—Penchaszadeh (1992, p. 291)

Escraches are campaigns of public condemnation through demonstrations that aim to expose the identities of hundreds of torturers and assassins benefitting from amnesty laws. Marchers invade the neighborhoods where torturers live, and walk around the streets carrying banners and singing slogans.
—Kaiser (2002, p. 499)

Between 1976 and 1983, Argentina was ruled by one of the most cruel and despotic military dictatorships of the modern era. The state-sponsored violence of this era was noteworthy even in comparison with what had taken place during numerous other coups and bloody dictatorships in Argentina (Arditti, 1999). In addition to the hundreds of thousands of political prisoners who suffered at the hands of the state security apparatus, tens of thousands of people "disappeared." Despite extensive and continuous follow-ups by their families, human rights activists, and others, most of the disappeared have not yet been traced. We now know that in some cases the victims were stripped naked, sedated, and thrown from flying military aircraft into the waters of the Atlantic Ocean or the Rio de la Plata. Horacio Verbitsky, a military officer who confessed to the crime of pushing victims out of aircraft, also explained that this was church-supported policy and that priests comforted the executioners after killings (Verbitsky, 1996).

DOI: 10.1037/14138-003
The Psychology of Dictatorship, by F. M. Moghaddam
Copyright © 2013 by the American Psychological Association. All rights reserved.

Like many other repressive dictatorships, the rulers of Argentina in the period 1976–1983 were creative in finding novel ways to make their numerous victims suffer. As Penchaszadeh (1992, quoted at the beginning of this chapter) explained, the victims of the state repression not only lost their lives and their material possessions but also lost their children. In many cases the infants and young children of political activists were handed over to be brought up as part of the families of those who had tortured and assassinated the parents. This has meant that even when, with the availability of new technologies, DNA testing is used to identify the kidnapped children of the disappeared and the skeletons of their biological parents (Corach et al., 1997), a deep moral dilemma confronts those seeking justice: whether and how to tell the children that their foster parents are responsible for the torture and murder of their biological parents.

The ruling power elite in the Argentine dictatorship developed and aggressively enforced alternative norms for behavior, one of them being that political activists opposed to the dictatorship did not have the right to raise children or even to live. They reasoned that such children would grow up to become part of the opposition (the persecution of entire families as a result of the "wrongdoing" of an individual is common to a number of dictatorships, most notoriously the Soviet Union under Stalin [Montefiore, 2003], but also in dictatorships in smaller countries such as Cambodia under Pol Pot's Khmer Rouge [Ung, 2000]). The solution, they concluded, was to have such children "cared for" by those who are fully dedicated to the regime—sufficiently so to torture and kill opposition members. The military rulers received support for the norms they developed and the cruel actions they undertook, often directly and explicitly, from the Catholic Church hierarchy in Argentina (Mignone, 1988).

But just as the military dictators in Argentina developed alternative norms to help them try to stamp out opposition, there evolved an oppositional set of norms among those civilians who were brave enough to seek justice and to continue the struggle for a more open society. For example, mothers and grandmothers of the disappeared began to silently gather in public. Throughout Argentina and the outside world, these women became known as the mothers and grandmothers of the Plaza de Mayo (Arditti, 1999) because of the location where they first began to demonstrate in public. Although their numbers were small, the continued public appearance of these women was enormously important because it kept alive the issue of the disappeared. Through the emotional power of the human rights catastrophes they spotlighted, such as their concern to get back the infants born to pregnant women who died in concentration camps, the mothers and grandmothers of the Plaza de Mayo influenced the discourse in and about Argentina both within and outside the country (a similar role was played by the Black Sash White women who displayed their opposition to apartheid in South Africa from 1955 until 1994 by appearing in public wearing their mourning clothing, see Burton, 2010).

More recently, those seeking justice have developed a new social behavior, *Escraches*, as described by Kaiser (2002, quoted at the beginning of this chapter). This new behavior has been a reaction to the general postdictatorship amnesty enjoyed by former torturers and assassins of the 1976–1983 era. After a former torturer or assassin is identified; people flood his neighborhood (these individuals are almost all male) and publicize his presence. This public outing is intended to keep alive the issue of the disappeared and place pressure on former torturers and assassins to collaborate in finding out what really happened to victims of the dictatorship.

The behavior of both supporters and opponents of the dictatorship in Argentina raises important questions for psychological science. What psychological processes enabled the dictators in Argentina to create a sociopolitical system that justified torturing and killing parents and giving the children of victims to be looked after by torturers and assassins? What psychological processes enabled the grandmothers and relatives of the disappeared to continue the struggle against dictatorship even when the only action they could take was to make brief appearances in public silently demonstrating their opposition? I argue that both the establishment of dictatorship and the dismantling of dictatorship in Argentina and elsewhere are achieved through people's capacity for meaning making, both intentional and otherwise. This capacity for meaning making also enables torturers and assassins to construct justifications for why they should take care of their victims' children.

TRENDS IN PSYCHOLOGICAL SCIENCE

> But cognitive science in its new mood, despite all its hospitality toward goal-directed behavior, is still chary of the concept of agency. For "agency" implies the conduct of action under the sway of intentional states. (Bruner, 1990, p. 9)

The modern science of psychology has undergone a number of important intellectual swings since its beginnings in the 19th century (see Moghaddam, 2005). The traditions established by Wilhelm Wundt (1832–1920) and Edward Titchener (1867–1927) of using introspection to explore elements of the mind in the latter part of the 19th century were swept aside early in the early 20th century by John Watson's (1878–1958) behaviorist manifesto in 1913 and later by B. F. Skinner's (1904–1990) radical behaviorism. The behaviorists dispelled mind, self, and other subjective phenomena they claimed were not directly and objectively measurable and could not be part of a science of behavior. The behaviorist argument that psychology must concern itself only with what is objectively observable, overt behavior, held sway in academic psychology for almost half a century.

In turn, behaviorism was gradually (although never completely) pushed from center stage by the cognitive revolution pioneered in the 1950s by Jerome Bruner, George Miller, Noam Chomsky, and others. With the cognitive revolution came a return to the mind, and more specifically, there evolved the metaphor of the mind as a computer, a "thinking machine." Although academic psychology had now once again focused on thinking, and not exclusively concerned itself with overt behavior as the behaviorists demanded, there was continuity in the adoption of a deterministic, causal model, but now the causes were assumed to be the workings of mental mechanisms.

Throughout this entire period, Freudian psychology remained a powerful influence, particularly in the clinical arena and in the broader culture and also to some extent on academic psychology (e.g., in research domains such as displaced aggression; N. Miller, Pederson, Earlywine, & Pollock, 2003). A foundational similarity between behaviorism, Freudian psychology, and traditional cognitive psychology is the causal model and the assumption that human behavior is causally determined at the individual level with no room for human free will. For behaviorists the causes are stimuli in the environment; for psychodynamic psychologists the causes are in the unconscious; and for traditional cognitive psychologists the causes are in mental mechanisms.

The emergence of neuroscience and the new brain imaging technology brought a new focus to the search for causes in specialized parts of the brain. As Bruner (1990, quoted at the beginning of this section) noted, the result has been a rejection of intentionality and conscious will (see Wegner, 2002, for a traditional view on this). Interestingly, some leading neuroscientists have begun to backtrack and rethink and to conclude that agency and personal responsibility and even free will do exist (Gazzaniga, 2011). Next, they will, I hope, discover the collective processes of meaning construction (i.e., how through social interactions people engage in meaning making) and the power of meaning systems to regulate thought and action.

But another group of researchers, part of a second cognitive revolution that includes Bruner (a pioneer also in the first cognitive revolution), have looked for answers not inside private individual minds but outside to the collective processes that characterize social life (Harré & Moghaddam, 2012). This new movement in psychology can be better understood by distinguishing between two types of human thought and action, the next topic I discuss. Meanings, as Wittgenstein (1953) showed, are necessarily social, patterned, and collective in character.

Performance Capacity and Performance Content

Imagine you are sitting in a dentist's waiting room and you hear a loud bang from outside in the street. You look at the only other man in the waiting room, and he does not show any reaction to the noise. You anxiously ask him, "Did you hear that noise?" He is an elderly gentleman and responds, "What did you say? My hearing aid doesn't seem to be working . . . battery too low. Talk louder!" His diminished auditory capacity has to do with that I call *performance capacity* (to do with human abilities), how well human beings can do things, how well their senses work, and how well they hear and see, for instance. Behavior in this domain is causally determined. For example, if I am in a car accident and receive a sharp blow to my head and lose my hearing, there is a causal relationship between the blow to my head and my hearing loss.

Now imagine if the dentist rushes out of her office and says to me, "Did you hear that sound? I think it was a gun firing! Isn't that what it sounded like to you?" This is a question concerning *performance content*, or the way behavior is carried out and the meaning given to it (adapted from Moghaddam, 2002). The question now is, What was the meaning of the noise? (referring to performance content). This is a very different question from, Did you hear a noise? (referring to performance capacity).

Whereas performance capacity is causally determined, performance content is regulated by normative systems: norms, rules, values, and other characteristics of the practice of culture. That is, in this case how I interpret the sound I heard depends on my cultural experiences, my knowledge, and the context in which I am at present. I might reply to the dentist, "I have a lot of experience with gunfire and am certain that was something other than a gun. Perhaps it was a car backfiring." Or, I might respond, "I have no idea what a gun sounds like, but the noise was very loud and I can't think what else it could be. How scary to think it probably was a gun!"

Meaning systems and the style in which people behave, the realm of performance content, are not adequately explained through mechanistic, causal models. The behaviorists were wrong in assuming that they could explain all such behavior through reference to stimulus–response (cause–effect) associations. However, having finally ended the dominance of behaviorism in academic psychology, psychologists are confronted by a new behaviorism in the form of simplistic and incorrect interpretations of neuroscience research. Even social behavior that is normatively regulated is being causally explained by reference to activities in specialized parts of the brain (see Bennett & Hacker, 2003; Harré & Moghaddam, 2012; as well as Doise, 1986, 2012, on levels of explanations).

Of course, some types of behavior, what I have referred to as performance capacity, can be explained causally with reference to biological processes. For example, human auditory capacity is limited to sound waves ranging from about 15 to 20 Hz to about 15,000 to 20,000 Hz. With aging usually comes a decline in the upper limit of hearing; continued exposure to loud noises also diminishes the range. Thus, aging and exposure to loud noises can accurately be discussed as causing a change in auditory capacity. The older man sitting in the dentist's waiting room was not able to hear the loud bang that sounded in the street because aging had diminished his hearing ability (hearing and interpretation are intimately connected, as in practice are performance capacity and performance content).

But almost all of the behavior I am concerned with in this book is about meaning making and conforming to and obeying meaning systems. This behavior falls into the domain of performance content and is normatively regulated. Next, I consider the example of dictatorship in Argentina, which represents the kind of complex social behavior one needs to understand in order to explain what happens in dictatorships.

Meaning Making in Dictatorships

The meaning making that took place within the circle of rulers during the 1976–1983 dictatorship in Argentina as well as within the circle of prodemocracy activists involved group and intergroup processes well-known to researchers who study conformity and obedience. These topics are discussed in greater detail in Chapter 6, but for now it is useful to highlight three points. First, in the context of a dictatorship, secrecy becomes of the highest importance for both the circle of rulers and the circle of prodemocracy activists. The first group wants to crush opposition to the regime and only divulges information that would serve this purpose. For example, the rulers wanted to keep secret the practice of throwing drugged opposition activists into deep waters where they would not be found but to spread fear by letting it be known that opposition to the regime would result in dire consequences. The activists, on the other hand, wanted to keep their membership and communications secret while at the same time publicizing human rights abuses by the dictatorial regime and the fact that there was an active opposition movement.

Second, the need for secrecy means that both the circle of rulers and the opposition activists become to a large degree insular and isolated. Both groups share information only with trusted ingroup members and restrict communications and interactions with those outside their ingroups. Of course, all political leaderships tend to experience some measure of isolation and secrecy, even in democracies in which there is a stronger tradition of public access to information and powerful decision makers. (A key difference between secrecy in democracies as opposed to in dictatorships is that in democracies critics can and do question even the top officials, inside and outside of government. An example from inside government is the Watergate affair that brought down the administration of U.S. President Richard Nixon in 1974; an example from outside government is the phone-hacking scandal that battered the global media empire of Rupert Murdoch in 2012.) Also, even grassroots movements are to some extent insular and closed to outsiders. However, in dictatorships such as that experienced by Argentina 1976–1983, the secrecy and isolation of both the rulers and their opposition groups reached extreme levels. Such extraordinary levels of secrecy on the part of the dictators are meant to safeguard the regime, and on the part of the opposition, such secrecy is intended to safeguard the activist ingroup.

Third, this self-imposed isolation and secrecy sets up the optimal conditions for conformity and obedience within the ruling elite in the dictatorship, a topic discussed in greater depth in Chapter 6. Also discussed further in Chapter 6 is the phenomenon of groupthink in dictatorships. The policies of the dictatorship in Argentina 1976–1983 were associated with the kind of collective cognition processes that lead to each member of the junta endorsing the tragically flawed norms that had evolved—such as giving the children of killed opposition activists to the torturers and assassins responsible for the annihilation of the biological parents of the same children.

Within the larger society, the self-imposed secrecy and isolation of the ruling elite, and the severe restrictions on freedoms for the masses, result in rumors taking a central place in social life. Within the Western context, from the pioneering studies (Allport & Postman, 1947) to contemporary research (e.g., Rosnow, 2001; Stadler, 2003), rumor has been viewed as aversive, as something that has a negative role in society. Rumor has been shown to have a particularly prominent role among African American communities in the United States (P. A. Turner, 1993) and to be a factor in sometimes keeping minorities back. However, in the context of dictatorship, rumor can serve the important constructive role of spreading information uncensored by the government and helping antigovernment movements gain momentum.

The case of rumor suggests that a strictly functional explanation of the survival of norms is inadequate. Rumors can serve a functional purpose and help the survival of a group in some contexts but prove to have no functional value in other contexts. This mixed role becomes clearer with respect to norms when one asks, How did torturers and assassins develop norms that enabled them to see it as correct to take care of the children of their victims? How do norms sustaining increasingly deviant behavior develop? A functional view of norms suggests that if the behavior they support fails to serve a survival function, such behavior would become extinct. But there are examples of norms that have little survival function; indeed, some norms seem arbitrary and incorrect (on an objective basis). In Chapter 6, I review experimental evidence demonstrating that arbitrary and incorrect norms can influence individuals. Related to this is the evolutionary concept of *runaway selection* (R. A. Fisher, 1915, 1930), which seems counterintuitive because it suggests that under certain conditions behaviors evolve that make little or no contribution to human survival. However, this counterintuitive explanation is powerful and of the highest importance because it explains how norms that have no objective value can thrive in societies and have widespread influence on behavior. Most important, the power elite can shape such norms and in this way influence the everyday behavior of ordinary people. I turn next to the kind of psychology that can explain such meaning making in societies.

TOWARD A PSYCHOLOGY CAPABLE OF EXPLAINING DICTATORSHIP

The focus of this book is on the psychological factors and processes that influence the emergence and continuation of dictatorship. I begin with the proposition that how humans behave and construct meaning collectively and also as individuals has a profound impact on the kind of political system that emerges and is sustained. Some styles of thinking, doing, and meaning construction support dictatorship. This is not only because of how the leadership behaves and constructs meaning but also because of how ordinary people behave and construct meaning in their everyday lives, in addition to their explicitly political actions (e.g., attending a political rally, voting in an election). For example, it is true that a major factor in the continuation of dictatorship in postrevolution Iran was Khomeini's style of behaving and constructing meaning, but another vitally important factor was the meaning construction and behavioral style of the Iranian population and different factions within this population.

A psychological approach to the understanding of dictatorship runs the risk of being *reductionist*, that is, attempting to explain macro societal and intergroup processes through a reliance on intraindividual processes such as personality traits. In the past few decades a great deal has been written about the so-called Big Five personality traits (Agreeableness, Conscientiousness, Extroversion, Neuroticism, Openness to Experience) and their supposed universality (see Moghaddam, 2005). Unfortunately, mainstream researchers have once again fallen into the trap of assuming that so-called psychological processes within independent individuals cause certain types of behavior. In this case, universal traits serve as assumed causes.

Such traits are, of course, derived from verbal self-reports, which themselves arise from the normative system—out there in society, not in private minds. For example, consider the case of participants in a study making ratings on paper-and-pencil measures of agreeableness. On a scale of 0 (*very low*) to 5 (*very high*), Jill rates herself as 4 on agreeableness. Her rating of 4 arises through her interactions with others, the knowledge she has of how others view her, the way she would like others to see her, and a host of other factors to do with the changing social world she inhabits. The 4 rating does not arise from the properties of an isolated mind making decisions in private but arises out of Jill's experiences in collective, public, social life.

Solutions are at hand because recent developments in psychological science have led to an emphasis on psychological phenomena as the properties of the meaningful activities of people (Harré & Moghaddam, 2012). For example, recognizing, remembering, deciding, conforming, obeying, and the like are best understood not with reference to assumed processes in private minds but in the context of the ongoing activities of people, usually in interaction with others.

Unfortunately, the conceptual foundations and current trends in neuroscience have added further to the confusion of mainstream research. The emergence of brain imaging technology has mesmerized psychologists in large part because it seems to provide a path to scientific respectability. Psychology has always labored under the shadow of the "real sciences," and brain imaging technology has been heartily adopted as a means to establish the scientific credentials of psychology. Thus, just about any study, no matter how poorly formulated, now seems more scientific when it involves brain imaging.

TWO FALLACIES: THE MEREOLOGICAL AND THE EMBRYONIC

Conforming, obeying, and all other such activities are carried out by persons and not by bits of persons. For example, it is a person who feels jealous of another person and not an amygdala that feels jealous of another person or another amygdala, just as it is a person who shoots a gun and kills another person and not a hand that shoots and kills another person or hand. Psychologists must avoid the *mereological fallacy*—the attribution of the properties of wholes to parts (Bennett & Hacker, 2003). Persons are intentional beings, and each person must be treated as an integrated whole, not as bits and parts. The tendency to try to explain behavior in relation to bits of the brain or some other part of the human body is misguided. As the psychologist Daniel Kahneman (2011), who won the Nobel Prize for economics in 2002, pointed out, "cognition is embodied; you think with your body, not only with your brain" (p. 51). Moreover, as Greek philosophers pointed out 2,500 years ago and as has been repeated ad nauseam by modern researchers (Aronson, 2007), humans are social animals and can only be understood in social context.

Although the idea of humans being social animals is often repeated, its full implication is not well recognized in contemporary mainstream psychology. It is common for researchers to start with the statement that humans are social animals and then move on to explain behavior in relation to a part of the human body. Furthermore, in traditional research, particular bits of behavior are often studied in isolation, independent of the rest of society. Thus, bits of bodies (e.g., the amygdala) are put forward as the source of bits of behavior (e.g., jealousy), as if bits of bodies and behaviors existed independent of persons and contexts (Harré & Moghaddam, 2012).

To make progress applying the new psychological approach to dictatorship, one must also go beyond the *embryonic fallacy*—the assumption that as soon as life begins, the individual becomes the source of psychological experiences (Moghaddam, 2010). According to the embryonic fallacy, just as the individual is given personal legal rights at birth as an independent, self-contained entity, he or she is ascribed the power to act as an independent, self-contained psychological source. The fallacious nature of this viewpoint becomes clear when one takes into consideration the three basic points discussed in the sections that follow.

Individuals Are Thrown Into the Social World

The individual is "thrown into" a world that is already structured and directed in particular ways (following Heidegger, 1996). The newborn infant is immediately surrounded by a preexisting physical and cultural socialization system, one that shapes the life of the newcomer in particular ways and gives the infant selected, "biased" directions. Far from being neutral, the environment into which the infant is born is politically, socially, economically, psychologically, and in every other way, including architecturally, designed to bring about socialization in particular biased manners and toward particular biased goals. The infant arrives in a world preprogrammed to give shape to particular types of psychological citizens (Moghaddam, 2008c).

The family, the neighborhood, and the school are the primary socialization agents during the first 2 decades or so of life. Having arrived in the world utterly helpless, the newborn has little choice but to conform and obey and to take shape in accordance with the local normative structure. This structure includes (a) informal values, norms, and rules, such as those regulating the behavior of men and women; (b) formal *black letter* law, such as national and state or regional laws stipulating the duties and rights of citizens; (c) religious systems (e.g., Christianity, Islam, Judaism) that set out the framework for "good" and "bad" behavior; as well as (d) the built environment, which establishes the physical "container" for social behavior, structuring and guiding what can be done and thought (Bechtel & Churchman, 2002). During the initial few decades of life, despite being inquisitive and explorative (Gopnik, Meltzoff, & Kuhl, 2000), the individual has very little opportunity and resources to actually influence the normative structure. Later, depending on how much economic and political power individuals acquire, some people are able to influence their surroundings beyond the scope of their immediate and personal lives. However, the regular and routinely reported pattern for most human beings most of the time is to conform to local norms and rules for correct behavior and to obey authority figures.

Individuals Take on Worldviews of Their Cultures

Through socialization processes within a socially constructed and collaboratively upheld world, individuals take on the worldview of the collective within which they have been trained (Moscovici & Duveen, 2001; Valsiner & Rosa, 2007). This collective worldview takes shape on a foundation of inherited characteristics but transforms the individual well beyond what is biologically inherited. Thus, despite the strong possibility that humans are "prewired" to learn language (Chomsky, 1965), the language they learn depends on their surroundings: Those born into an English-speaking family will learn English; those born into a Chinese-speaking family will learn Chinese; and so on. Similarly, even if humans are born with an innate moral grammar (Hauser, 2006), the particular morality they learn to follow depends on which society they are born into. For example, a boy born into a Muslim family in Saudi Arabia is likely to grow up to believe that it is morally correct for a man to be able to have more than one wife at the same time, whereas a boy born into a Swedish family is more likely to view polygamy as immoral.

Of course, this does not mean that people necessarily always conform to and obey black letter or formal law that is on the books. Rather, the informal normative system is much more powerful. For example, during the time of Prohibition in the United States (1919–1933), countless Americans broke black letter law by drinking alcohol. The Eighteenth Amendment of the U.S. Constitution banned the drinking of alcohol but was never in danger of being obeyed and surviving.

The socialization process through which individuals take on the collective worldview begins even before birth. In a study of the crying patterns of 3- to 5-day-old French and German newborns, Mampe, Friederici, and Wermke (2009) demonstrated that French newborns cry with rising and German newborns with falling melody contours. This suggests that even before birth, the fetus is learning melodic features of the ingroup language, an action that helps the baby bond more effectively with the mother after birth. This process of culture acquisition continues throughout childhood, resulting in cross-cultural differences in thought and action. Such differences are reflected in the traditional cross-cultural journals (e.g., *Journal of Cross-Cultural Psychology*) and texts (e.g., Berry, Poortinga, Segall, & Dasen, 2002).

But the traditional literature misses an important point: The source of human worldviews is out there in the socially constructed and normatively regulated world and not in the private minds of individuals (Harré & Moghaddam, 2012; Moscovici & Duveen, 2001; Valsiner & Rosa, 2007). The individual acquires from the social world the various attitudes, values, attributions, beliefs, prejudices, and all the other psychological characteristics that social psychologists measure through their instruments and experiments. Such psychological phenomena are not created independently by individuals in their private minds, they are constructed collaboratively through the participation of the individual in social life. This is what being a social animal means, a meaning neglected in traditional psychology.

Individual characteristics do set some limits on how cognition and action come to be shaped and can be changed. For example, categorization is a universal cognitive process that leads humans to group social and nonsocial phenomena (see Moghaddam, 2008b). It is inconceivable that humans today would or could function without using categorization to process information. However, even this universal is in major ways influenced by culture; for example, the content and boundaries of categories are culture dependent.

Thus, although there are certain limits to the psychological malleability of humans, the normative system shapes thought and action in line with local expectations. The child born in St. Petersburg, Russia, will grow up speaking Russian and acquiring a Russian worldview, whereas a child born in Beijing, China, will grow up speaking Chinese and taking on a Chinese worldview. This very simple pattern has profound and often overlooked implications.

Conformity and obedience are normal human behaviors; all humans conform and obey to a great degree. I have argued that most humans do the right thing according to local normative systems: Most people are rule and law abiding even when the police and security forces are absent. Extensive psychological research discussed in Chapter 6 attests to this. It is more accurate to view nonconformity and disobedience as abnormal than to view conformity and obedience as abnormal. In October 2011, small groups of young people were taking part in the Occupy Wall Street sit-ins as a way of protesting the enormous inequalities that are part of the American economic and political system. For the first time in recent American history, most young people are facing a less prosperous future than their parents. Despite the enormous debts young people accrue to gain university qualifications, despite the housing crisis they face, and despite their bleak job prospects, they have for the most part conformed and obeyed. They have done the right things according to a set of norms and rules constructed by their elders in a world that enormously benefits a small number of their elders. The Occupy

Wall Street protestors, the nonconformists, constitute a tiny group of young people.

The natural human tendency to conform and obey means that there is always a great danger of dictatorships continuing, and democracies drifting away from the democratic moral base to become dictatorships. This is particularly so because there is a tendency for some leaders to want to subvert democratic procedures and continue their own rule even when they themselves came to power through popular vote. A prime example of this is President Hugo Chavez of Venezuela, a former military officer who was first elected to power in 1998. Since then Chavez managed to change the constitution so that he can run for the presidency indefinitely. There is a serious danger of Chavez becoming president for life. In February 2012, President Abdoulaye Wade of Senegal was also making moves to become president for life, starting with an attempt to run for a third term in office, even though the Senegalese constitution sets a two-term limit. Of course, there is a tradition of this kind of extended presidency in Senegal: Since gaining independence from France in 1960, Senegal was ruled for about 40 years by only two presidents, first Léopold Sédar Senghor and then Abdou Diouf (Gellar, 2005). These minor political figures pale in comparison with Vladimir Putin, who is continuing the tradition of the ancient tsars and the communist dictators in Russia (of course, it could be claimed that Putin has won popular elections in Russia, but the fact is that these were not free and fair elections, and opposition candidates were not allowed to campaign and compete).

Prediction and Normative Psychology

Normative systems regulate and make behavior more predictable in probabilistic terms. One of the avowed advantages of using a causal, mechanistic model in psychology is that it allows for the prediction of behavior: Causes (independent variables) predict effects (changes in dependent variables). In contrast, normative accounts of behavior allegedly have low predictive ability. However, I argue that normative psychology does not suffer a deficit in terms of predictive power.

With respect to the predictive power of traditional causal and alternative normative accounts in the domain of performance content (dealing with meaning systems), it is incorrect to assume that traditional causal accounts are superior. Human behavior in the domain of performance content is not predicted 100% by cause–effect accounts; this includes the classic experimental studies in which independent variables are manipulated and their impact on dependent variables is measured. For example, in the seminal studies of obedience to authority conducted by Milgram (1974), typically about two thirds of the participants obeyed the instructions of the teacher, but roughly one third did not obey (this is discussed in more detail in Chapter 6, this volume). In just about all experimental studies of this genre, there is variance in the behavior of the participants, meaning that behavior was not 100% predicted by the manipulation of the independent variable(s). The percentage of variance accounted for in many experimental studies is far, far lower than 100%, meaning that prediction was far from perfect.

This is obviously very different from prediction in the domain of performance capacity: Jim's auditory nerve has been damaged as a result of prolonged exposure to very loud music, and as a result he suffers nerve deafness. Unfortunately, his nerve deafness is so severe that he is not helped by wearing hearing aids. In such cases, there is a direct causal link between nerve damage and auditory (in)capacity. This is fundamentally different from asking a person the meaning of a noise that is heard (Was that a gun firing?) or from a person refraining from listening to a noise because he or she does not like it (e.g., Hettie refuses to listen to Mozart because she prefers hip hop).

Given that traditional experiments interpreted causally often account for far less than 100% of the variance in a population, do normative accounts have predictive power? The answer to this question is a resounding yes. Normative accounts have very good predictive power. This includes normative accounts developed by laypeople in everyday life; otherwise their social lives would be completely chaotic. People continually make predictions about the behavior of other people in their daily lives, and most of the time these predictions prove to be correct. This is because most of the time, most people behave correctly; according to the local normative system, they do the right thing. Of course, a great deal of behavior is routine and habitual (Duhigg, 2012), so people do not need to be conscious of what they are doing as they follow well-worn paths of thinking and action.

A normative approach to understanding behavior requires that people give special attention to the local normative system, and psychologists can assume that individuals will for the most part follow local norms and rules for behavior. However, psychologists do not treat the normative system as causes; rather, they assume that individuals have agentic power and can choose to behave in one way or another. This is in line with the adoption of a P-grammar (Person grammar) in which persons are taken to be morally responsible for the consequences of their actions (Harré & Moghaddam, 2012). A main feature of P-grammar is that in the socialization processes, as the individual develops from child to adult, she or he is assumed to take on increasing responsibility and to acquire agentic powers. It is not bits of his brain or his personality traits that are responsible for the crimes against humanity committed by Bashar al-Assad in Syria in 2012; it is the person of Bashar al-Assad himself who is responsible.

NORMATIVE PSYCHOLOGY AND DICTATORSHIP

One fact was evident throughout the GDR's history: a lot of people did not like the GDR. That there was mass discontent with the political constraints and material shortcomings of life in the GDR is indisputable. (Fulbrook, 1995, p. 151)

In his seminal analysis of the East German dictatorship, Fulbrook (in the preceding quote) made it clear that this dictatorship never gained popularity. There was a great deal of discontent among the majority of people, and it was for this reason that such an extensive security apparatus was needed to keep control and prevent a total collapse of the system. In the fight to keep control, the East German regime had one important asset, unity in leadership, "from the later 1950s until the late 1980s elite groups (in the GDR) were relatively united and lacking in any outwardly visible factional splits which might have provided political space . . . for exploitation by dissent from below" (Fulbrook, 1995, p. 31). Solidarity at the top enabled the East German dictatorship to focus on regulating behavior at the everyday level as well as to shape national policy toward controlling the normative system.

From the perspective of normative psychology, the challenge of understanding dictatorship becomes one of understanding the processes through which meaning making comes to be monopolized throughout society by the dictator and his henchmen. This monopoly comes about first through the development of a springboard, which enables the potential dictator to spring to power. The dictator then uses his power monopoly to shape the normative system in society, ascribing meaning to things and behaviors. Of course, many people will attempt to resist this new normative system, but sheer force and intimidation is used to crush opposition.

Just as dictatorial power is enforced through manipulations of the normative system, so opposition to the dictatorship often succeeds through reconstructing the meaning of things and behaviors. For example, Fulbrook (1995) described how in the 1980s the opposition to the dictatorship in East Germany adopted a number of *symbolic carriers* to identify their cause, such as the swords-to-ploughshares badge. This badge had communist credentials, so it was difficult for authorities to object to it. Accompanying this symbolic carrier was a picture of the statue donated by the Soviet Union to the United Nations building in New York. Again, this was something the East German authorities could not object to, at least immediately, "What they did object to, however, was the way in which this symbol caught on as a badge of protest" (Fulbrook, 1995, p. 111). Eventually, the protestors were able to use these revised carriers to help transform the normative system in East Germany, to topple the regime.

The struggle, then, in the competition to establish and maintain a dictatorship is to control the normative system that regulates behavior, most directly by sheer force. To understand dictatorship, psychologists must attend to the factors that enable the dictator to spring to power.

CONCLUDING COMMENT

Traditional psychology in the shape of behaviorism, psychoanalysis, cognitive psychology, and now neuroscience has adopted a mechanistic, reductionist, causal model of behavior. The standard paradigm involves the manipulation of independent variables (assumed causes) to test their effect on dependent variables (assumed effects). This model is suitable for behavior that falls under the umbrella of performance capacity but not behavior that involves performance content, which is primarily about meaning construction. The creation and maintenance of dictatorship is fundamentally about monopoly over the means for the construction and maintenance of meaning systems. Through power monopoly, the leadership in dictatorships forces the rest of the population to live according to a normative system dictated from above. Traditional causal models are incapable of explaining such behavior, central to which are intentionality and collective processes.

3

THE SPRINGBOARD MODEL OF DICTATORSHIP

Not, then, men and their moments. Rather moments and their men.
—Erving Goffman, *Interaction Ritual* (1967/2005, p. 3)

Hitler not only filled a power vacuum, but soon won patriotic acclaim for systematically tearing up the humiliating peace settlement of 1919 and for restoring, almost overnight, what many Germans felt was their "rightful" place as the dominant power on the continent. He managed to do so almost without an army.
—Robert Gellately, *Backing Hitler: Consent and Coercion in Nazi Germany* (2001, p. 1)

Dictatorship first and foremost arises out of the characteristics of context. These characteristics come about in part through historic accident but also in part through the efforts of the potential dictator and his supporters. The exact combination of contextual and leadership factors varies to some degree from case to case, but the general pattern is consistent: Context creates the springboard, and the availability of the potential dictator who takes advantage of the situation to spring to power completes the shift to or continues the dictatorship. In the case of Hitler, the historical opportunities were created for him by the Treaty of Versailles peace settlement following World War I (1914–1918), which most Germans considered to be a national humiliation and a continued disproportionally unfair burden on the country. The Treaty of Versailles imposed massive reparations on Germany, set restrictions on the German military, and also redrew the frontiers and substantially reduced the territorial size of Germany. The

DOI: 10.1037/14138-004
The Psychology of Dictatorship, by F. M. Moghaddam

resulting discontent among Germans was enormous and amplified in the context of the 1930s, when German society was characterized by political and economic instability.

Germany in the early 20th century provides a case of a country that moved from democracy to dictatorship. In other cases, such as Iran in 1978 and Russia in 1917, a dictatorship collapsed and there was a real but relatively brief opportunity for the country to seriously begin to move toward democracy. This opportunity proved to be brief because many of the important situational factors that supported dictatorship before the collapse once again reappeared through cultural carriers that enabled the momentum of culture and the resilient continuation of everyday cultural practices and narratives (Moghaddam, 2002) as well as the tendency for people to reaffirm familiar meaning frameworks when an established meaning framework is threatened (Proulx & Heine, 2006). In the context of a dictatorship, a revolution and the collapse of established order may still result in a reaffirmation of beliefs in strong leadership, creating the possibility for the emergence of a new dictator. Also, the availability of a charismatic leader motivated to take advantage of the springboard to reestablish a dictatorship, such as in the case of Khomeini in Iran and Stalin in Russia, completes the shift back to dictatorship.

The main purpose of this chapter is to outline the *springboard model of dictatorship*. As a step toward describing the two-stage process of the springboard model, I first discuss various background factors associated with the nature of continuity and change associated with the springboard to dictatorship. These include the so-called paradox of revolution and change (whereby people experiencing revolution often feel that power relations have actually not changed, whereas from the outside it is often assumed that historically change is toward greater democracy), the stability of a cycle of rights and duties associated with revolutions, the control of the surplus in dictatorships, and the conditions in which leader personality can exert greater influence in dictatorships.

Next, I describe the two main stages of the springboard model: In Stage 1, a set of factors combine to create the opportunity for a potential dictator to spring to power; in Stage 2, a potential dictator emerges to take advantage of the created opportunity to spring to power. The springboard model assumes that there are potential dictators in every population at all times, in the sense that there are always present individuals with the necessary appropriate personality characteristics to serve in the position of dictator if and when the opportunity arises. What potential dictators need to actually spring to power and become dictators in practice is the opportunity. This opportunity becomes available when the necessary situational factors combine through historical accident, intentional design, and other influences to create the springboard to dictatorship.

FACTORS ASSOCIATED WITH CHANGE AND CONTINUITY

Prior to describing the two main stages in the springboard model of dictatorship, I examine some of the factors that are associated with change and continuity in the context of dictatorship.

The Paradox of Revolution and the Democratic Dictatorship

The turban has replaced the crown. (Arjomand, 1988, p. 173)

The nature of the preexisting regime shapes the dynamics and outcomes of political transitions . . . contemporary political changes are conditioned by mechanisms of rule embedded in the ancien régime. Authoritarian leaders in power for long periods of time establish rules about who may participate in public decisions and the amount of political competition allowed. Taken together, these rules constitute a political regime. Regime type in turn influences the likelihood that a political challenge will arise and the flexibility with which incumbents can respond. It also determines whether elites and masses can arrive at new rules of political interaction through negotiation, accommodation, and election, that is, whether any transition will be democratic. (Bratton & Van de Walle, 1994, p. 454)

Tsar Peter the Great (1672–1725) moved the capital of Russia from Moscow to the newly established city of St. Petersburg in 1712 after he wrested control of the region from the Swedes (Massie, 1980). Over the next 2 centuries, St. Petersburg developed into a refined city with grand palaces and elegant boulevards. Because the city was the center of aristocratic power, it also became the center of antigovernment political activities leading to the 1917 revolution that toppled the tsar and eventually brought the communist state into being. After Lenin's death in 1924, the city was renamed Leningrad, and from then it became a favorite target for Stalin's political programs. Leningrad achieved heroic stature when it survived the onslaught of Nazi German attacks during World War II, and the siege of Leningrad (September 8, 1941, until January 27, 1944) now stands next to the blitz of London and a few other such collective experiences as reflecting almost superhuman societal suffering, courage, and resilience. In 1991, the name of the city was changed from Leningrad back to St. Petersburg. As the birthplace of President Putin, it is again a city receiving special attention and support.

Thus, St. Petersburg has seen the transition from tsar to Stalin to Putin through historic revolutions over a century and symbolizes a paradox central to revolutions in dictatorial societies. That is, despite what seem to be fundamental political, economic, and social changes, these revolutions often result in little actual change in the most important areas of power sharing and genuine political choice for the masses. The dictatorship continues: One man continues to rule, often with an iron fist behind the cloak created by "democratic dictatorship." This paradox of revolution (Middlebrook, 1995) has to be addressed by students of dictatorship because it lies at the heart of the challenge to escape from dictatorship. Of course, rule by Stalin was in some respects very different from rule by Putin, but in other important respects the style of rule remains the same: ultimate decision-making power concentrated in the hands of a single individual.

Ra'anan's (2006) examination of how succession took place in Russia during four crucial transfers of power—from Stalin (1953), from Khrushchev (1964), from Gorbachev to Yel'tsin (1991), and finally to Putin (1999)— revealed that the system of power succession in place in Russia has encouraged plots and political maneuvering within an elite group of rulers, distant from the masses. This system of power transfer is associated with continuity in leadership style. In discussing *The 18th Brumaire of Vladimir Putin*, modeled on Karl Marx's (1852/1979) *The Eighteenth Brumaire of Louis Bonaparte*, Blank (2006) saw this system of power transfer as pointing to continuity and more of the same in the future:

> Much like the subject of Marx's . . . analysis, Putin has acted to concentrate power in himself and misuse democratic forms for what is increasingly recognized as an authoritarian regime, with the only putative guarantee of an open society resting on the personality of the man in the Kremlin and the balance of forces there . . . closer analysis shows that this system and Putin's own program resembles that of the last Tsarist reformer Peter Stolypin who, for all his reforming zeal, was no democrat. (p. 160)

This pattern of closed power transfer is repeatedly found in dictatorships, often remaining resistant to change even when historic revolutions occur, such as the Russian revolution of 1917, the revolution that led to the People's Republic of China in 1949, and the Iranian revolution of 1979.

Another feature of social life that tends to support continuity involves the priority given to rights and duties by power minorities and majorities, a topic I discuss next.

Assumptions of Rationality and Unidirectional Change

The social and economic origins of dictatorship have been examined in their different aspects, and some agreement has been reached following Barrington Moore's (1966) seminal study and related developments (e.g., Dahl, 1971; Rueschemeyer, Stephens, & Stephens, 1992). The political development of societies has been viewed as integrally linked with their economic development so that, for example, democracy is seen as far less feasible in a primarily agricultural society that has an elite that relies on land as its main source of power. A major weakness of these political and economic assessments, from a psychological point of view, is the assumption of human rationality and stability, which is very different from what psychologists know about actual human behavior. This was pointed out by Kahneman (2011):

> To a psychologist, it is self-evident that people are neither fully rational nor completely selfish, and that their tastes are anything but stable. Our two disciplines seem to be studying different species, which the behavioral economist Richard Thaler later dubbed Econs and Humans. . . . Unlike Econs . . . their [Humans] view of the world is limited by the information that is available at a given moment . . . and therefore they cannot be as consistent and logical as Econs. They are sometimes generous and often willing to contribute to the group to which they are attached. And they often have little idea of what they will like next year or even tomorrow. (p. 269)

This rational model underlies economic assessments of the origins of dictatorship and democracy. For example, Acemoglu and Robinson (2006) presented such a rational model, with elites and the masses assumed to be able to correctly calculate their own interests, inputs, and outcomes in a political struggle in which each group supposedly attempts to maximize ingroup profits. Thus, elites agree to democracy when they are threatened by revolution and the cost of revolution would be greater than the cost of allowing some form of democracy. But actual historical development does not proceed along such rational unidirectional paths.

Again and again one finds historical examples of dictatorships being overthrown by revolutionaries, only to find that soon afterward another dictatorship has been established—on a basis that is far removed from rational behavior and the maximization of rewards. Often the dictatorship that follows the revolution is even harsher and more destructive and has even more ruthless leadership than what came before: Stalin following the tsar in Russia and Khomeini following the Shah in Iran being prime examples. The continuity of dictatorships, even after the violent destruction of a dictatorial regime, is as prevalent as it is puzzling. A decade after the Iranian revolution that swept aside the Shah's corrupt dictatorship, Arjomand (1988, quoted at the beginning of this section) correctly and succinctly summed up the situation in Iran by declaring that the dictatorship of the mullahs had replaced the dictatorship of the Shah, the "turban for the crown." I now consider the factors that enable such continuity.

Of course, the availability of a potential dictator is an enormously important factor; such availability is necessary but not sufficient for the reemergence of a (new) dictatorship after revolution and the collapse of the old regime. There are always potential dictators present in every group, as suggested by research on individuals high on both support for group-based inequalities and authoritarianism (Altemeyer, 2004). The key question here has more to do with the situational factors that enable a potential dictator to resuscitate and perpetuate the dictatorship.

The Cycle of Rights and Duties During Revolutions

The processes of social comparison and relative deprivation characteristic of societies during times of revolution have another feature that is psychologically important: a cycle of priority given to rights and then to duties by revolutionaries who succeed in coming to power (Moghaddam, 2004). Moghaddam and Riley (2005) put forward a more general proposition characterizing this cycle:

> In relationships that are (a) changing, so that the norms and rules of behavior are uncertain or (b) adversarial, so that conflict is actual or very possible, those with equal or less power will give priority to rights and those who enjoy greater power will give priority to duties. (p. 79)

This proposition can be further clarified using the example of the relationship between children and parents, a relationship that is characterized by change and, as both children and parents discover, can involve at least moderate levels of conflict. As the child grows up, he or she demands more and more rights: "That's not fair! I should be allowed to go out and play." "All my friends are at the party, you have to let me stay out with them!" On the other hand, the parents give priority to duties: "You can't go out because you have to do your homework." "You have to take responsibility for cleaning your own room." Eventually the child grows up and has children of his or her own, so that he or she is now the parent facing demands for increased rights from his or her children. As the parent, he or she now reminds his or her own children of their duties: "You must be back home by 9 o'clock, no later!" The cycle of rights and duties experienced by children and parents is characteristic of minority and majority groups during times of change and/or conflict.

Minority groups typically protest and mobilize using a rights rhetoric: For example, during the 1960s the focus was on women's rights, Black rights, and gay rights (rather than women's duties, Black duties, and gay duties). During major revolutions, opposition groups rally around calls for the upholding of what they see to be their rights. In the lead-up to the Iranian revolution, millions of Iranians of all political persuasions packed the streets of Tehran, Shiraz, Mashhad, Isfahan, and other major cities, demanding their rights. Khomeini and other leaders used the rhetoric of rights to blast the Shah's dictatorship. But after the revolution, once Khomeini took control of the reins of power, he changed his rhetoric to that of duties: People now had a duty to obey the Islamic government, and those who disobeyed were treated even more harshly than under the previous dictatorship.

The Control of the Surplus and Dictatorship

The springboard model of dictatorship is concerned with how democracies sometimes move back to dictatorship and how dictatorships continue to survive. The springboard model is not directly concerned with the origins of dictatorship, although it is important that the emergence of a surplus in human societies originally created a means through which dictators could become more powerful. Around 12,000 years ago, humans underwent the transformational change from living in hunter–gatherer nomadic groups numbering a few hundred to living in more complex agricultural settlements numbering in the thousands. This change was also associated with the domestication of animals and some specialization in tasks; for example, some individuals were able to serve as professional soldiers or priests rather than as farmers. What made this specialization possible was the emergence of a surplus in food and some other products.

The emergence of a surplus was transformational in major ways. For the first time in their evolutionary history, humans did not immediately consume what they had available but accumulated a surplus substantial enough to feed and equip large numbers of people occupied in nonfarming activities for long time periods. The availability of a substantial surplus meant that some people could be hired in professions that did not require their direct participation in production. Most important, some people could be hired as full-time soldiers and some as full-time priests, the first to provide military enforcement of a particular political order and the second to provide moral and "legal" justification for the political order. Strongmen emerged—chiefs, lords, kings, emperors—who controlled the surplus and distributed benefits to their supporters. As a general rule, these strongmen ruled as dictators (according to the definition I provided in Chapter 1), with a few brief periods in ancient Greece and ancient Rome being exceptional in that a limited form of participation by some people (free men) in decision making was permitted. Particularly since the 18th century, major revolutions, such as the American and French revolutions, have attempted to move societies from dictatorship to democracy, but this shift has been along an extremely bumpy road. Sometimes the road has circled back, influenced by the leader's personality.

Leader Personality and Degrees of Freedom

The personalities of leaders can have an important influence on national policies and international relations (Byman & Pollack, 2001; Greenstein, 2009), but this influence varies across situations (Greenstein, 2002, presented exceptionally insightful case studies of American leaders and their situations). To better understand the relationship between leader personality and the situation, it is useful to consider the role of degrees of freedom in situations (see Moghaddam, 2005). When the degrees of freedom in a situation are low, the personality of leaders has less of an impact on outcomes. Consider the example of a Catholic priest leading his congregation in mass. The degrees of freedom are low, meaning that both the leader and his followers have to behave according to a strict set of rules about how one should conduct mass in a Catholic church. However, in other situations, the degrees of freedom are relatively high, meaning that the leader has more freedom and can display a wider range of behaviors and decisions. For example, imagine a situation in which considerable instability has been created (by a natural disaster, or a terrorist attack, or war, or economic collapse, or some other catastrophic event). In the midst of the havoc in such an emergency, the leader will have a greater range of behavioral options, and the personality of the leader will have a greater impact on the outcome of events (Greenstein, 1975, discussed in more detail the conditions in which leader personality becomes more important).

In discussing the springboard model of dictatorship, I first focus on perceived threats that lay the ground for the rise of dictatorship. The threats are associated with economic and political insecurity and external and internal enemies. Other important components of these threats are perceived impending decline, collective helplessness and lack of trust, and threatened collective identity. These processes result in a society that experiences a high level of collective distress.

A second set of factors, discussed later in this chapter, focuses on situational characteristics, particularly institutional and cultural forces, that support dictatorship as the best solution to societal distress and perceived decline. These include the support of dictatorship on the part of resourceful elites (e.g., the business community) and on the part of powerful institutions (e.g., the church, the military), the growth of a bureaucracy compatible with dictatorship, the presence of cultural practices that support dictatorial leadership, and the occurrence of crisis incidents—events that give the potential dictator the opportunity to use the springboard and spring to power. The first and second sets of factors, then, together help to create and set in place the springboard to dictatorship: the first by leading to a high level of societal distress and perceived instability and the second by supporting dictatorship as the best solution available for society being resurrected and rising successfully out of its crisis.

I also discuss the charismatic leader and the "moral revival" that enables him to spring to power. Most important here is the moral mission of revival that the charismatic leader spreads and activates in society. This moral mission enables him to inspire followers who develop faith in his version of their resurrection, and a fanatical and irrational association develops between the dictator and his followers.

THE FIRST COMPONENT OF THE SPRINGBOARD MODEL: PERCEIVED THREATS AND THEIR CONSEQUENCES

In this section, I am concerned with threats that increase risk and lead to heightened uncertainty and psychological distress in a population. An impressive array of psychological theory and empirical research illuminates and supports the idea that people who feel uncertainty and threat tend to react by becoming more ethnocentric, intolerant of dissent, and supportive of ideologically orthodox leadership. Research programs that line up with this include the classic research of Stouffer (1955) and Sherif and his associates (Sherif, Harvey, White, Hood, & Sherif, 1961) as well as more recent research on the model of compensatory conviction (McGregor, Prentice, & Nash, 2009), uncertainty-identity theory (Hogg, 2007), right-wing authoritarianism (Altemeyer, 1988), the need to belong to groups and nations (Baron, Crawley, & Paulina, 2003; Staub, 1997), the need-for-closure model (Kruglanski, 2004), and the uncertainty management model (van den Bos, 2009). It is impressive that researchers from diverse theoretical perspectives and using different research methods have converged on this viewpoint (this is important for my thesis because these perceived threats and their consequences are one part of the springboard that under certain conditions can lead to dictatorship).

For example, whereas Billig (1982) illuminated the link between uncertainty with extremism through narrative analysis of human discourse, McGregor and his colleagues have examined how, through goal-regulation processes that humans share with dogs, pigeons, and other vertebrates, uncertainty and associated perceived threat can lead to religious extremism (McGregor, Haji, Nash, & Teper, 2008). According to this model, goal frustration can result in high-anxious uncertainty, and religious zeal is a path to cope with the arising discomfort. Whereas rats might adopt compulsive running or grooming to cope with such discomfort, humans adopt religious zeal. Although the interpretation of devotion to religious ideals after goal frustration as a way to reduce anxiety finds support among enlightened academics, fortunately McGregor does not have to have his research peer reviewed in Iran or Saudi Arabia—the fundamentalist regimes there would not be positively disposed to his viewpoint. Tackling uncertainty from a different perspective, Hogg (2007) argued that one way in which people attempt to escape the aversive feelings associated with uncertainty and threat is through self-categorization and identification with a group. Building on the identity tradition pioneered by Henri Tajfel, John Turner, and others, Hogg (2012) presented evidence to suggest that the anxiety-provoking experience of uncertainty can lead people to extremist groups.

A number of researchers looking at long-term evolutionary and historical evidence have also concluded that difficult, uncertain societal conditions are associated with gravitation toward ideologies that provide certainty. For example, surges in Judaism, Christianity, and Islam have tended to coincide with historical periods of uncertainty, disruption, and distress (Armstrong, 2000). Adopting an evolutionary perspective, I have argued that rapid industrialization, societal changes, and accelerating globalization have resulted in large scale "sudden contact" between groups with insufficient preadaptation. The psychological impact has included threatened collective identities, the rise of radicalization, extremism, terrorism, and support for strong, aggressive leadership (Moghaddam, 2006, 2008c). The accelerating pace of change, sudden contact, and the possibility of *catastrophic evolution*, the sudden decline or perceived possible ingroup extinction of particular human groups, has resulted in a greater sense of insecurity in many parts of the world (Moghaddam, 2010).

This contextual or situational approach follows the tradition of Milgram (1974), Zimbardo (2008), and others who presented evidence showing that under certain conditions even people with normal psychological characteristics can behave in extreme (and violent) ways. A different approach was adopted by Altemeyer (1988), Kruglanski (2004), and others who used individual difference measures (e.g., right-wing authoritarianism and need for closure) to show that some individuals are particularly likely to become more extremist in the face of uncertainty and threat, and that "certain personality types have a tendency to cope with a collective threat, one that involves high levels of uncertainty and induces various negative emotions, by expressing less tolerant, more rigid, and more punitive attitudes toward fellow individuals" (Merolla, Ramos, & Zechmeister, 2012, p. 212).

Uncertainty in the Direction of Political Change

There is some disagreement about the exact direction in which people change (see the discussions in Hogg & Blaylock, 2012): One group of researchers believes that uncertainty and threat necessarily result in a shift toward right-wing ideology (e.g., Jost et al., 2007), whereas other researchers argue that the shift could be toward identifying with extremist groups of the political left or right (e.g., Hogg, 2009). Once again, the available empirical research is extremely limited, and most of it has involved Western undergraduates as participants. It is questionable how much paper-and-pencil tests with undergraduate students in New York, Boston, London, and other such Western, relatively liberal cosmopolitan urban centers can tell researchers about the behaviors of ordinary people struggling to survive in dictatorships such as North Korea, Iran, Russia, China, and Saudi Arabia.

Historical experiences indicate that dictators can espouse ideologies of the political left or right, and people experiencing uncertainty and threat can end up "taking shelter" in the arms of extremist groups and dictators of the political left or right. Bullock's (1993) brilliant analysis of the parallel lives of Hitler and Stalin underlined this point. However, whether the public shifts to support the extreme political left or the extreme right depends on the local circumstances, cultural conditions, and the available leadership.

This point is illustrated by research conducted in the context of the Middle East conflict and studies on how Israelis have reacted to the *intifadas* (Arab word for uprisings) waged by Palestinians (Arian, Shamir, & Ventura, 1992; Shamir & Sagiv-Schifter, 2006). Public opinion in Israel after the first intifada (1987–1993) shifted to support more investment in military power and more aggressive policies toward the Palestinians (Arian et al., 1992), and the majority of Israelis thought the intifada would work in the favor of Likud, a right-wing Israeli political party. After the second intifada (2000), Shamir and Sagiv-Schifter (2006) assessed the results of five national surveys conducted in the early 2000s and concluded that "general political tolerance in Israel declined during the Intifada, while political tolerance toward Arabs declined even more, about twice as much" (p. 588).

Thus, in the Israeli context, increased external threat has resulted in greater intolerance among Israeli Jews and higher support for right-wing extremist leadership in line with the shift in public sentiments. In a context such as Cuba, the leadership of the Castro family and the Communists' domination of politics means that the rally-around-the-flag and ingroup cohesion resulting from uncertainty, insecurity, and threat, such as threat from the American military, is more likely to result in higher support for left-wing extremist leadership.

I have argued, then, that there is a link between perceived uncertainty and threat, on the one hand, and support for strong, aggressive leadership, on the other hand, This leadership can be extremist to the political left or right, and if a society is already not dictatorial, the probably of dictatorship increases in such conditions. But what kinds of uncertainty, insecurity, and threat are most important in creating the springboard to dictatorship? I start by considering economic and political instability, assessing the role of external and internal threats and the perception of impending ingroup decline.

Collective Economic and Political Insecurity and Relative Deprivation

In 1980, a series of events occurred while I was researching in Tehran that made life in Iran even more politically and economically unstable than it had been since the turbulent 1978–1979 revolution. The invasion of the American embassy in Tehran by pro-Khomeini activists and the hostage-taking crisis that began in November 1979 had already created a lot of additional uncertainty, with rumors that there would be an American military attack to rescue the embassy hostages (an attack that eventually took place and failed, as I discuss later in this chapter and in Chapter 5). Additionally, the so-called Cultural Revolution launched by pro-Khomeini factions targeted academics, professionals, and university-educated people in general and forced the closure of all higher education institutions, which were seen as not being Islamic enough (whereas in Iran the Cultural Revolution targeted Islamic enemies, in China class enemies were targets during the Cultural Revolution; Chang & Halliday, 2005). The faculty and students were forced out of their university campuses with the avowed goal of helping them become educated in the real world. Then, in September 1980, the Iraqi military invaded Iran, and wild rumors spread that Tehran would soon be overtaken by marauding Iraqi soldiers. The value of the Iranian rial plummeted further, and there was a huge outflow of capital from Iran. Also, the brain drain out of Iran accelerated.

But in the midst of the confusion and uncertainty, the life-and-death threat posed by Iraq concentrated the minds of both the leaders and the masses in Iran (I am reminded of Dr. Samuel Johnson's remark that "when a man knows he is to be hanged in a fortnight, it concentrates his mind wonderfully"; Boswell, 1791/1980, p. 849), and a nationalist revival swept Tehran and the rest of the country. People of very different political persuasions, many of whom had been fighting one another in the postrevolution era, banded together to fight the Iraqi invaders. Millions of women, children, and men cooperated to fill buses with clothing, food, and all kinds of equipment to rush to the front, even though the exact location of the front was not clear to most Iranians.

Neighborhoods organized groups of men and supporting equipment and sent them rushing to the front in minivans. Most important, the members of different political factions—and there were many of these in Tehran at that time, ranging from the extreme left to the extreme right (although almost all of them have since been wiped out by the Islamic fundamentalists)—agreed to collaborate and pull as one to help the war effort. The extraordinary concentration of energies and support for the central government brought about during the 8-year war with Iraq meant that the central government became a stronger and far more expansive and intrusive force in society, crushing opposition voices in the name of the war effort. Those who dared oppose the Islamic fanatics who took over the government were accused of being traitors. Indeed, young men suspected of being part of anti-Khomeini forces were particularly likely to find themselves sent to the most dangerous part of the war front, never to return alive.

The 1980–1988 Iran–Iraq War intensified economic and political uncertainty in Iran, and it served the purposes of the pro-Khomeini movement because the external threat galvanized people and harnessed support for Khomeini's dictatorial rule. Again and again, researchers have found in such situations that societies experiencing serious economic and political uncertainty and threat turn to a savior who they hope will lead them out of the crisis. There is no doubt that the economic and political crises of the post-World War I era in Europe were in large part responsible for the rise of dictators in Germany and Italy as well as the increasing strength of fascism in a number of Western nations, including England, where Sir Oswald Mosely's Blackshirts held sway for a period in the 1930s (Blum, 1998, provided an excellent succinct discussion of the historical background to this period). Similarly, the turmoil of the World War I era enabled the Russian communists, who were numerically a relatively small group at the time, to grab the reins of power and eventually for Stalin to emerge to take on the role of savior.

Varieties of Relative Deprivation

My emphasis here is on perceptions and relative evaluations of the economic and political situation in society, rather than on the actual objective situation. I see relative deprivation, a concept that was first applied to interpret studies carried out during World War II (Stouffer, Suchman, De Vinney, Star, & Williams, 1949), as playing a particularly important role in the process through which people come to assessments about how well they are doing individually and collectively. Relative deprivation has been found to play an important role in a wide range of behavioral domains (H. J. Smith, Pettigrew, Pippin, & Bialosiewicz, 2012), including life satisfaction and health. For example, in organizations, satisfaction and well-being are influenced more by income rank in an organization than by absolute income (Brown, Gardner, Oswald, & Qian, 2008), and greater wealth inequalities have detrimental consequences for the health of those at the bottom of the societal status system (Marmot, 2004; Subramanyam, Kawachi, Berkman, & Subramanian, 2009). People feel and do better (in terms of health) when they earn \$5,000 in a society in which the top 1% earn \$100,000 on average than when they earn \$5,000 in a society in which the top 1% earn \$10,000,000 on average.

In his seminal study on relative deprivation, Runciman (1966) introduced the important distinction between *egoistic deprivation*—feeling relatively deprived because of one's own situation in a group, and *fraternal deprivation*—feeling relatively deprived because of the situation of one's ingroup in society. Fraternal deprivation has been found to be particularly predictive of support for collective action in the face of perceived injustices (Guimond & Dubé-Simard,

1983). But how does one explain revolutions such as the one in Iran in 1978–1979 when the 1973 oil price increases resulted in a huge boom to the Iranian economy? I was a student in England at the time and regularly visited Iran in the 1970s; the economy was rapidly expanding. Why did a revolution come about in an expanding economy? This gets at the heart of another paradox discussed by various researchers (J. C. Davies, 1974; Runciman, 1966): Revolutions often take place during periods of economic growth.

The key to this paradox seems to be feelings of relative deprivation arising out of rising expectations. A central psychological component of this process is the social comparisons people make (Corcoran, Crusius, & Mussweiler, 2011), particularly at the intergroup level (Taylor, Moghaddam, & Bellerose, 1989). In assessing their own situation, people make comparisons with particular others, but they also make comparisons with themselves as they expected to be. For example, Ahmed compares himself with particular others around him, but he also compares his situation with the situation he expected to have (as Lamiell, 2003, demonstrated, people often come to assess their situation by comparing themselves to the persons they could be). When what Ahmed expected to have is far better than what he actually has—for example, he expected to be driving a new car but is instead taking the bus—he feels relatively deprived. Leaders can manipulate feelings of relative deprivation by influencing the social comparisons people make.

Manipulating Relative Deprivation

In Iran during the 1970s, expectations were rising faster than actual income, so that feelings of deprivation grew despite improving standards of living. The Shah and his cronies actually speeded up this process by suggesting that Iran was becoming the Switzerland of the Middle East. This was a fatal mistake because rising expectations among Iranians resulted in discontent with the Shah's regime. In contrast, Khomeini seemed to have a natural instinct for dealing with such situations when he came to power. Instead of trying to meet expectations, or raise expectations with lofty promises, he dramatically lowered expectations after the revolution.

This was a reversal of course because before the revolution, Khomeini had raised expectations and highlighted how Iranians were deprived and how the Shah's regime was failing to provide adequate services to the Iranian population. In taped speeches that were smuggled into Iran and circulated widely (I personally listened to a number of these tapes), Khomeini made exciting promises about how living conditions would improve for Iranians after the revolution and how they would receive free government services and enjoy a higher standard of living (these early, prerevolution speeches have been wiped clean from the postrevolution records within Iran).

But after the revolution and the consolidation of his monopoly on power, Khomeini radically changed his message: This world is of no value, and material things are worthless! We must strive to please God and only think of our fate in the next world! The material life is not of value; we must dedicate ourselves to the spiritual life! By dramatically lowering expectations about material conditions and living standards in this material world, Khomeini shifted the discourse and lowered expectations among Iranians.

External Enemies

> Be it thy course to busy giddy minds
> With foreign quarrels (Shakespeare, *Henry IV*)

There is a long history of the presence of an external threat being magnified and used by those who want to establish or to continue or to expand dictatorship. As the king advises his heir in Shakespeare's *Henry IV*, "giddy minds" can be kept occupied with "foreign quarrels." This external threat can be real, but it can also be manufactured and manipulated by would-be dictators. Even when the threat is real, what matters most is how it is subjectively interpreted. Irrespective of the real or imagined nature of the threat, the message conveyed to the general population is, "A dangerous enemy is at our gates and intends to attack and destroy us; we cannot afford to have dissent and disunity at home." A function of an external threat has been to help achieve a number of goals that strengthen prodictatorship causes. These goals include keeping national attention focused on external threats (and not being distracted by internal problems), allowing authorities to crack down on internal critics, and also increasing support for the restriction of freedoms and the establishment of a more closed society. This last goal is related to a trend that is vitally important for the ambitions of extremist, authoritarian leaders: External threat tends to result in greater support for strong, aggressive leadership.

The idea that external threat leads to internal cohesion is associated with a functionalist tradition of intergroup relations (e.g., Coser, 1956). In his classic realistic conflict field studies, Sherif (1973) demonstrated that as boys went through the transition from group formation to intergroup competition to intense intergroup conflict, their support for aggressive leadership also increased. When the conservative British politician Margaret Thatcher was in trouble and likely to lose the next national elections, the so-called Falklands effect came to her help. The invasion of the Falklands Islands, which were under British protection, by the Argentine military in 1982 galvanized the British public, and Thatcher found herself winning another general election in 1983. President George W. Bush had lackluster public support during his initial period of presidency, but immediately after the 9/11 terrorist attacks the

American public "rallied around the flag" and gave President Bush enormous support. Malici (2005) showed that as long as France and Britain shared a common perception of terrorist threats after 9/11, they remained in the Bush-led coalition, but once their perceptions of the external threat diverged, they stopped their collaboration (France did not participate in the U.S.-led invasion of Iraq in 2003).

A shared perception of external threat and imminent danger is often associated with diversion away from problems and divisions internal to the group. But, of course, this does not mean that war can be best explained as a diversionary tactic (Levy, 1989) or that external threat reliably results in internal cohesion: A necessary condition is that all the main groups perceive the threat as also directed at them (Stein, 1976). When only a section of society sees the threat as directed at them, cohesion does not result.

In the 21st century, a number of dictatorships in smaller non-Western countries have used the United States as an external threat, the sole superpower of the world intent on crushing independent countries such as Iran, North Korea, and Cuba. Positioning the United States as the external threat has been made possible by the history of the United States in each of these countries. In the case of Iran, in 1953 the United States intervened to overthrow the only democratically elected government in the country's history and helped to reestablish the dictatorship of Mohammed Reza Shah (de Bellaigue, 2012). The United States helped South Korea in the 1950–1953 war against North Korea and has maintained trade embargoes against the latter. In the case of Cuba, since Spain lost Cuba as a colony after the Spanish—American War in 1898, the United States supported a series of corrupt dictators, most recently Fulgencio Batista (1901–1973), and then pressured the communist state, overtly and covertly. Thus, it has not been difficult for Iran, North Korea, and Cuba to target the United States as an external enemy.

It is in the Iranian dictatorship that one finds the most consistent and creative use of the United States as external threat. The Shah was identified by just about all Iranians as an American puppet, but it was Ayatollah Khomeini who took the lead in focusing on the United States as the external threat by labeling America and Israel as the "Great Satan" and the "Little Satan," respectively. Throughout the months and days leading up to the actual overthrow of the Shah, Khomeini (who had taken refuge in Paris) repeatedly warned that the United States was plotting and interfering in Iran. During the spring of revolution in 1979, I was back in Tehran and witnessed repeated warnings that the Americans were interfering to bring back the deposed dictator Shah or his son.

All of these explicit warnings and implicit rumors about American plots against the revolution, with repeated reminders of what antidemocratic

American interventions had done in Iran and other revolutionary countries in the past, resulted in an atmosphere of near hysteria. Both pro- and anti-revolution forces were expecting an American intervention any time soon. The American embassy in Tehran, as well as all pro-American companies and individuals, were the center of much suspicion. Almost every evening, there would be new allegations against the Great Satan. It was in this atmosphere that on November 4, 1979, a group of hotheads, mostly students, climbed over the walls of the American embassy in Tehran and launched the 455-day hostage-taking crisis during the presidency of Jimmy Carter (this is discussed further in Chapter 5). The hostage-taking crisis served the cause of the religious fanatics in a number of ways, the most important being that it put the spotlight directly on the United States as external threat number one.

Despite all of their efforts to avoid being positioned as Iran's number one enemy, the Carter administration fell deeper and deeper into the trap set for them by the religious fanatics who had grabbed the reins of power in Iran. The climax of the calamitous policies followed by the Carter administration was the enormous folly of attempting to rescue the American hostages on April 24, 1980 (Operation Eagle Claw). Apparently, the idea had been to land American troops in a stadium across the road from the American embassy in Tehran, then storm the embassy and rescue the hostages. During the time of this ill-conceived rescue attempt, I awoke one day in my home in Tehran to hear news about American helicopters having been brought crashing to the ground in the deserts of Iran. It was through divine intervention, according to the government officials in Iran. At the time, residents initially dismissed the reports as Iranian government propaganda. After all, no one could believe that the Carter administration would attempt to implement a rescue plan that was so seriously flawed in just about every possible way. The failed rescue mission had given the fanatics what they needed: proof that the United States was plotting to intervene militarily in Iran. The fanatics felt justified in cracking down on dissenting voices even harder after this point.

During the time of the hostage-taking crisis, I used to drive past the American embassy in Tehran almost daily, and it was clear that enormous numbers of religious fanatics guarded the building night and day. The hostages would have been killed before any rescuers could get to them. Second, the location of the stadium and the American embassy in a central, heavily populated, well-guarded location meant that the rescuers were likely to be captured, even if they had managed to land in the stadium across the road from the embassy. Third, the fact that several of the helicopters crashed into each other in a sandstorm suggests that the American planners did not even have enough information about local conditions at the initial landing location.

Of course, the tactic of magnifying external threat to create internal cohesion and support for the leader is also used in democracies. For example, leaders in the United States have sometimes used external threats to limit access to information as well as to decrease the means by which opposition voices can veto leadership policies (Gibler, 2010). The rally-around-the-flag tendency means that following increased external threat, the American public supports more hawkish foreign policies as well as more restrictive policies at home. It is not so much that those high on authoritarianism become more so but that ordinary Americans take on a more authoritarian behavioral style (Hetherington & Suhay, 2011).

Internal Enemies

All dictatorships attempt to crush internal opposition and end basic liberties, but there is considerable variation with respect to the dynamic relationship dictatorships work out between external and internal threats. For example, in Nazi Germany, the focus of Hitler and his followers was first to destroy all internal opposition forces and silence all domestic critics and only then embark on wars with external enemies. Similarly, throughout the Long March and the struggle for power of the 1930s and during much of the 1950s and 1960s, Mao's intent was first and foremost to gain absolute control of all that went on within Chinese society. The external threats of capitalist America and subversive Soviet Union, which from Mao's perspective had deviated from the true Marxist path, were treated as secondary to the challenge of gaining absolute internal control through continual revolution. In contrast, in Iran and North Korea, the main tactic of dictatorship has been to use external threat (of a supposed international conspiracy spearheaded by the United States) to both mobilize the internal base and crush the internal opposition.

The peculiar dynamic between internal and external threat is best understood within the cultural–historical context and particular leadership of each dictatorship. For example, the priority Hitler and the Nazi movement gave to wiping out internal threats derives from their interpretation of why Germany was defeated in World War I and had to suffer a humiliating peace treaty. Hitler believed that German defeat in World War I had been as much a result of internal traitors as it had been at the hands of external enemies. According to this interpretation, while the best Germans sacrificed their lives on the front lines during World War I, traitors of all kinds profited from the war back home. To ensure that this treachery was not repeated, Hitler ordered extreme repression and mass executions of subversives back home during World War II.

The most important groups targeted as internal threats have been deviants, and those who are different from societal norms. As a religious minority, Jews have been prime targets in many dictatorships, including Nazi Germany, the

Soviet Union, and of course Iran and other Islamic dictatorships. Authorities have been able to target Jews and other minorities mainly because of two sets of factors. First, in many instances the persecution and expulsion of minorities has resulted in short-term material gains for some majority group members, as when minority group members are forced to abandon their belongings and flee for their lives. For example, this was the fate of some, although certainly not all, Zoroastrians, Bahais, Jews, and Armenians in Iran after the revolution. Second, the targeting of minorities is made possible by normative factors: Dissimilar others can be more easily positioned as a threat; this is because at both the intergroup level and the interpersonal level, people tend to be more positively disposed toward more similar others (Osbeck, Moghaddam, & Perreault, 1997).

Perceived Impending Decline, Collective Helplessness, and Lack of Trust

> For Italy, being the least of the great powers remained a vexing fate. Bureaucrats in the colonial ministry had entertained themselves during the war with extravagant expansionist "plans" for the nation to take over not just all of East Africa but the Portuguese colonies and a great deal of Turkey into the bargain. (Bosworth, 2006, p. 91)

World War I had raised images of the glorious past, the Roman Empire, in the minds of some Italians, and the reality of the 1920s was a bitter struggle. Raised expectations brought into sharp relief the actual situation in the post–World War I era in Italy: political and economic fragility and the sense that things should be a lot better than they were. The atmosphere in Germany at the time was in key respects similar; most people "were weary of the Weimar experiment in democracy, with the endless elections, the countless demonstrations and lawlessness in the streets, the long lines before the welfare offices, and the scale of the social chaos" (Gellately, 2001, p. 10). The 1929 global financial crisis intensified the sense of decline and helplessness, and the state of the German economy became disastrous:

> Over the winter of 1931–2, bankruptcies began to eat away at the fabric of German business. After the summer crisis of 1931, all the major banks were under state control. There were spectacular failures in the insurance and the engineering industries. (Tooze, 2006, p. 22)

In the crucial period immediately after the collapse of the Shah's dictatorship in Iran in 1979, there was initially a feeling of exhilaration and excitement, but parallel to this there grew a sense of instability, lawlessness, and chaos. All government officials, including the prime minister and cabinet members, had the designation *temporary* attached to their titles, there seemed to be nobody ready to take responsibility, and the police acted hesitantly—and sometimes not at all—to stop lawbreakers. Entire streets in Tehran were illegally overtaken by stall vendors of various kinds, and anytime the authorities attempted to stop traffic violators they were met with jeers and shouts of "We had a revolution to be free." The students who returned to universities in 1979—many of them had not been able to take regular classes for several years because of revolutionary disruptions—were not ready to accept the authority of the university administration and faculty. I remember almost every student received an A that first semester because professors dared not give anyone a lower grade. I witnessed several final examinations in which students demanded (and received) a different, easier set of exam questions, ones they could answer! Of course, the better students recognized that this was unfair to them because in the chaos of postrevolution Iran their superior performance was not being recognized.

The same general sense of instability and lawlessness can be found prior to the rise of many dictators, including Napoleon, recognized by many historians as a precursor to modern dictators (Rowe, 2009). Terror and counterterror created havoc in postrevolutionary France at the end of the 18th century:

> Republican officials; army officers; members of departmental administrations; conspicuous militants of the popular societies; and, in the south, Protestant farmers and merchants—all became prey for the *sabreurs* of the year III. Corpses were dumped in front of cafés and inns in the Midi or thrown into the Rhone or Saône. In many areas, the Counter-Terrorists would gather together at an inn as if for the day's hunting, and go off in search of their quarry. (Schama, 1989, p. 852)

The chaos that follows major disasters of all kinds, from earthquakes and other natural disasters to terrorist attacks and wars, creates an opportunity bubble for leaders to exert themselves (Moghaddam & Breckenridge, 2011), and in some instances dictators can spring to power in these situations to fill the power vacuum.

Threatened Collective Identity

Perhaps the factor that has the most important role in creating the springboard to dictatorship is a collective sense of threat to the ingroup identity. Again, this is a subjective experience based on perceived and not necessarily actual threat. The question of identity is often misunderstood as asking, Who am I? Of course, this is not the question of identity because (if for some reason I need to) I can immediately determine who I am by looking at my driving license. A person who asks, Who am I? is probably experiencing memory loss or has some other serious cognitive impairment. On the other hand, a person who asks, What sort of person am I? and What sort of group do I belong to? is addressing the issue of identity.

Since the 1970s, identity has become a central topic of psychological research through an experimental program pioneered by Henri Tajfel, John Turner, and their students (see Moghaddam, 2008c, Chapter 5). Tajfel's group began with an intriguing empirical finding that merely categorizing individuals on the basis of what objectively is a trivial criterion can result in intergroup bias and ingroup favoritism (Tajfel, Flament, Billig, & Bundy, 1971). Thus, even when all Joe knows is that he is in Group X and some other unidentified individuals are in Group Z on the basis of a trivial criterion (e.g., a dot-estimation task), and he does not and will not know the identity of others in the ingroup and outgroup or the reason he is allocating points or what the points mean and the points he allocates do not accrue to himself, he still has a tendency to allocate more points to himself. Social identity theory (Tajfel & Turner, 1979) interpreted these findings by proposing that humans are motivated to achieve a positive and distinct identity, and they will adopt a variety of individual and collective strategies to achieve this goal and to respond to threats to the thwarting of this goal. An impressive body of research has endorsed and elaborated this viewpoint (Abrams & Hogg, 2010; Postmes & Jetten, 2006).

Subsequent research has shown that threats to collective identity are particularly important because of the dependence of individual identity on collective identity. Threats to collective identity can result in a range of reactions, from a sense of helplessness and decline to radicalization and violent actions (Breakwell, 1986; Moghaddam, 2008c; D. Rothbart & Korostelina, 2006; Taylor, 2002). The significance of threats to collective identity become clear when one considers situations in which *sacred carriers* representing the ingroup are threatened (Moghaddam, 2002). For example, the Islamic veil worn by women in some countries is only a piece of cloth, as is the American flag (Old Glory), but both pieces of cloth serve as sacred carriers and have defenders who are willing to lay down their lives to prevent their desecration (this is discussed in more detail in Chapter 5, this volume). Threats to collective identity also play a central role in setting up the springboard to dictatorship: The perception that one's ingroup is seriously threatened and in decline can be associated with collective helplessness. In desperation, people in this situation can end up supporting dictators who come in the shape of saviors, from Hitler to 21st-century dictator saviors.

Thus, the first set of factors that help create the springboard to dictatorships tend to magnify threat, instability, and relative deprivation. I now turn to a second set of factors, situational in nature, that help further complete the construction of the springboard.

THE SECOND COMPONENT OF THE SPRINGBOARD MODEL: SITUATIONAL FACTORS SUPPORTIVE OF DICTATORSHIP AS THE SOLUTION

The springboard to dictatorship is also created through the influence of a number of situational factors, including the support of important elites, institutions, and bureaucracies as well as crisis incidents. The potential dictator can play a pivotal role in bringing these factors into play, for example, by courting the support of resourceful elites and helping to bring about crisis incidents.

Elites Supporting Dictatorship

All governments reflect a tension between "the will of the people" and "decisions by leaders on behalf of the people." In genuine democracies, this tension is addressed through regular, free, and fair elections so that the people get to choose their political leaders. Of course, there are enormous challenges in democracies, such as when voter turnout and trust in government is low (as it is in the United States at the start of the 21st century). Although free and fair elections for important political offices are not held in dictatorships, dictators do use other means to try to show that they are supported by the people. For example, rigged national and local elections are held in which people are coerced to participate (as in Russia and Iran), and mass demonstrations of support for the Great Leader are held in which people "spontaneously" express their deep feelings of love for the Great Leader (as in North Korea, when in December 2011 the Great Leader died and his son, the Great Successor, took the reins of power). Although dictators are for certain periods of time able to coerce mass expressions of support, they can only do so through support from key elites. Similarly, elite support is necessary for dictatorship to spring to power in the first place.

Two theories are particularly useful in understanding the role of the elite in the springing to power of a dictator. Pareto's (1935) elite theory, which was discussed in Chapter 1 of this volume, and in some respects follows the tradition set by Nicollò Machiavelli (1469–1527), is particularly applicable. From Pareto's perspective, the dictator will be challenged by talented counterelite members who are first and foremost motivated to move up the social hierarchy individually and join the ruling elite. However, if talented members of the counterelite are not permitted to move up individually, they will rabble rouse and help to mobilize the nonelite masses. This collective mobilization could lead to a revolution and the toppling of the current dictatorship. Thus, to maintain power, the ruling dictator must allow talented individuals to rise up individually and join the ruling elite.

From Pareto's (1935) perspective, the dictator springs to power through the support of counterelites, and his demise comes about when social mobility is blocked, talented potential elite members are prevented from moving up, and a new counterelite mobilizes the masses to revolution. Case studies of the demise of dictators show that another factor is competition between members of the existing elite. For example, Grafton and Rowlands (1996) pointed out that the Duvalier dictatorship in Haiti collapsed not so much because of popular movements "but from fellow members of the elite seeking a larger share of the spoils of power" (p. 267).

The role of the elite, as discussed by Pareto (1935), is similar to Marx's idea of the vanguard of revolution, people who tend to be from the middle and upper classes but use their intellectual and other resources to organize and lead the proletariat to revolution. Resource mobilization theory (discussed in Chapter 1, this volume) places even greater emphasis on the role of the elite in helping the dictator to power because from this theoretical perspective a collective movement becomes possible only when people with material, intellectual, and other resources support the movement (McCarthy & Zald, 1977). Resource mobilization theory proposes that psychological feelings of discontent, deprivation, and dissatisfaction generally can be manufactured through resources—just as the "need" for a new perfume, dress fabric, hair style, or any other product is manufactured through resources invested in marketing.

Thus, dictatorships come about and are sustained in key respects through the activities of elites: First, elites sustain dictatorships by providing strategic and resource support; second, elites bring about revolutions and changes in dictatorship regimes by organizing and leading mass revolts.

Institutions That Support a Dictatorial System

As I review the progress of the Arab Spring, the phrase that most immediately comes to mind is, Le Roi est mort, vive le Roi! ("The King is dead, long live the King!"). One by one, the dictators in Tunisia, Egypt, and Libya were toppled, but after the revolution little seems to have changed. For example, early in 2012, Doctors Without Borders found that torture is continuing in Libya, but now it is the revolutionaries who are torturing supporters and members of the former dictatorship (Worthington, 2012). In Tunisia and Egypt, the draconian laws set by dictators might be changed, but the new rulers seem to be set on implementing Sharia law, which will be a serious setback for democracy and particularly for minorities and women. In explaining why it is so difficult to progress beyond dictatorship, it is important to keep in mind the role played by certain institutions that support dictatorship.

All major 21st-century societies began as dictatorships and have at their roots institutions and practices that potentially support dictatorship. This includes the societies of North America, which began as British colonies ruled by monarchs across the Atlantic Ocean. Although in some situations, such as Poland in the 1980s, the church can play an antidictatorship role, the historical influence of organized religion, particularly Christianity and Islam, has been in support of dictatorship. Devoutly religious people often find themselves asking the kinds of questions raised in Mario Vargas Llosa's (2000) novel *The Feast of the Goat* about the dictatorship of Rafael Trujillo (1891–1961) in the Dominican Republic in 1930–1961: "Why did the Church of Christ support a regime stained with blood? How could the Church shelter with its moral authority a leader who committed abominable crimes?" (p. 181). Even when organized religion has been instrumental in destroying one dictatorship, as happened in Iran in 1978–1979, the nature of organized religion is such that it often supports the reestablishment of dictatorship in another shape, as happened in Iran after 1979. This is because in organized religion and dictatorship the same priorities are endorsed by authorities: absolute obedience based on faith in a Supreme Being or Supreme Leader, acceptance of certain truths without objective proof, and willingness to forgo questioning and research outside of a framework provided by authorities.

For similar reasons, the military is another institution rooted in dictatorship and potentially always a force for reestablishing dictatorship in countries that have progressed to democracy. There are certain periods in history and certain situations in which the military has been a liberal force relative to the conservatism of political institutions and the general population, such as in the case of the Israeli military in the 1970s, but historically the military has acted as a prodictatorship force. Indeed, the quintessential dictatorships in South America for much of the 20th century involved a marriage of the church and the military.

The Arab Spring has reinvigorated organized religion and placed it in an advantageous situation relative to the military in many Arab societies. This is because Mubarak (Egypt), Bin Ali (Tunisia), Qaddafi (Libya), and other recent dictators have relied heavily on the military and wiped out all secular opposition groups within their societies but did not have the power to close down mosques (just as Eastern Bloc communist regimes never achieved the power needed to shut down religious activities prior to the collapse of the USSR). As a result, opposition forces could only use mosques as their sanctuaries and bases, and subsequently the antidictatorship revolutions of the Muslim world have taken on a religious character. This is what took place in Iran: The secular opposition to the dictatorship of the Shah was wiped out in the 1950s and 1960s, with the result that the only place for the opposition to gather and organize was the mosque, which the dictator Shah could not close down. As a result, the anti-Shah revolution had a religious leadership and character, and secular politicians had almost no organization to compete with the mosque-based movement of Khomeini's followers.

Hierarchies of Dictatorships and Cultural Traditions
That Support Dictatorship

In her analysis of corruption and government, Rose-Ackerman (1999) paid particular attention to *kleptocracy* in which "corruption is organized at the top of government" (p. 114), pointing out that "corrupt rulers will support policies that produce personalized gains even if they result in lower overall social wealth" (p. 115). I agree that the main motivation of dictators is to retain power, irrespective of whether the overall social wealth suffers. However, in such systems there must be some relative benefit for *little dictators* if they are to continue to support the Supreme Dictator. Although the Supreme Dictator ignores overall social wealth, he cannot ignore the interests of the rest of the ruling elite and the factions, particularly the security services, that support his rule.

Dictatorial tendencies are replicated in hierarchies of dictatorships so that in the family, the school, the office, the work group, and at many different levels little dictators can thrive. Whereas the major dictators must gain power over the state, little dictators need only gain power at the small-group level. Thus, although my primary concern in this text is with the state as a unit, in order to better understand the dictatorial state, because this state tends to nurture and function through a strong hierarchy of dictatorships, I also concern myself with little dictatorships.

The relationship between the elite power group and local dictators is illustrated by the case of two controversies in China in 2012, the first involving the former Communist Party politburo member Bo Xilai and the second, the blind dissident lawyer Chen Guangcheng (Richburg, 2012). The case of Bo Xilai illustrates how a rabble-rousing provincial leader will be tolerated and even encouraged up the hierarchy of the national system despite widely circulating stories of the little dictator's corruption. What forced the central Chinese authorities to take action to control Bo Xilai was that his former right-hand man, Wang Lijun, took refuge in one of the U.S. consulates in China and retold tales of corruption and possible murder of a British businessman by Bo's wife. The mistreatment of Chen Guangcheng by local authorities was highlighted by the world news media when he managed to escape house arrest and take refuge in the U.S. embassy in China. Clearly, the central authorities already knew of his mistreatment by local officials when Bo advertised his plight after escaping house arrest, but it serves the purposes of central authorities to use little dictators to crack down on dissidents and keep order.

Hierarchies of dictatorship can thrive even in subsections of democratic societies and serve as a part of the potential for dictatorship that always threatens democracies. Even within the largest contemporary democracies, there are subcultures that are dominated by hierarchies of dictatorships with numerous little dictators. Some such cases involve colorful and well-documented little dictators, such as the long-term FBI director J. Edgar Hoover (1895–1972), who wielded extraordinary power within the bureau and in the larger American society (Gentry, 2001). Another example is Huey Long (1893–1935), the populist governor of Louisiana (1928–1932) and U.S. senator (1932–1935), who enjoyed supreme control in Louisiana until his assassination in 1935 (LeVert, 1995). But in most cases the little dictators work anonymously within gray bureaucracies.

The influence of the little dictators is in the continuation of narratives and cultural traditions at the micro level, often below the radar of national and even regional concern. For example, the little dictator father raises his child in an authoritarian manner and in this way is likely to pass on some features of authoritarianism to the next generation. The little dictator in an organization such as the FBI sets into place patterns of behavior that continue to survive as "the way we do things around here" for many decades after his actual departure.

Bureaucracies and Dictatorships

> If bureaucracies can run off on their own in a democracy, then they can really "fly" in a communist system. For here the bureaucrats are safe from exposure, questioning, and criticism unless the leaders of the party apparatus turn against them. However . . . Why should the party deal harshly with the basis of its power? (Ryavec, 2003, p. 92)

Ryavec's (2003) insightful analysis of the runaway nature of bureaucracy in a communist system can be extended to dictatorships in general. His analysis was specifically focused on the USSR, a communist system that never really progressed beyond the historical stage of development known in communist ideology as "the dictatorship of the proletariat" (in the case of the Soviet Union, the proletariat were not well represented by their dictators!) in which a vanguard group would govern as dictators on behalf of the proletariat. Thus, Ryavec's analysis was focused on a dictatorship that used the ideology of communism to justify dictatorial rule and developed an extensive bureaucracy to enable that rule. However, I argue that all national dictatorships necessarily develop and sustain a vast and tangled bureaucracy and nurture *bureaucratization*, the arbitrary use of rules and regulations to organize and pattern behavior in organizations, with the ultimate goal of protecting the dictator and other members of those organizations. Indeed, the bureaucratization of everyday life is among the most profound psychological influences and foundations of dictatorial regimes.

First I consider how bureaucratization comes about in dictatorships. Of course, bureaucratization is found to some degree in all large modern societies, but the extent is far greater in dictatorships. This is mainly because in more open societies the users of bureaucratic services, the ordinary citizens, can give critical feedback and can express their level of satisfaction with the services received. Local newspapers, Internet blogs, radio call-in shows—there are multiple ways in which ordinary people can get the word out about the services provided by a bureaucracy. Of course, such checks on the power and efficiency of bureaucracies are not completely successful even in the most open democracies. Despite such limitations, the critical feedback provided by ordinary people ensures some level of accountability and a higher probability of improvement in services. But such checks are almost completely missing in dictatorships because dictators do not allow an open critical assessment of any major section of society for fear that criticism would spread to other sectors.

A common feature of dictatorships is that they have a zero-tolerance policy against anyone criticizing the regime and its associates, including the bureaucracy. Because of the lack of openness and information about how things work and who is supposed to do what in dictatorships, it is far more difficult to actually criticize bureaucrats. A complaint about bureaucratic inefficiency can quickly be repositioned by bureaucrats into a political threat and an attack against the regime (I expand on this point in Chapter 5).

On several trips I took in the mid 1970s, it was normal for the police in Eastern Bloc countries to stop cars with foreign plates and fabricate an excuse to demand a fine, a bribe actually, so one could be left alone (of course, the local inhabitants suffered far greater punishments if they failed to conform with the corruption). In one incident in Yugoslavia, when I tried to complain at the police station, my local contacts refused to help for fear of reprisals, and my complaints were dismissed with threats of harsher reprisals if I persisted. It becomes much easier to simply conform and accept the corruption and inefficiency because to do otherwise is to risk persecution.

Crisis Incidents

> On 27 February (1933) the Reichstag in Berlin was set on fire by a young Dutchman of extreme left-wing opinions. Using this as a pretext to claim that Germany was threatened by a Bolshevik coup, Hitler issued a presidential decree "for the Protection of the People and the State." For many years this was to be one of the main foundations of Nazi tyranny. It swept away constitutional safeguards against arbitrary arrest and the suppression of free speech. A wave of arrests followed. (A. J. Nicholls, 1997, p. 45)

I have emphasized the role of the springboard to dictatorship and proposed that there are always potential dictators in society, but what makes a dictatorship possible is the availability of a springboard that a potential dictator can use. However, some potential dictators are more capable than others in helping to bring to life the springboard and in using it to grab power. One of the key characteristics that differentiates between potential dictators who come to power and those who do not is the ability to construct and use crisis incidents, such as the Reichstag incident used by Hitler in 1933 (there is some debate as to whether the young Dutchman of extreme left-wing opinions acted alone or whether the Nazis played some role in setting the fire) and the hostage-taking crisis used by Khomeini in 1979—1980 (discussed in more detail in Chapter 5, this volume).

In this chapter, I have discussed how the personality of the leader becomes more influential in situations with greater degrees of freedom. The uncertainty, unpredictability, and flux that characterize crises such as the Reichstag fire incident in Germany in 1933 and the hostage-taking incident in Iran in 1980 are associated with very high degrees of freedom and present exceptionally good opportunities for a leader's personality to exert influence. Even more extreme examples of this are found in societies engulfed in large-scale and longer term crises, such as the expulsion of most educated civilians from cities by Pol Pot's Khmer Rouge in the 1970s in Cambodia, the Great Leap Forward of the late 1950s in China, and the Cultural Revolution of the 1960s also in China. One interpretation of Mao's "perpetual revolution" is that it was intended to create a perpetual crisis with large degrees of freedom in which the leader could exert maximum influence.

THE DICTATOR SPRINGS TO POWER

The creation of the springboard to dictatorship provides potential dictators the opportunity to spring to power. There are always potential dictators in every context, but the situational demands present opportunities to potential dictators with particular characteristics. These situational demands are often linked to wider macro processes outside a particular country. For example, the intervention of major world powers, particularly the United States and Russia, has ensured the emergence, continuation, and/or end of particular dictatorships. During 2012, Bashar Assad was given the green light by Russia and China and was receiving material and other support from Iran to continue to kill Syrian civilians who were demonstrating to end the Assad dictatorship (Russia and China vetoed a United Nations resolution condemning Assad for his continued attacks on the Syrian civilian population). Bashar inherited his position as dictator from his father, Hafez Assad, who grabbed power in 1970 and killed tens of thousands of civilians to maintain his iron grip on power. Currently, the United States and its allies continue to support another set of dictators, the Saudi royal family.

Availability of Charismatic Dictator

Potential dictators are not equal in their ability to help manufacture and take advantage of the springboard to dictatorship; some are superior in their abilities to spring to power. What are the hallmarks of the successful potential dictators? What enables them to become actual dictators? A great deal of attention has been given by psychologists, historians, and others to the personality of dictators (as discussed earlier in this text). Gilbert (1950), author of the only other book titled *The Psychology of Dictatorship*, focused on the personalities of four Nazi leaders whom he came to know in person through his work as a psychologist to the court at the Nuremberg Trials (Gilbert, 1947/1995). Like some other psychologists who in the postwar era looked for answers to explain the horrors of World War II (e.g., Adorno, Frenkel-Brunswik, Levinson, & Sanford, 1950), Gilbert (1950) relied on psychodynamic interpretations (using concepts such as suppression, authoritarianism, paranoia) to explain the personality of Nazi leaders. Freudian ideas have also influenced historians in their case studies of dictators, but in his monumental parallel case studies of Hitler and Stalin, Bullock (1993) expressed skepticism about projects that place heavy emphasis on such interpretations of dictators. However, he did see value in particular insights, such as the idea that both Hitler and Stalin were high on *narcissism*, a state in which only the needs, feelings, wishes, and so on of the person are real (Bullock, 1993).

Rather than rely on a psychodynamic approach, modern research focuses more on the cognitive and personality styles of the dictator. For example, researchers might describe dictators in terms of their closedmindedness (Kruglanski, 2004) and their rejection of an open society (Altemeyer, 1988). But there are countless individuals high on narcissism, closedmindedness, and other psychological characteristics that supposedly mark the personalities of Hitler, Stalin, and other dictators. How does one explain the amazing success achieved by some dictators in springing to power? I argue that there is a symbiotic relationship between the dictator and the springboard he helps to construct, and it is this relationship that enables the spring to power to take place.

Shared Moral Mission for Revival

The coming to power and continuation of dictatorship are fueled by a launching of a moral mission, which serves particularly to motivate the ruling elite, keep them cohesive, and justify the punishments against dissenters, with the severest punishments being reserved for dissenters within the ruling elite itself. As Arendt (2004) pointed out, the totalitarian movement involves perpetual motion, so the moral mission is constantly shifting and everyone, particularly members of the power elite, has to keep alert to keep strictly in line with the latest changes. The moral mission can take on many different forms, from the Nazi ideology of the revival of the master race to the holy moral crusade of Stalin in the name of the people to Mao's perpetual revolution to maintain the purity of the people's revolution to the religious crusades of Khomeini and other Islamic dictators and would-be dictators.

The moral crusade is spread through the power of narratives, propagated through the education system and mass media. For this reason, dictators insist on total control of educational institutions and the mass media and come crashing down on resistance. The cultural revolutions spearheaded by Mao in China in the late 1960s and by Khomeini in Iran in the early 1980s were seen as necessary because the education systems and the intellectuals in Iran and China were not serving their proper roles as the ruling dictators demanded these roles be. In both cases, universities and important schools were emptied of professors and students, and there was an attempt to "reeducate" them according to the principles of the moral crusade.

The constantly changing nature of the moral crusade tends to be toward greater and greater radicalization, so that tests for purity and inclusiveness become more and more stringent. As a result, there is a continuous weeding out of impure elements from within the power elite, and to outsiders this seems like the revolution is eating its own children. The revolutionaries of yesterday are always in danger of being branded impure and cast out of the leadership, with dire consequences for themselves and their families. In Stalin's case, the purges were so drastic that very few of the original revolutionary leaders of Lenin's era survived. The same is happening in Iran, where even those who served in the highest offices of the land under Khomeini (e.g., Hussein Mousavi, former prime minister, and Akbar Hashemi Rafsanjani, former president) have not been safe from persecution for having stepped outside the shifting and exacting ideology of the moral crusade.

In addition to serving its primary function of keeping the power elite cohesive and at the ready, the perpetual moral crusade serves to keep the rest of society on the move, unnerved, and less capable of organizing and mobilizing resistance. The constant harassment of the masses is enabled through the moral crusade, starting with children in schools as targets. These children are forced to pass ideological school tests, including the contents of important ideas condoned by the Supreme Dictator. In order for their children to gain entrance to universities, colleges, job openings, and opportunities for advancement in general, parents find they have to support their children as they try to succeed in the continually changing ideological tests. Even when parents themselves oppose the moral crusade, they often find themselves helping their children to absorb the state-sponsored morality as a necessary step to survival in the dictatorship. Thus, many parents who despise dictatorships and who dream of achieving genuine democracy in countries such as Russia, China, Iran, and North Korea find themselves helping their children learn the ruling regime's version of truth and morality merely to try to open better opportunities for their children.

CONCLUDING COMMENT

I have argued that in terms of personality characteristics, such as narcissism, authoritarianism, and the like, there are potential dictators in every context (you probably know this from your experiences in work and school contexts!). Most of these potential dictators never realize their dictatorial potential, or at most they become little dictators within a subculture that supports them within a limited space. The coming into being and perpetuation of dictatorship at the national level requires a springboard from which the potential dictator can leap to the highest level of power. Once the springboard comes into being, there are always potential dictators ready to try to use it. But some potential dictators are particularly skilled at helping to create the springboard and using it to spring to power.

The springboard to dictatorship is helped into being by a number of characteristics that are still present in all societies because all contemporary societies, including the democracies of Western Europe and North America, began as dictatorships. Thus, the potential dictator finds natural allies in a number of deeply rooted institutions, the church and the military being the main ones, followed closely by the major business institutions. Within the springboard model, I identified other factors that help to create the springboard, and the relative importance of these factors may well vary across time and across contexts. Consistent across these factors is the proposition that context is of paramount importance, and to understand dictatorship one must look first and foremost to the socially constructed world out there, rather than to the characteristics of isolated individuals.

The springboard model leads one to look to collective meaning-making processes and the construction of a social reality that reinforces and perpetuates the hierarchy of dictatorship. Most important, the constructed social reality enables the power elite to maintain cohesion on the basis of a continually moving but identifiable ideology and through this cohesion to use brute force to subjugate the majority. This bidirectional action of absolute subservience to the Supreme Dictator's ideological line combined with the dictator's utter ruthlessness in enforcing obedience and conformity among the masses is a hallmark of dictatorship.

II

PSYCHOLOGICAL
PROCESSES IN
DICTATORSHIP:
THE HISTORICAL CONTEXT

All contemporary societies began as dictatorships and have within them the elements that could once again reproduce dictatorships in new, adapted forms. No society is immune from this danger. I have discussed sacred carriers as one means of sustaining continuity. For example, human sacred carriers such as the Emperor and physical sacred carriers such as Mount Fuji for long periods helped sustain continuity in Japanese dictatorship. They lie dormant now that Japan is a democracy, with the potential to germinate and recreate Japanese dictatorship in new forms.

However, it would be a grave mistake to envisage the potential for the reproduction of dictatorships as lying in individual psychology. For sure, the psychological characteristics of individuals are influential in how this potential for dictatorship is manifested, but the characteristics of individuals are in large part the outcomes of socialization processes and become realized in cultural contexts. It is to the larger societal conditions and characteristics that one must look to understand the potential for dictatorship.

The larger societal context and macro collective processes are already out there when individuals are born into this world, and they continue after people individually exit. This continuity often takes place across very long time periods, with little change to key components. For example, the hierarchical command structure of the military and the church have remained essentially unchanged over thousands of years. Both institutions continue to profoundly influence political and sociocultural life in the 21st century, even in democratic societies. Indeed, the role of the military in American life has increased and become more rather than less central since World War II, so that President Dwight Eisenhower's warnings about a military-industrial complex have come to fruition. Lasswell, Horowitz, and Stanley's (1997) prophetic discussions about the garrison state have been followed up by recent research (e.g., Bernazzoli, 2010) exploring how militarization and a siege mentality pervade the United States and many of its major institutions (Unger, 2012).

Whereas the roles of the church and the military are explicit in supporting dictatorships in states such as Iran and Saudi Arabia, the potential roles of these institutions in strengthening tendencies toward dictatorship, or even possibly one day reproducing dictatorship, are far more subtle in democracies such as the United States.

In Part II of the book, my focus is on psychological processes that play an important role in the emergence and continuation of dictatorship. The processes considered range from various cultural carriers that help to sustain collective narratives in support of dictatorship to seemingly individual-level processes such as displacement of aggression, conformity and obedience, coerced participation, leadership, and styles of thinking. I say *seemingly* because traditional research has assumed the source of such processes to be inside the individual. In reality, the source of such processes is out there in social relationships and the wider culture.

4

SACRED CARRIERS AND NARRATIVES: THE PUZZLE OF CONTINUITY IN DICTATORSHIPS

> Police have sealed off a southern Chinese village and cut its food supplies in an attempt to crush an uprising by villagers angered by government land seizures and the death of a man in police custody. . . . The protests in Guangdong province are part of a growing trend of confrontation between Chinese and their government over the seizure of land for business development projects.
>
> —Wong (2011, p. A21)

This newspaper report is one among many that have appeared in recent years, reflecting the anger of local villagers at their treatment by corrupt government officials in China in the 21st century (Page & Spegele, 2011). The economic boom in China of about 8% to 10% growth each year in the early 21st century has been accompanied by enormous increases in the price of land, particularly in coastal areas of the eastern part of the country. Protected by the closed government system and the lack of accountability, local and even national officials have worked hand in hand with entrepreneurs to take over and develop land owned by farmers (for a critical examination of problems in the closed Chinese system, see Lemos, 2012, who based his assessment on recent empirical evidence and highlighted lack of health care as particularly problematic for the Chinese masses). Again and again, local villagers have demonstrated that they know very well what their interests are and how they are being cheated, but in most cases they simply have not been

DOI: 10.1037/14138-005
The Psychology of Dictatorship, by F. M. Moghaddam

able to resist the brute force of the government security crackdown. Their villages have been cut off, and they have been isolated, starved, and beaten into submission. These 21st-century village protests are in a long line of attempts by ordinary Chinese people to get more accountability in their local and national governments. The personal stories of the victims are harrowing, as I discovered during my visit to China, where I met students from rural areas who whispered about their families being cheated out of their land by local officials back home. The students dared not speak out for fear of reprisals.

DICTATORSHIP IN CHINA

Since the beginning of the 20th century, there have been successive collective movements in China toward overthrowing dictatorship. The old imperial order was swept aside at the start of the 20th century by the so-called Boxer Uprising, a nationalistic movement that was brought under control by Western military intervention. The Manchu dynasty was overthrown and a republic declared in 1911, but over the next few decades no single power managed to gain control of the entire Chinese territory. The Chinese Communist Party was established in 1921, inspired by and initially modeled on the Soviet example. However, its leader, Mao Zedong (1893–1976), eventually recognized that China and Russia were two very different contexts, and in China the revolution would have to be fueled by rural working populations rather than urban workers as in Russia. Mao led communist forces to victory and established the People's Republic of China in 1949, although the Nationalists did manage to escape to Taiwan and continue to enjoy independence as a capitalist state with some measure of democracy.

Having come to power through revolution and with the promise of fundamental change, Mao actually went on to rule China in the style of the old emperors (Salisbury, 1992). The aspect of continuity that most concerns me is the concentration of absolute power in the hands of a single leader who had complete control of decision making and could not be opposed. Although power was supposed to be in the hands of the Chinese Communist Party, and particularly its politburo, in practice while Mao was alive he wielded absolute power.

Mao and the Continuity of Dictatorial Leadership in China

The so-called Great Helmsman actually led China down terribly destructive paths, resulting in the needless deaths of millions of people. This was particularly so during the Great Leap Forward (roughly 1958–1961) when China was supposed to bound ahead and industrialize and the Cultural Revolution (roughly from 1968 to the early 1970s) when as part of perpetual revolution Chinese society was supposed to cleanse itself, get rid of antirevolutionary elements, and make progress "for the people." In addition to these catastrophic domestic programs ("Close to 38 million people died of starvation and overwork in the Great Leap Forward and the famine, which lasted four years," Chang & Halliday, 2005, p. 438; see also Benton & Chun, 2010), Mao's foreign policy resulted in the strengthening of horrific dictatorships such as the one that continues in North Korea. Mao's monumental mistakes are typical of what happens when a single person has absolute power in a society.

Since Mao's death, China has continued as a politically closed dictatorship ruled by a clique with an economically more open market. Thus, Chinese society has benefited from more openness only insofar as the financial market is concerned. Those Chinese citizens who assumed that economic liberalization would be accompanied by political liberalization have been rudely awakened again and again. Of course, those outside China are aware of the bloody crackdown that took place in Beijing's Tiananmen Square in summer 1989, but there are also the thousands of crackdowns—little acknowledged in the rest of the world—that have taken place against local people attempting to speak out against the corruption that infects China (Lemos, 2012). Unfortunately, there is not enough focus in the rest of the world on the lack of political freedom in 21st-century China.

On the one hand, the supposed open economic system means that people in China have the opportunity to buy into the illusion of economic meritocracy; on the other hand, the closed political system means that ordinary Chinese people are forced to put up with the injustices of enormous economic inequalities coupled with government corruption at all levels. Thus, in 21st-century China two parallel illusions and their associated "benefits" for the people are being upheld: first, the illusion of meritocracy and genuine economic openness and, second, the illusion of dictatorship on behalf of the masses. When Chinese people rebel and declare their rejection of these illusions, the suffocating hand of the state "corrects" their behavior.

The puzzle of the continuity of dictatorship has profoundly affected me personally from the time that as a young researcher and fervent supporter of the revolution I rushed back with the revolution in Iran. The euphoria of experiencing the shackles of dictatorship being broken—in hindsight, I would say I only saw the visible shackles being broken—was the most exhilarating experience of my life. Witnessing a people chained by the Shah's security apparatus break free and, for the first time in living memory, dare to speak out openly was a great moment for any human being to experience. But just as the giddy heights of postrevolution euphoria were unforgettable, so were the terrible torments that followed as Iran plunged back into dictatorship and darkness. Once again, Iran is ruled with an iron fist by one unelected man.

Why have so many revolutions failed to break people free from dictatorship? Why is the Arab Spring proving to be such a struggle for those who support open societies in Egypt, Tunisia, and Libya, where dictators have fallen yet new forms of dictatorship are on the rise under new guises? Why did the collapse of the Soviet Union and the move toward democracy in Russia, Ukraine, and some other Eastern Bloc countries lead back to Putin and other "democratic dictators"?

In addressing the puzzle of the continuity of dictatorship in this chapter (following the approach outlined in Chapter 2), I focus first on the role of narratives and the normative system that is already out there before each individual comes into this world and continues in important respects unchanged after each individual leaves the stage. Of course, change can only be understood in relation to constancy, and my first step is to clarify varieties of change and constancy.

First-Order, Second-Order, and Third-Order Systems

Behavior in each society is regulated by two sets of rules and norms (see Finkel & Moghaddam, 2005): The first is *informal*—what people think is correct behavior (related to subjective justice); the second is *formal* law—what the authorities state is correct behavior (related to black letter law). The informal normative system and formal law do not always agree. For example, consider how people (particularly students and professors) behave in everyday life with respect to photocopying copyrighted material from journals and books—they break formal laws every day! But as Ellickson (1991) demonstrated in his study on how order is kept without formal law in everyday life, although most professors "would flunk if quizzed on the details of legal restrictions on copying for classroom use" (p. 261), they do behave within the constraints of informal rules. For example, professors routinely copy entire journal papers but not entire books.

Changes in formal black letter law can come about without necessarily accompanying changes in the informal normative system. It is useful to distinguish between three levels of systems (an adaptation from Moghaddam, 2002). A *first-order system* is one in which both formal law and the informal normative system endorse group-based injustices—examples being the time of slavery in the southern states of the United States and the time of apartheid in South Africa. In a *second-order system*, the formal law has been reformed to support group-based justice, but the informal normative system has not changed in the same direction and to the same degree. For example, although on paper race discrimination has ended in the United States and South Africa, in practice racial prejudice continues in some ways and in some areas in both countries. A *third-order system* is one in which both formal law and the informal normative system support justice and equality—this is an ideal not achieved by any major society so far.

Change within each of these levels, *within-system change*, is far easier to achieve than change from one level to another, *between-systems change*. The difference between these two types of change can be clarified using ideas from the so-called Palo Alto group (Watzlawick, Weakland, & Fisch, 1974). Imagine you are having a nightmare in which you are swimming in a crocodile-infested river. You swim as fast as you can, terrified of the crocodiles gliding toward you. You finally get to the riverbank and scramble to safety. This is within-system change: You are still dreaming, but now you feel safer because you escaped from the crocodile-infested river. Between-systems change takes place when you dream you are swimming in the crocodile-infested river and are so frightened that you suddenly wake up. The change from sleeping to being awake is a change from one system to another. This between-systems change is extremely difficult to achieve for societies, even through violent revolutions.

Most revolutions involve an attempt to move from a first-order to a second-order system, to transform a system in which both formal law and the informative normative system endorse group-based injustices to a system in which at least formal law forbids group-based injustices. Unfortunately, this change from first-order to second-order system has proved to be extremely difficult in many countries, and so has the postrevolution plight of people in Iran, Russia, China, and so on. For example, in Russia, Putin's maneuvering from president to prime minister to president again is perfectly legal according to formal black letter law. Similarly, the constitution of Iran permits a single male Supreme Leader to determine everything for everyone else in the country. In China, the closed and secretive procedures for leadership selection in which the masses play no role are in accordance with formal law. To achieve between-systems change from a first-order to a second-order system in Russia, Iran, China, and other such dictatorships, it is necessary to transform the formal law of the country as well as the informal normative system.

The barriers to achieving such change are subtle and resilient, a topic I discuss next.

SACRED CARRIERS AND NARRATIVES

I want him to understand that this stunt that he is talking about pulling could greatly endanger our young men and women in uniform who are in Iraq, who are in Afghanistan. We're already seeing protests against Americans just by the mere threat that he's making. (President Barack Obama quoted in Stephanopolous, 2010)

On September 8, 2010, the president of the United States spoke publicly on television about the danger posed by the planned action of an until then little-known pastor in Gainesville, Florida, with a church congregation of about 50 people. Around the same time, local and national religious leaders, national religious organizations, major newspapers such as the *The New York Times* and *The Washington Post*, U.S. embassies in the Near and Middle East, General David Petraeus (the top U.S. and North Atlantic Treaty Organization commander in Afghanistan), Hillary Rodham Clinton (U.S. secretary of state), and notable American politicians (including Republicans John Boehner and Sarah Palin) spoke out against the planned action of this pastor. Very soon this pastor was no longer little known, despite having only a handful of followers. He was interviewed on national television, and his every move was reported in the press. On Friday, September 10, 2010, Asif Ali Zardari, the president of Pakistan, criticized the planned action of the pastor, and there were violent demonstrations against the pastor in Afghanistan and Pakistan with injuries and deaths reported. The formerly unknown pastor, who still had only a few dozen followers, had become world news.

What shot this unknown pastor into the international spotlight? What was he planning to do that was so controversial and the cause of so much concern and conflict at national and international levels? The answer is that the pastor had threatened to burn the Koran. On the one hand, the pastor was only threatening to burn a book, and so one might be puzzled by all the fuss. On the other hand, the Koran is not just any book—it is what I have described as a *sacred carrier*, a means through which vitally important values are sustained and passed on in cultures and something true believers are willing to die for (Moghaddam, 2008a). In this chapter, I am particularly focused on the role of carriers generally, and sacred carriers specifically, in bringing about the continuity that is characteristic of cultures.

Perhaps the most important yet often overlooked feature of culture is its continuity: Culture is in place when an individual arrives into this world and continues—albeit to some degree changed—when the individual exits from this world. How does one explain the profound mystery of cultural continuity? How does one understand the overwhelming power of this continuity to sweep aside plans and slogans for change? Revolutionary leaders, firebrand politicians, economic reformers, community activists, religious fanatics, even major dictators—all kinds of people find themselves in a similar quagmire: Having promised radical change, they find that "the more things change, the more they remain the same." Despite what Heraclitus observed over 2,500 years ago, that one cannot step twice into the same river and that change is constant and unstoppable, there is the other side of the coin: the great challenge of achieving foundational between-systems change. I clarify this idea further by examining the so-called paradox of revolution and types of change.

The Paradox of Revolution and Between-Systems Change

Even the most radical and widespread movements for societal change have been confronted by the paradox of revolution, for example, as discussed by Middlebrook (1995) in the Mexican context: The change that was assumed to happen through revolution often does not come about in the areas that matter most, such as leadership style, justice, and group-based resource inequalities. After a brief period of euphoria and surface change, the postrevolution society reverts to old ways. Of course, some change does come about in some areas, but it is often too little and excruciatingly slow. What was assumed to be between-systems change proves to be within-system change. Why is this?

For example, revolutions as historic and dramatic as those in France (1789) and Russia (1917) and more recent ones such as in Iran (1978–1979) did not result in a between-systems change in the vitally important area of leadership style. After these seemingly foundational revolutions, the tradition continued of one man ruling with an iron fist: Napoleon Bonaparte in France, Stalin in Russia, and Khomeini in Iran. This rule of despotism continued a trend that had been present before the three revolutions. All three revolutions had raised expectations that liberty and the will of the people would find ample room for expression and growth, but all three resulted in the crushing of basic freedoms and the mobilization of the masses against their own basic freedoms and against their own interests. The same continuity in leadership style is present in China, where the new emperors follow the same path as the prerevolution emperors (Salisbury, 1992). Although there is a lot of freedom for entrepreneurs in the financial market of China, despotism and lack of liberty continue in the political sphere.

Change and Continuity in Postrevolution Iran

Life in Iran after the revolution made me acutely aware of the paradox of revolution. When the Pahlavi regime collapsed and the Shahs with their supposed 2,500 years of continuous history were swept aside, on the surface at least the expectation on Iranian streets was that people would now enjoy basic freedoms. Like hundreds of thousands of other Iranians who had studied in the West, I eagerly rushed back to Iran in the spring of revolution to participate in the rebuilding of the country. Everything seemed to have been transformed—the government was toppled; all the heads of major corporations, banks, universities, and even the leadership of charities had been pushed aside, had been imprisoned, or had escaped abroad. The vast majority of officers in the army, navy, and air force were either in hiding or had fled; some had been killed. Even some ordinary police officers had taken off their uniforms and melted into the general population. During the first few months after the revolution, it seemed that the old regime had evaporated and the old ways of doing things had completely disappeared. The revolution had given birth to a new world with transformed people and new behavior patterns.

Dress codes also changed dramatically, from emulation of the latest fashions in Western societies to emulation of the simplest styles of common people on the streets in Iran. Certain clothing styles were taken to be symbols of the Western decadence and impurity, and people wearing such clothes were shunned and even mistreated. It became dangerous for a man to wear a tie, and a bow tie was even more demonic. The safest path for men was to be disheveled and unshaved. The most drastic change in clothing requirements was reserved for women, who were now obligated by law to cover themselves with the Islamic hijab. Thus, the most immediate and visible sign of revolutionary change was the veil covering women in Iran.

Iranians even seemed to speak differently after the revolution. The Shah-era titles and figures of speech were stripped from communications, so that everyone became *brother* and *sister*, and speaking and writing in a common and folksy manner was commended. The tone was set by Ayatollah Khomeini, who made rambling, lengthy speeches using everyday language to communicate in ways that matched the speech style of less educated people on the streets. Intellectuals mocked him, but he connected immediately and directly with the masses and moved them this way and that—rather as Chairman Mao had done in the heyday of the 1960s Cultural Revolution in China (I witnessed the same charismatic rabble-rousing leadership in Venezuela—I was teaching at the University of Caracas at the time—where Hugo Chavez attempted to gain a power monopoly in the early 21st century). Whereas prior to the revolution, the Shah had given press interviews in English and French and refined Farsi, Khomeini spoke directly in common Farsi to peasants and workers, smattering his speech with Islamic quotations in Arabic that would set the crowd crying out Islamic chants in unison.

The names of streets, buildings, squares, and other public spaces; the faces of coins and monetary notes; national and local flags—everything and everywhere seemed to be transformed by the revolution. The breadth of this change matched that experienced in other historic revolutions. For example, after the French Revolution a variety of radical changes were attempted, such as the introduction of a revolutionary calendar with the month being divided into three 10-day periods with new names for the days (Schama, 1989). After the 1917 Russian Revolution also, the list of changes was extensive and included all names of places, modes of address in speech, and of course the rules of private ownership (Figes & Kolonitskii, 1999).

Carriers and Continuity

Thus, as Middlebrook (1995) and others have noted, revolutionaries from Mexico to Russia and from Venezuela to China have attempted to bring about between-systems changes, but invariably they have been confronted by the paradox of revolution. To explain this stubborn continuity, it is useful to consider the role of varieties of carriers (Moghaddam, 2002). *Carriers* can be physical objects, such as national flags and statues and uniforms, but they can also be psychological constructs, such as stereotypes. For example, skin color is a physical attribute that has served as a carrier, such as when most Black people in the United States were slaves and Black was synonymous with slavery. But long after slavery ended in the United States, stereotypes based on skin color persisted to function as carriers (Steele, 2010).

The power and nature of carriers can best be understood by clarifying the distinction between carriers and *symbols*, or things that represent particular meanings in a culture. For example, during World War II, Winston Churchill's famous V sign was a symbol for victory. The concept of carrier is broader and more dynamic than the traditional symbol in a number of ways. Most important, carriers are about the narratives that construct, sustain, and propagate meaning. For example, it is the narratives that underlie a national flag, rather than the national flag itself, that are the important part of a carrier. Similarly, it is the carriers that sustain a dictator that are most important, not the dictator himself.

This explains why a dictator can be toppled in an antidictator revolution but replaced by another dictator because there has been no serious change in the narratives supportive of dictatorship. In practice, it turns out to be easier to change a dictator than to change the narratives supporting dictatorship. Recently there has been some attention to this continuity in language, as in a series of studies published on the lingering of prerevolution narrative styles in postcommunist discourses (Andrews, 2011). For example, Levintova (2011) explored official ideological discourse in pre- and post–communist Russia, concluding that "in Russia the conservative political discourse, first articulated during the Brezhnev era, is more durable, immutable, and recurring, a finding that does not bode well for the liberal alternative on the political elite level" (p. 174). This conservative political discourse includes authoritarianism, state-controlled media, and selective application of law—the hallmarks of continuity from the tsars to the communist leaders to Putin.

Distinct Roles of Sacred Carriers in Dictatorships and Democracies

Admiration for Mussolini verged on adoration, at times suggesting a strange symbiosis of fascist and Catholic mentalities in the production of a kind of political demi-god. Very often fascist "faith" was intimately linked to the figure of Mussolini. Corner (2009, p. 139)

There is a fundamental difference between the role of sacred carriers in dictatorships and democracies. The difference is not in the importance of sacred carriers because in both systems sacred carriers play a vitally important role. For example, consider the role of the American flag (Old Glory) in the United States or the role of the office of the president of the United States. Physically, the American flag is just a piece of cloth, but there are Americans who would die for the flag because it is a sacred carrier of the highest order for American values. The office of the president of the United States is also a sacred carrier, with both Democrats and Republicans honoring this office (this is different from honoring the person in office). Sacred carriers play an equally important role in dictatorships, but this role is different, and the difference is hinted at in the quotation from Corner (2009) at the beginning of this section.

In dictatorships, the dictator himself becomes the most important sacred carrier. This is why cults of adoration mixed with faith and the divine arose in the cases of Mussolini, Hitler, Stalin, Mao, Khomeini, and many other dictators. These dictators were not only obeyed, they also became infallible. To question their word was equivalent to questioning the word of God. Disobeying them was equivalent to sin.

In the case of Khomeini, who was already a major religious leader in the world of Shi'a Islam before he climbed to political power as dictator in Iran, it seems easier to understand how the religious and political elements of adoration became fused in the minds of his followers. Even with Mussolini, this fusion seems understandable because he was dictator in a country that at that time was strongly Catholic, and he managed to incorporate the Catholic Church within his regime, gaining strong backing from church leaders, initially at least. But the same trend of faith and divine being infused in the person of the political dictator is evident in the case of Stalin, Mao, and some other officially secular dictators. The acknowledgement of this fact leads to the recognition that it is not the church proper but faith, worship, the construction of a divine, and other features of religious behavior that characterize the relationship between dictators and their followers. Of relevance here is the terror management theory perspective (Pyszczynski, Solomon, & Greenberg, 2004), according to which the masses in dictatorships are made acutely aware of their own mortality (by continued threats of violence, repression, and death), and heightened mortality salience leads them to apparently embrace the ideology of the regime, including embracing the Supreme Leader as semidivine.

The Dictator in Everyday Social Lives

The dictator's role as sacred carrier is reflected in the ever-present image of the dictator in the form of photographs, paintings, statues, film, and other types of representation. Every business, office, school, university, train station, and sports stadium—all public spaces—is required to have images of the Great Dictator. The pressure from the public space often intrudes into the home, so that even supposedly private space also has to have images of the so-called Supreme Leader.

This pervasive presence of the Supreme Dictator has a profound impact on everyday life, including how people think on matters that seemingly have nothing to do with politics. "Can there be any doubt that the ubiquitous portraits of the national leader in dictatorial societies not only convey the feeling that 'Big Brother is Watching' but also lead to an actual reduction in spontaneous thought and independent action?" Kahneman (2011, p. 56) made this observation in the context of discussing research on how even subtle cues in the environment can influence people's behavior, such as cues that remind people of money leading to more individualistic, more selfish, and less cooperative behavior (Vohs, 2006). Kahneman's concern with spontaneous thought and independent action is laudable, but my concern here is with an even more basic impact of the ever-present image of the Supreme Dictator: the transformation of the Supreme Dictator into a divine being.

Because in dictatorships the dictator becomes a sacred carrier, and because as sacred carrier his value and divinity become absolute, any form of disobedience to his dictates become unacceptable, just as turning one's back to Christ or Mohammed or other divine messengers is unacceptable in the eyes of Christian and Muslim believers. In line with this trend, commentators have discussed criticism or disobedience toward Stalin and other dictators in religious language. For example, this is how R. C. Tucker (1979) discussed the tragic situation faced by people in Stalin's Russia:

> To confess to heresy was not enough; the heretic had to join the inquisition. Only by entering the ranks of the accusers could he expect to have his recantation taken seriously. To denounce Trotskyist contraband on the part of others demonstrated the genuineness of one's own "real" Bolshevism—that is, Stalinism. Recantation followed by denunciation was becoming a ritual of Soviet political culture. (p. 362)

Words such as *heresy, recantation,* and *inquisition* demonstrate the religious flavor of the processes.

The same process was evident in Iran, where to show that they were not deviating from the line of the Imam (i.e., the position taken by Khomeini on any and every issue), the children of the revolution went through waves of recantations and denunciations so that yesterday's president (e.g., Abdulhassan Banisadre, 1980–1981), prime minister (e.g., Mehdi Bazargan, 1907–1995), and cabinet minister (e.g., Sadegh Ghotbzadeh, 1936–1982) became today's enemy. In Iran the denunciations have been more explicitly religious, so that anyone daring to speak up against the corruption of the state is branded "un-Islamic" and a "heretic." The core power elite in Iran has ruthlessly sliced away at its own body to ensure cohesion at the top. Any member of the Iranian power elite who criticizes the regime or supports greater political openness is immediately branded, ousted, hunted, and silenced. This "purity" at the top of the power elite enables the regime to act with even more extreme harshness toward dissent among the masses, bringing about a silence and loneliness in the wider society.

Silence, Ideology, and Terror

> In regimes of authentic terror, silence reigns. (Kula, 2009, p. 150)

What is the role of ideology in dictatorships? Important contributions have been made to understanding the nature and role of ideology in democracies through experimental, survey, and narrative research methods (Altemeyer, 1988; Billig, 1991; Duckitt, Wagner, du Plessis, & Birum, 2002), but the picture in dictatorships is foundationally different. I argue that the most important role of ideology in dictatorships is to enable the ruling elite to remain cohesive and feel themselves justified in crushing the opposition by killing, maiming, imprisoning, and intimidating ordinary people who actually or potentially form opposition groups. Some of the important misconceptions about the role of ideology in keeping the masses in their inferior position have arisen because researchers working in Western democracies have assumed, sometimes explicitly, that group-based inequalities are maintained in dictatorships in the same way that they are maintained in democracies.

Again and again, there is clear evidence that dictatorships are maintained first and foremost by force exerted by a cohesive power elite. Again and again, people living in dictatorships have shown that what is keeping them from overthrowing dictatorial rule is the guns held to their heads and not primarily the ideologies that dictatorial powers are attempting to impart to them. For example, consider events around elections in Zimbabwe in 2008 and in Iran in 2009. After the first round of presidential elections in Zimbabwe in 2008, it looked as if the popular vote would put opposition leader Morgan Tsvangirai in power. But there was a huge and immediate mobilization of Zanu-PF party gangs of thugs as well as various security forces, sometimes in uniform, intended to terrorize the opposition and ensure the continued ruling of Robert Mugabe. One observer reported that

> now the murders here are accompanied by torture and rape on an industrial scale, committed on a catch-and-release basis. When those who survive, terribly injured, limp home, or are carried or pushed on wheelbarrows, or on the backs of pickup trucks, they act like human billboards, advertising the appalling consequences of opposition to the tyranny, bearing their gruesome political stigma. (Godwin, 2010, p. 109)

After systematic abduction, rape, castration, torture, and killing of the opposition, and even ordinary people who had little to do with the elections, Mugabe was declared the winner (Godwin, 2010).

A similar pattern of events unfolded after the 2009 presidential elections in Iran, when the opposition leader, Mr. Mousavi, seemed to have won the popular vote, but Mr. Ahmadinejad was "miraculously" declared the winner by Iran's Supreme Spiritual Leader only hours after the end of voting. This was a surprise because all indications were that the popular vote had gone to Mousavi and because there had not been enough time to count the votes! There was widespread belief, both nationally and internationally, that the election had been robbed. Even though Mousavi had previously (1981–1989) served as prime minister with Khomeini's blessings, he was now regarded by the fundamentalist clique ruling Iran as too liberal relative to Ahmadinejad.

Huge protests erupted against the rigged election results throughout Iran, with millions of people venting their anger and using electronic communications to try to thwart the security clampdown (Kamalipour, 2010). The backlash from the government, backed by the Supreme Leader Khamenei, was a devastating orgy of killing, rapes (of both men and women), and terror. The *basij* (an irregular paramilitary force well-known for its violent and corrupt methods) was let loose, and in many instances this force acted with ferocious zeal to brutalize the unarmed protesters, with the consequence that the public outcry were fairly quickly muffled. Protesters ran out of air and suffocated.

The cases of elections in Zimbabwe (2008) and Iran (2009) demonstrate how the masses can clearly perceive the unjust nature of the political system they live in, and even summon up the courage to demonstrate their desire for reform, but find themselves strangled by the brute force of dictatorial power. For those who have not experienced this suffocation, it is difficult to even imagine the intensity of the pressure exerted by dictatorships.

Culture of Silence

> Among acquaintances there was a tacit agreement not to talk about political events. Anyone could be arrested and forced by the police to incriminate his friends by reporting such conversations as evidence of their "counter-revolutionary" activities. In this climate, to initiate political discussions with anyone except one's closest friends was to invite suspicion of being an informant or provocateur. (Figes, 2007, p. 252)

A common feature of life in dictatorships is a particular form of silence in the public sphere. This silence was described by Figes (2007) in his brilliant analysis of private life in Stalin's Russia. There are informers everywhere, and perhaps one in five Russians was in one way or another serving as an informer at the height of the terror. Even within the family, parents dared not speak openly in front of their children, and sometimes even in front of one another because of the fear that their own family might, mistakenly or intentionally, inform on them. In Iran since the 1980s, government authorities have improvised new ways to coax children to inform on their parents. For example, in one case I encountered, children in a classroom were shown unusual items and asked if they could guess their use. Inserted in the string of items were bottles used to store wines and spirits. Eager to show off how much they knew, some children fell into the trap of relating how they knew about the bottles because they had seen bottles like them at home—not remembering that alcohol was forbidden and their homes would be raided. Of course, in most cases the banned substances confiscated from homes ended up as part of the black market controlled by state security forces.

Perhaps one of the most frightening aspects of life in dictatorships is that the forced silence means it is extremely difficult to know what to do when a relative or friend disappears. Has the person been mugged by robbers? Been killed in an accident? Been kidnapped by gangsters? Or taken by the security forces? It is often very difficult to even explore the truth, and sometimes it can take weeks to get to some kind of certainty. In Iran the authorities typically do not confirm where an individual is being held or why the person was arrested. After a person is taken by authorities, often telephone calls are received by relatives and friends, purportedly from people who can help for the right price, but it is never clear who is asking for the money and whether they really can help free the disappeared. In cases in which the disappeared has been killed, the authorities do not allow a funeral ceremony or any kind of independent inquiry. Silence in dictatorships such as Iran reigns supreme, even after death.

It became routine in Stalinist Russia for the close relatives of dissidents, particularly their spouses and children, to be arrested as well and often also sent to the Gulag and executed. The reasoning for this terrible action was that a person either confided in his or her spouse and close family or at least could have been reported for antirevolution sentiments by the spouse and close family; either way, the most efficient strategy was to include the spouse and close family in the punishment. Besides, it was dangerous for the dictatorship to have more disgruntled people running around in society.

Because of the intense focus of the revolutionary regime on spies and traitors in the midst of the population, as well as the regime's propaganda about hidden spies and traitors, there is a retreat from the public sphere. Complaints about the corruption and ineptitude of the regime are not aired and gradually only find expression in private diaries (Figes, 2007). Each person living in the dictatorship literally becomes an isolated island, unable to connect with other islands; Arendt's (2004) brilliant analysis highlighted the loneliness and individual isolation that enables totalitarian systems.

An important element sustaining this culture of fear in dictatorships is the presence of widespread and sometimes false rumors, encouraged by the authorities, about the power and reach of the state security apparatus. In the German Democratic Republic, by the 1980s the Stasi had files on about six million citizens, using a hierarchical and specialized network of informers (Fulbrook, 1995). The outcome was that East Germans retreated into the privacy of their own lives and after the uprising of June 1953 were not able to collectively act against the regime until the late 1980s. A climate of suspicion and distrust pervaded social relations, and some strange ideas circulated about the activities and power of the Stasi. Of course, some of these ideas were true! For example, in addition to the usual surveillance procedures adopted by security forces in dictatorial regimes (e.g., bugging devices, telephone tapping), the Stasi even collected the smells of people in jars so as to help police tracker dogs locate suspects (Fulbrook, 1995). An interesting variety of such Stasi tactics is now on display in the DDR Museum in the rebuilt Berlin.

RETHINKING FALSE CONSCIOUSNESS AND SYSTEM JUSTIFICATION

> The ideas of the ruling class are in every epoch the ruling ideas: i.e., the class which is the ruling material force of society is at the same time its ruling intellectual force. The class which has the means of material production at its disposal, consequently also controls the means of mental production, so that the ideas of those who lack the means of mental production are on the whole subject to it. (Marx & Engels, 1848/1967, p. 59)

This famous passage from Marx and Engels encapsulates the important idea of the ruling class dominating the ruling ideas of a society. Of course, mechanistic interpretations of this passage have resulted in overly simplistic depictions of how ideas are caused by material conditions. But this is a misreading of Marx and Engels and misses the two main points they explore: First, ideas arise out of the relationships people have within the production process and in the material world; second, the ruling class has far greater means to produce, disseminate, and appropriate ideas.

The political and economic dominance of the ruling class has led many researchers to adopt what Abercrombie and Turner (1978) referred to as the *dominant ideology thesis*, the idea that an identifiable, cohesive set of beliefs dominates society, infuses particularly the consciousness of the lower classes, and inhibits class-based collective rebellion against those in power (see also Abercrombie, Hill, & Turner, 1990). In contemporary psychology, the dominant ideology thesis is reflected most directly in system justification theory (Jost, Banaji, & Nosek, 2004; Jost & van der Toorn, 2012) and a number of other intergroup theories that place emphasis on the beliefs, values, perceptions, and psychological orientation of people that justify the prevailing group-based inequalities (see Moghaddam, 2008b).

In a powerful critique of the dominant ideology thesis, Abercrombie and Turner (1978) proposed that there is little evidence that the lower classes are dominated by one cohesive ideology that keeps them in their place. Their analysis endorsed the idea that the target of the dominant ideology is actually the dominant class; it is the rulers rather than the ruled who require a cohesive ideology for the system to survive.

The lower classes in capitalist societies are necessarily engaged in the routines of economic activity, toward making ends meet. The conformity and obedience that characterize the actions of working class people are not arising out of an ideology coming down from the top but are more the result of the compulsion of economic necessities. Because working class people have so few resources and so little time, and because they find themselves struggling to make ends meet, the most important factor shaping their actions is sheer economic necessity. It is the bills that have to be paid—being behind with the rent and the loan payments—that shape working-class consciousness and actions.

The dominant ideology critique rings even more true in the context of dictatorships than it does in the context of Western capitalist democracies. The initiatives for maintaining and extending the existing group-based inequalities come from those in power, and it is the members of the ruling groups who are in need of ideological cohesion to maintain their superior positions. If those in power fail to uphold group-based inequalities, then the social order is in danger. They have access to power and resources and can challenge the status quo. This is unlike those in the lower classes who have access to little power and resources. Even when they perceive the existing order and reward distribution as unjust, which they invariably do, they do not have the means to force between-systems change.

Of course, some exceptions are available, as when unarmed people manage to mobilize and overthrow entire regimes, such as happened in Burma, China, Nepal, South Africa, the Philippines, and Thailand (Schock, 2005) and more recently in Tunisia and Egypt (in 2011). But in many such cases, there is simply a circulation of elites and within-system change in line with Pareto's (1935) elite theory. In the few cases in which popular uprisings manage to result in a more democratic state, as in South Africa, the role of external forces for change is vitally important (e.g., Western countries had decided to stop supporting apartheid). On the one hand, new electronic communications systems and international human rights consciousness are assisting ordinary people to revolt, but on the other hand, the apparatus of repression in the hands of states has become more formidable.

CONCLUDING COMMENT

Most revolutions have achieved within-system rather than between-systems change, and this limitation underlies the paradox of revolution—after each revolution, a feeling arises that the more things change, the more they remain the same. I have argued that this paradox is explained in large part through the roles of various types of carriers, particularly sacred carriers, which sustain continuity in the most important features of culture. Sacred carriers are particularly important in achieving cohesion in the ruling elite because through this cohesion the rulers are able to use devastating force to brutalize the masses into submission—as evident in contemporary dictatorships, including those that parade the ideology of Islam (e.g., Iran), communism (e.g., North Korea), and various other ideologies (e.g., Syria, Russia, China). In Chapter 5, I explore another tactic used by dictatorial regimes to maximize cohesion, a tactic well-known to psychologists: displacement.

5

DICTATORSHIP, DISPLACEMENT OF AGGRESSION, AND GROUP COHESION

Now is the winter of our discontent
Made glorious summer by this sun of York;
And all the clouds that lower'd upon our house
In the deep bosom of the ocean buried.

—Shakespeare, Richard III

Shakespeare's play *Richard III* begins with these lines describing how the gloom of war has been buried. But instead of being happy about the arrival of peace, the speaker, Richard (at the time, Duke of Gloucester), laments that these times of peace and merriment are not made for one such as he:

I, that am curtail'd of this fair proportion,
Cheated of feature by dissembling nature,
Deform'd, unfinish'd, sent before my time
Into this breathing world scarce half made up,

Richard's deformity is more of character than of body. He convinces himself that he cannot thrive in a time of peace and "idle pleasures," so he must create dissent and disorder. He feeds off chaos, eventually becoming king through intrigue and murder. Richard retains power as long as he can play people against one another, using lies and deceit to ferment suspicion and dissent. Modern dictators often share a similar intuition in that they sense they

DOI: 10.1037/14138-006
The Psychology of Dictatorship, by F. M. Moghaddam

can only survive through continuous conflicts, both internal and external. A tragic example of this is Robert Mugabe, who began his political life with considerable promise but is ending it through turmoil and conflict.

Mugabe played a significant leadership role in the struggle to end White minority rule in what used to be named Southern Rhodesia and then Rhodesia and is now Zimbabwe, a mineral-rich country of about 15 million people in Southern Africa. In many respects his early years represent much that one would hope to find in the life story of a national hero and liberator. He was born in 1924 into a poor Black Catholic family; his father was a carpenter who abandoned the family for many years. Young Robert took advantage of Jesuit education and became qualified to work as a schoolteacher. He went to Ghana, the first British African colony to gain independence (in 1957), to teach and to learn from the experiences of the first liberated African state. There he married a Ghanaian teacher, and they went back to what was then Rhodesia in 1960 and became involved in the political movement to end White minority rule. The vast majority of arable land in Rhodesia was owned by White farmers, and the benefits of the rich mineral mines went almost exclusively to Whites. The political, legal, and military apparatuses of the state were also under White control. But the Black liberation movement was gaining momentum across Africa.

After a period in exile, Mugabe returned to Rhodesia in 1963, only to be arrested and jailed, where he was to remain until 1974. During his time in jail, Mugabe earned more university qualifications through correspondence and gave lessons to his fellow inmates. When he was finally released, Mugabe and his family took refuge in Mozambique, which had recently gained independence. Increased violent opposition eventually led to the collapse of the White government in Rhodesia, and in 1980 Mugabe's political party won the majority of seats of the assembly, and he became the first prime minister of the newly established independent country of Zimbabwe. Thus, Mugabe's early life fits the liberator story line: Born into a poor Black family in an African country ruled by a White minority, the hero climbs up the ladder of success through education and hard work, becomes a political leader, is thrown in jail for many years, is freed and goes into exile, and then returns to win national leadership through popular vote. Unfortunately, Mugabe's story line eventually ends up much more like Khomeini's than Mandela's, throwing Zimbabwean society into a dark period of dictatorship.

Since the 1980s Mugabe has clung to power and become absolute dictator of Zimbabwe. He has shown himself to be just as brutal and eager to use force to retain power as the White minority government he overthrew. He has used assassinations, torture, kidnappings, rape, and imprisonment to repeatedly thwart democratic movements and continue his monopoly on power. Over the past 30 years his opponents have included different politicians as well as student and labor movements, but he has consistently relied heavily on one particular tactic: *displacement of aggression*, action intended to harm others by a person who feels provoked against a third-party target who is not responsible for the provocation. The immediate target of Mugabe's tactic of displacement of aggression has been the White population of Zimbabwe; a secondary target has been Great Britain and other (former) colonial powers. Ordinary Black Zimbabweans have been encouraged to see the White population of Zimbabwe and next Great Britian and other (former) colonial powers as the source of all their problems and not see the corrupt Mugabe regime as a problem.

The targeting of the White minority was certainly legitimate at the time of the struggle to end apartheid in Rhodesia, but Mugabe has continued to use the Whites as a target to redirect attention away from the problems created by his own corrupt and despotic regime. Any individual or any group that has dared to oppose his rule has been branded as a traitorous front for the Whites or the British or the Americans, or all of these. In the name of Zimbabwean nationalism, he has launched widespread campaigns of terror, throwing hundreds of thousands of both Black and White people out of their homes and businesses. The process of displacement of aggression, used effectively by Mugabe and other dictators, has been the focus of intensive psychological research.

DISPLACEMENT OF AGGRESSION

The concept of displaced aggression was first formalized by Sigmund Freud (1856–1939) and used particularly to explore conflict (Freud, 1955, 1961). At the root of this concept is Freud's view about the processes through which individuals become "civilized" and the psychological costs involved in this process. Individuals are born with basic instincts that clash with the morality dominating society, particularly in the domains of sexuality and aggression. The behavior of human infants is initially guided by the pleasure principle, driving infants toward instant gratification. Gradually, the child learns to repress thoughts and actions that are unacceptable according to societal norms. For example, the child learns that particular parts of the body are associated with shame and guilt and should not be touched or exposed in public.

But basic instincts and motives that are pushed into the unconscious because of societal pressures do not evaporate. Rather, they are continually pushed up and tend to creep through the defense mechanisms, rather like water seeping through cracks and crevices. The primary defense mechanism is repression, but there are also secondary defense mechanisms, and these include displacement of aggression. Associated with displacement of aggression are two other secondary defense mechanisms: *rationalization*, whereby individuals reinterpret their own thoughts and actions to make them more acceptable (the dictator enforces strict censorship, explaining, "We must protect the people from those who want to mislead them"); and *projection*, attributing one's own desires, thoughts, and motives to others rather than to oneself (the dictator claims, "Those foreign powers want to deprive our people of basic freedoms"). Often in dictatorships the displacement of aggression takes place in association with rationalization and projection: For example, the dictator argues, "We have to be vigilant and aggressive against our enemies who desire to mislead and repress us by sowing dissention. Our loyal people will silence dissenting voices before they can cause mischief among our ranks."

Freud's insights into displaced aggression arose from his own experiences of life as a Jew living in Vienna (the apartment where Freud lived for most of his professional life in Vienna is now a museum, very much worth visiting because of its intimacy and small scale) through the wars of the late 19th and early 20th centuries, particularly the 1914–1918 "Great War" and the rise of Nazis in Germany from the 1920s. Freud escaped the Nazis and died as a refugee in England at the start of World War II. Thus, he had direct experience with dictatorship and associated destruction. For Freud, the destructive urges in humans are intimately connected with the constructive urges, as hate is connected with love.

All relationships, even those between long-term lovers and husbands and wives, involve libidinal ties characterized by ambivalence and complexity. Lovers who feel pain when they are apart can also fiercely argue and experience anger and hate when they are together. Husbands and wives who raised children in loving families can divorce and fight one another in angry and destructive divorce proceedings. In Freud's psychology, love and hate are two sides of the same coin, which can easily turn, so that fierce love can turn to fierce hate.

In group contexts also, libidinal ties between the ingroup members involve both positive and negative sentiments, and the challenge for the group leader is to manage the jealousies, rivalries, hatreds, and other potentially destructive sentiments group members experience toward one another. Freud's answer is that leaders redirect such negative sentiments onto dissimilar targets outside the group. Thus, every religion is "a religion of love for all those whom it embraces; while cruelty and intolerance towards those who do not belong to it are natural to every religion" (Freud, 1955, p. 98). Freud's ideas on displacement of aggression served as the foundation of frustration–aggression theory, which postulated that aggression is "always a consequence of frustration" (Dollard, Bood, Miller, Mowrer, & Sears, 1939, p. 1).

More than 8 decades of research (N. Miller, Pederson, Earlywine, & Pollock, 2003) has shown that the precursors and correlates of aggression are far more complex than assumed by frustration–aggression theory. First, frustration can, but need not, result in aggression. Second, more powerful agents can show aggression more openly, but less powerful agents can also act aggressively in indirect ways (e.g., lower status workers in an organization can sabotage projects as acts of aggression against the bosses). Third, a series of relatively minor frustrating experiences can cascade and build up to increase the probability of aggression.

Research in social sciences broadly, and not just in psychology, has for some time supported the idea that there is an association between external threat and internal cohesion. As Sumner (1906, p. 12) stated in his classic work *Folkways*, "The relation of comradeship and peace in the we-group and that of hostility and war towards out-groups are correlative to each other." The ploy that successive dictatorships have used to increase internal cohesion by displacing aggression onto an outgroup threat has been the subject of study in anthropology, political science, sociology, and of course psychology (see related discussions by Feldman & Stenner, 1997; Stein, 1976).

The value of this research is that it helps to highlight the terrible harm that dictatorships can inflict using displacement of aggression. For example, at the time of the 1978–1979 revolution in Iran, Iranian women had made tremendous progress toward equal rights, and female students were competing openly for university places. Women did so well in academic competition that by the 1990s they constituted about 60% of undergraduates in Iran. However, this was not to the liking of the fundamentalist regime in Tehran, and they used strings of labels, such as *Westernized women*, *Western values*, and *Western spies*, to manufacture a problem and to try to drive women out of the public sphere and back into the home. Educated women, particularly those advocating equal rights, became a major target of displacement. Any women opposing the regime were labeled either *sexual deviants* or Western spies or both. Women have now been excluded from studying many of the major subjects in Iranian universities, a move much to the liking of the religious fundamentalist men who support the regime (many of whom could not have competed with women for university places on a level playing field). Of course, one possibility is for Iranian women to study abroad, but the regime rarely gives exit visas for single women to leave Iran, and besides, the permission of a guardian man is needed for a woman (married or unmarried) to travel abroad.

By targeting women, then, the Iranian regime has maintained the support of fundamentalist men who believe that men should make all important decisions for women. Besides, any time there is a problem, from natural disasters to shortages in food and services, religious fundamentalist men are encouraged to blame immoral women. Of course, indications of the same behavior are evident in some Western societies, where natural disasters, the tragedy of 9/11, and all kinds of other problems have been blamed on homosexuality and other deviances from the "true path."

Displacement of aggression can best be understood in the larger context of the relationship between outgroup threat and ingroup cohesion, a relationship that figures prominently in the functioning of dictatorships.

OUTGROUP THREAT AND INGROUP COHESION

> The relation of comradeship and peace in the we-group and that of hostility and war towards other-groups are correlative to each other. The exigencies of war with outsiders are what make peace inside. (Sumner, 1906, p. 12)

One of the oldest ideas in group dynamics is that external threat results in ingroup cohesion. In Aesop's fable about the shepherd boy who cried wolf, the danger from an external threat resulted in the villagers rushing to the aid of the shepherd boy (until they discovered he was deceiving them). This basic relationship between external threat and internal cohesion was set out perhaps most darkly by Freud (1930/1961), who argued that it is always possible to "bind together a considerable number of people in love so long as there are other people left over to receive the manifestations of their aggressiveness" (p. 114). Dictators use external threats as a means of achieving internal cohesion and displacing aggression. Although my focus is on dictatorships, I argue that the basic relationship between external threat and internal cohesion has also been used by democratically elected leaders to win support for themselves. This is relevant to the topic of dictatorships because the greatest danger to democracy arises when a charismatic democratically elected leader maneuvers to increase domestic support by focusing the national attention on external threats and then even launching a war as a diversionary tactic.

The so-called diversionary theory of war has traditionally received mixed support from empirical studies, but in recent years there have been more focused tests of this theory, showing in more details the conditions in which it is valid (Pickering & Kisangarri, 2010). For example, there is evidence that territorial conflicts are particularly effective at getting people to rally around the flag (Tir, 2010). Also, diversion works particularly well when a leader uses force against ethnic minorities as a distraction from domestic problems (Tir & Jasinski, 2008). Most important from the perspective of the thesis of this book, there is evidence that diversionary tactics are adopted by leadership when there is a threat of losing support from domestic groups important to the rulers (N. H. Nicholls, Huth, & Appel, 2010). That is, the rulers are focused on maintaining cohesion in the ruling elite, and they are more likely to use diversionary tactics when they feel that this is needed to help keep the ruling elite stable.

As illustrative examples, I discuss in more detail the case of hostage taking in Iran and the Iran–Iraq War (1980–1988), events that helped to move the country away from democracy after the 1978–1979 revolution and strengthened the forces of dictatorship in that country. Both the hostage crisis and the Iran–Iraq War represent diversions that were unplanned by the Khomeini regime but were opportunistically used to eliminate internal competition and move the country toward an Islamic military dictatorship. Gellately (2001) insightfully commented that the war "revolutionized the revolution" (p. 261) in Nazi Germany from 1939, and the same is true in Iran from 1980.

The cases of hostage taking in Iran and the Iran–Iraq War are important illustrations of how in at least some circumstances the main goal of dictatorial leadership in using external threat is to streamline and make uniform the ruling group. In the case of Iran after the revolution, the ruling group consisted of a fairly broad array of people, including Western-educated liberal Muslims who supported democracy. The presence of these moderates in leadership positions posed a challenge to the hard-line Islamic fundamentalists, who believed in societal obedience to a Supreme Leader and rejected democracy. The hostage-taking crisis and the Iran–Iraq War were used by the hard-liners in Iran primarily to push their rivals out of leadership positions.

Hostage Taking in Iran

The hostage-taking crisis has shaped U.S.–Iran relations since 1979 and, apart from the Iranian revolution itself, was the most important single event to shape politics in Iran. I was working in Tehran at the time of the hostage taking, and I interviewed some of the students who took part in the event. Consequently, my views on the hostage-taking crisis are influenced by personal experience as an Iranian present at the event, as a researcher who interviewed some participants on the spot, and as an academic later working in the United States and reading American accounts of what took place. What I find missing most from American accounts is an understanding of the vitally important functions served by the hostage crisis in the long term-goals of those seeking dictatorship.

The Iranian revolution that toppled the Mohammad Reza Shah (1919–1980) and ended the Pahlavi dynasty (1926–1978) involved an enormous uprising of a wide spectrum of Iranian society of many different political persuasions. Included in this revolutionary movement were millions of university-educated middle-class professionals, many with experience of life in

Western democracies. There were many factors that led to the revolution, but among these was a desire for greater political and social freedoms—freedoms that from a global perspective were in line with democratic aspirations. In addition to the millions of people who marched under an Islamic banner against the Shah, there were millions of others who had secular and democratic aspirations.

I started teaching at Tehran University and the National University (later renamed Beheshti University) in the spring of revolution immediately after the universities opened in 1979. University campuses in Iran had become very exciting places because a very broad array of political and cultural groups were taking advantage of the new freedoms available. Every imaginable political perspective was represented on campus, from Marxism–Leninism to Islamic fundamentalism, from liberal democratic to right-wing nationalist. Only the monarchists were banned. In the immediate postrevolution period, all other groups freely continued with their meetings and pamphlets and newspapers. Even within the Islamic movement, there were many different perspectives. Those who followed the line of the Imam, Khomeinists, were very different from the Mojahedin Khalgh, or what the Shah had called Islamic Marxists who were influenced by the left-leaning cleric Ayatollah Mahmoud Taleghani (1911–1979). No group had a power monopoly in the months immediately after the revolution, and women were free to be active in public life without the *hejab* (veil). Female professors and female students were fully active in universities.

The Continuity of Religious Traditions

But within the free atmosphere of Iran in that giddy postrevolution period, it was obvious that there were huge differences between the views of political factions. I was among the prodemocracy advocates, and I recall distinctly realizing that my views contradicted those of the pro-Imam Khomeini followers. To understand this clash, one needs to delve into some traditions in Shi'a Islam, the religion of well over 90% of Iranians. Every Shi'a Muslim is obligated to select a cleric worthy of serving as a source of imitation (*marja-i-taqlid*), an authority figure who will serve as a guide in all of the choices one makes in life, including in business and also personal decisions such as marriage and gender relations. Shi'a Muslims typically also pay their religious taxes (e.g., *khums*, *Zakat*) to this same marja-i-taqlid. The important clerics who have reached the lofty position of ayatollah, which means they have the authority to interpret the Koran, are selected as marja-i-taqlid by millions of followers. Important ayatollahs write *risala*, or detailed guides spelling out how their followers should think and act in every sphere of life (this is similar to the system of ordinary Chinese asking for instructions in Mao's China, to "secure the concordance of every action with Mao Zedong Thought" Leese, 2011, p. 198). In 1979 in Iran, Ayatollah Khomeini served as the marja-i-taqlid for tens of millions of Shi'a Muslims. His views about government and his support for an Islamic republic, headed by an Islamic jurist, had been known since the 1960s (Abrahamian, 1993). There was a direct contradiction between Khomeinism, the line of the Imam, and democracy.

Khomeinism

On the one hand, Khomeinism is based on the idea that a knowledgeable cleric, a marja-i-taqlid of the necessary caliber, knows what is best for the people and serves as their guide, as a shepherd guides a flock of sheep. This leader interprets the word of God for the people, in light of contemporary conditions. He helps them make the right choices in political, economic, social, and personal affairs. On the other hand, there is the idea of democracy as government "for the people, by the people." Again and again, I came across followers of Khomeini who dismissed democracy as a Western import, not suitable for Iran.

Khomeinism raises critical questions, such as whether the ordinary people can make important political decisions when they are ignorant of what God desires them to do according to the holy Koran. The role of the Supreme Leader is to show people the right path according to holy scripture. It would not matter if all of the people in Iran voted because the word of Imam Khomeini would be more important. Indeed, those following Khomeinism argued that the West had gone wrong exactly because of democracy, the people not having an absolute leader such as Imam Khomeini to lead them in the correct direction. Obviously, from the perspective of prodemocracy critics, Khomeinism maps directly onto the political system of dictatorship: one unelected leader making decisions for everyone.

But in the period immediately after the revolution, there still were prodemocracy advocates who hoped and openly spoke up for a more open, tolerant society. These advocates (myself included) seem naive in hindsight because they failed to recognize how effectively extremism coupled with violence can gain control of an entire society.

Khomeini's views about an Islamic republic, and Khomeinism in general, seemed so radical and out-of-date that the vast majority of university-educated Iranians did not consider them seriously. There seemed to be too many diverse prodemocracy, left-leaning, and liberal groups for the Khomeini line to succeed. However, Khomeini began a step-by-step line of attack, starting with a referendum in March 1979 asking people to simply choose between an Islamic republic and monarchy. The outcome of the referendum was a foregone conclusion given that the revolution had been antimonarchy, but the vast majority of people did not know what they were voting for. Next, Khomeini dismissed attempts to develop a constitution along democratic lines, building on the 1906 Iranian constitution, and instead set up a 73-member assembly to develop a new constitution for an Islamic republic. The constitution that emerged established that all law had to be in accordance with Islamic principles, and the ultimate interpreter of such principles and all laws was a Supreme Leader, *velayat-e-faghih*. In circumstances in which a single cleric was not recognized as having such leadership qualities, then a group of Supreme Leaders would guide the country.

In essence, velayat-e-faghih means that in the Iranian constitution the elected representatives of the people are subservient to the clerical leadership, either single or plural. It is as if the elected president and representatives of Europe were subservient to the Pope or a group of bishops if they failed to agree on a Pope.

But opposition to the constitution was deep, including among the members of the revolutionary government and even among some clergy. The idea of velayat-e-faghih was not generally agreed on, and at that time in Iran I came across many people inside and outside of universities who had helped to bring down the monarchy but were adamantly against the proposed constitution. At that time, Khomeinism was not strong enough as a movement to impose the principle of velayat-e-faghih. It is in this context of competing interests within Iran that one can best understand the important role that came to be played by the invasion of the U.S. embassy in Tehran and the taking of embassy staff as hostages.

Hostage Taking and the Prodemocracy Groups

My early childhood was spent in a house located close to the U.S. embassy in Tehran, and I knew the neighborhood very well and frequented it often. During and after the revolution, the embassy was routinely targeted by anti-Shah and anti-American demonstrators, and the first time it was physically attacked and taken over was on February 14, 1979. But after a few days, the government of the interim prime minister Mehdi Bazargan (1907–1995) managed to persuade the attackers to both free the embassy staff and to clear out of the embassy. Bazargan was married to one of my extended family; he was a devout Muslim, but he had been educated in France, and his long career as a political activist reflected a deep respect for human rights. Inevitably, his support for international law and human rights resulted in a direct clash with Khomeini.

In the period following the temporary takeover of the U.S. embassy, Khomeini kept his focus of attack on the United States. In speech after speech, he called the United States the "Great Satan," and he warned that the

American government was plotting to overthrow the revolution and bring back the monarchy. These warnings sounded highly plausible to Iranians because it was common knowledge that in 1953 the Central Intelligence Agency (CIA) had orchestrated a coup against Mohammed Mossadegh (1882–1967), the democratically elected prime minister of Iran, and reinstated the Shah as absolute dictator. Thus, Khomeini's constant accusations about American plots were highly persuasive in an Iranian context rife with rumors about CIA saboteurs and American spies. There were strong rumors in Iran at the time that most of Bazargan's political associates, particularly Abbas Amir-Entezam, Abol-Hasssan Bani-Sadre, Sadegh Ghotbzadeh, and Ibrahim Yazdi, were CIA operatives. (All of these early revolutionaries were later either assassinated, executed, or driven out of political life. Khomeini had himself appointed Bazargan as prime minister, and Khomeini's eventual outing and ousting of Bazargan was a clear example of a revolution eating its own children.)

Khomeini needed to find a means to drive out of power the Bazargan types, the prodemocracy, Western-educated Muslims who rejected his views on the Islamic republic and particularly the idea that society had to be subservient to a Supreme Guide, velayat-e-faghih (of course, Khomeini saw himself as this all-powerful guide). The hostage crisis provided such a means, and later the war with Iraq helped to complete the task of putting into place a dictatorship justified by Khomeini's interpretation of Islam. The actual takeover of the U.S. embassy on November 4, 1979, was not a planned event. I am convinced of this because I was close by at the time and spoke with some of the young people who climbed over the embassy wall. In hindsight, the attack against the U.S. embassy seemed to have been encouraged by Khomeini in speeches that demanded that the United States return the Shah to be put on trial in Iran, but in actuality Khomeini was opportunistic and he recognized he could use the hostage-taking crisis to consolidate his own power. He immediately sent his son Ahmed to lend support to the embassy invasion.

The Bazargan government collapsed almost immediately after Khomeini declared his support for the hostage taking. Along with this collapse, the more moderate, prodemocracy politicians and political movements were in retreat. The vanguard of the revolution was now headed in a different direction, involving direct radical action that flouted international law. Khomeini and his followers kept the focus of the nation on the American enemies by providing continuous coverage of the "plots" they had discovered in the captured "nest of spies," as they called the U.S. embassy (see Taheri's, 1988, lively account of the hostage crisis). Embassy personnel had not managed to shred all of the documents in the embassy, and even the shredded documents were now painstakingly put back together by "students of the line of the Imam." Every day there was a new revelation from the radicals inside the captured embassy so that the media headlines were continuously shaped by the Khomeinists. Moderate politicians found themselves attacked as pro-American, particularly if they attempted to argue that capturing an embassy and taking embassy staff as hostages was against international law. The radicals freed all Black and female hostages, and they accused the rest of the hostages of being spies intent on defeating the revolution and bringing back the monarchy.

Impact of the Doomed Rescue Mission

The position of the radicals became even stronger and that of the moderates even weaker when the Carter administration embarked on a seriously flawed and disastrous rescue mission (as discussed in Chapter 3, this volume). This mission has been discussed in detail from the perspective of the U.S. government and people (e.g., Ryan, 1985), but little attention has been given to the perspective from inside Iran. During my walks around the neighborhood of the captured U.S. embassy, it was clear that any American rescue attempt would end in large numbers of people being killed, probably including all of the hostages. If President Carter's main goal was to bring the hostages out of Iran alive, military force would fail. However, if the goal was to punish Iran and set an example so that other revolutionaries would not attack U.S. embassies around the world, then a huge military force and all-out war were needed.

The actual rescue mission was suicidal and doomed from the start. There was not ever a realistic possibility that the plan would work. Desperation was the main reason the plan was put into effect; the hostages were front-page news in the United States, and President Carter had no possibility of being reelected as long as the hostages remained in Iran. In the end, two of the eight helicopters involved in the rescue mission had to turn back because of mechanical failure, and eight American crew members died in a third helicopter that crashed at the desert site that was supposed to have served as the launching pad for the mission. The five remaining helicopters turned back, and the mission was aborted. Later, President Carter was to quip that if he had sent an additional helicopter, the mission would have been successful and he would have been reelected, but this assessment was utterly mistaken. There were simply too many Islamic fundamentalists inside and around the captured U.S. embassy for several truckloads of American troops to be able to carry out a surprise attack and rescue the hostages.

News of the failed American attack galvanized public attention inside Iran and helped Khomeini pinpoint attention on the external threat posed by the Great Satan. The rescue mission was presented as a direct attack on the revolution and evidence that America was determined to bring back the "CIA Shah." The Iranian public gave almost no attention to the threat posed by the Soviets, who had invaded Afghanistan and now shared a much longer border with Iran. Instead of being seen as an ally against the Soviets, the United States was seen as the only real enemy. Khomeini sent his henchman Sadegh Khalkhali (1926–2003), known as the "hanging judge," to the site of the crashed American helicopter, and the Iranian media were full of images of Khalkhali rummaging through the charred corpses of Americans who had died in the desert sands. It finally took 444 days for the hostages to be freed, and by that time Khomeini had found another external threat to use against his internal rivals—Saddam Hussein.

War and Saddam Hussein as External Enemy

On September 9, 1980, Iraqi troops crossed into Iran and so began the 8-year-long Iran–Iraq War. Khomeini and his supporters had stretched the hostage crisis as far as they could, and now they dragged on the war against Iraq even longer. Initially the Iraqi military made some ground because the Iranian defenses were so disorganized. The Iranian military had been gutted during the revolution. When I returned to Iran from studies in England, like hundreds of thousands of other returning Iranians I attempted to report for national service duty because at that time the law required that all Iranian men serve 2 years of national service. But I found that the military was in disarray and not equipped to incorporate new national service recruits. Most of the military barracks were looted and empty. Like many other young people, I received a military exemption. When the Iraqi military invaded Iran a year later, Iranian defenses were still disorganized. However, within a few years after the invasion, the Iranian military had recovered. Moreover, in addition to the regular military, there had now developed several additional layers of revolutionary security forces.

The war with Iraq allowed Khomeini and his followers to use the external enemy as an excuse to build up their own Islamic security forces (of course, Saddam Hussein was motivated by the same need for an external enemy to achieve a firmer grip on power inside Iraq) consisting of the following:

- Committees were connected to local mosques and consisted of bands of young zealots who would keep control in the neighborhood and ensure conformity and obedience among locals. These Committees helped control ration cards and ration supplies in each neighborhood but also continued to serve as a crude frontline information-gathering service for the regime's security apparatus.
- Basij literally translated means mobilization, and the origins of the Basij go back to the early days of the Iran–Iraq War when

the Iranian population was mobilized to send men and supplies to the front to fight the Iraqi invaders. But Basij gradually came to mean the mobilization of pro-Khomeini, rather than nationalist, forces, and after the end of the war in 1988, Basij took on a more formal political meaning, with Basij members also serving as local Committee members. By the time of the 2009 elections, fraudulently "won" by Mahmoud Ahmadinejad, the Basij had become a plainclothes security force able to mobilize quickly to trouble spots. Basij members mercilessly attacked people demonstrating against the fraudulent elections and quelled the antigovernment movement.

- The Republican Guards (or Guardians of the Revolution) also took shape during the Iran–Iraq War. From the time of the revolution, Khomeini and his supporters did not trust the regular military, even though all the senior and almost all midlevel officers had been replaced after the revolution. To ensure that the military would not be able to overthrow the mullahs, the Republican Guards were created as a parallel military force. During the Iran–Iraq War, the Republican Guards developed an army, a navy, and an air force parallel to those of the regular military. The Republican Guards now number almost 150,000 and control important parts of the Iranian economy, including several foundations and banks. The 2009 presidential elections saw a major power shift from the traditional mullahs to the Republican Guards and a handful of radical mullahs who now serve as a religious front for what has in practice become the military dictatorship of Iran.

Thus, the tactic of focusing on an external enemy enabled Khomeini and his hard-line followers to eliminate their internal rivals and hijack the revolution away from democracy to establish a dictatorship ruled by a Supreme Leader. The power of the Supreme Leader is based on the Revolutionary Guards, the Committees, and the Basij, all of which took shape and gained strength in the long struggles against external enemies. But having come to power and taken shape as an anti-American force, the radicals were trapped by their own tactics. After the Iran–Iraq War, they were forced to continue the battle against the United States, most publicly and directly through confrontation on Iran's nuclear program. The entire justification for the revolutionary regime in Iran has been anti-Americanism, so it is impossible for the regime to come to agreement with the United States without weakening its own foundation.

The anti-American justification for the dictatorship in Iran means that in the future the Iranian regime will be forced to align itself even closer with

China. Signs of this shift are already apparent in Iranian markets, which have been opened up to a flood of goods from China (often to the detriment of local Iranian industry). But alignment with China is less risky for the current Iranian regime because there is far less likelihood of rifts in the leadership over alignment with China than alignment with the United States.

Purifying the Leadership

The same zealous concern to purify the leadership has also been evident in other dictatorships, the classic examples being Stalinist Russia and Nazi Germany. As long as the Soviet Union was engaged in World War II, there was less danger from splintering within the Soviet leadership. However, after the war, the threat from Stalin's viewpoint was that there would be expectations for political restrictions to be eased, and he became concerned that the people might support reform-minded leaders. Consequently, "Immediately after the end of the war, Stalin launched a new purge of the army and the Party leadership, where rival power-centres, formed by groups perceived as 'liberal' reformers, had emerged as a challenge to his personal authority" (Figes, 2007, p. 464). In particular, military heroes who might provide inspiring leadership for the people were targeted by Stalin. Within a few years, many of the high-ranking military war heroes had been jailed or killed.

For Hitler, the war against the internal enemies was a precursor for the war against external enemies, and he used both groups of enemies as a means to solidify his power base. Thus, the attacks on minorities at home and the purification of the German leadership was, from Hitler's point of view, a necessary step to victory over external enemies. If the internal enemy became dangerous then, Hitler instructed, "all opponents should be killed and everyone in the concentration camps executed, so that a revolution would be deprived of its leaders at one stroke" (Gellately, 2001, p. 70). Throughout his struggles to attain and maintain power, Hitler was keenly focused on ensuring that there would be no one to challenge his position and the Nazi leadership would remain unified behind him.

COHESION, LOYALTY, AND CORRUPTION IN DICTATORSHIPS

Dictatorships are by definition relatively closed political systems in which the vast majority of people have no voice and even the members of the ruling elite do not have freedom to deviate from the official line. Dictatorships survive by crushing opposition voices, particularly if dissent arises from within the ruling elite. The higher up the chain of command the voice of dissent, the more merciless the reaction from the dictator. The members of the power elite must be absolutely loyal to the Supreme Dictator to survive.

This take-no-prisoners absolutist approach creates a context that is highly conducive to the growth of corruption. In dictatorships, citizens rightly fear that if they voice complaints about any form of corruption, this will be interpreted as rebellion against the regime—a deadly sin. As a consequence, there is a deep and justified fear among the people of being identified as a dissident. The outcome is prevailing silence and reluctance to provide feedback to rectify faults in the system.

The silence prevailing in dictatorships is reinforced by the behavior and advice of family and friends, coworkers and neighbors, and everyone in one's social circle. This is because they are all keenly aware that when a person in their circle is branded as a troublemaker by security forces, they too could become "infected" by association.

People working in positions of authority in dictatorships are very aware of the reluctance of ordinary citizens to speak out and risk being branded a dissident. This leads to a greater and greater tendency for employees, including government officials, to become inefficient and corrupt and to accept inefficiency and corruption in others as well as to rebrand complaints about inefficiency and corruption as criticism of the political regime. This holds even in cases in which the complaint has nothing to do with politics— ostensibly at least. For example, in two separate instances I complained about the inefficiency of local bureaucrats in Iran in the early 1980s, and in each case my complaint was turned against me: I was complaining because of my opposition to the revolutionary government. I had the same experience when I travelled in Eastern Europe before the collapse of the USSR: My complaints against traffic police fines were relabeled as criticism against the communist regime.

The silence prevailing in dictatorships ensures that the long-term trend is always toward greater and greater inefficiency and corruption. Bribery and kickbacks become part of the normal way of doing business. Critics inside the country are jailed or killed, while critics outside the country are dismissed as lacking cultural understanding: "You outsiders do not appreciate that what you call bribery is not bribery but part of the local culture." The impact of inefficiency and corruption is to lower the quality of life for the masses.

People living in dictatorships recognize that their lives are polluted by corruption and inefficiency; this is particularly so in dictatorships such as Russia, Iran, China, and Saudi Arabia, where international travel and news are more common. Regimes such as North Korea and Cuba attempt to more strictly limit information, but the isolation only increases the ratcheting up of inefficiency and corruption. How is the regime to deal with the frustrations that arise among the masses living their daily lives in inefficient and corrupt systems? In the next chapter, I discuss one of the most important mechanisms used by dictatorships.

CONCLUDING COMMENT

The concept of displaced aggression continues to be highly influential in research (e.g., Vasquez, Lickel, & Hennigan, 2010) and indispensable in explaining the behavior of dictatorial regimes. The closed nature of dictatorships and their intolerance of criticism result in increasing inefficiency and corruption and a generally lower standard of living for the masses. To diffuse anger and frustration among the passes, the dictatorial regimes target internal and external enemies and displace aggression onto them. But this strategy is costly because aggression against internal minorities (including scientists and intellectuals) has high human and economic costs, wasting scarce human resources, and aggression against external targets results in the damaging of international relations and trade.

Displacement is a powerful means of behavioral control in dictatorships. In Chapter 6, I consider the processes of behavior regulation more broadly.

6

CONFORMITY, OBEDIENCE, AND BEHAVIOR REGULATION

> She arrived in a striped sweater, long-limbed and elegant despite a giant
> rip below one knee of her Prada trousers. The short haircut that invited
> comparisons to Audrey Hepburn was growing out. . . . She drove her
> Prius over to Venice, where she stood for a long time admiring a checked
> dress in the window of Pamela Barish's Abbot Kinney shop. . . . She
> chooses chic and often witty gala dresses from Prada, Lanvin, and Viollet.
> —Joan Juliet Buck (2010, p. 270)
> describing the actress Carey Mulligan in *Vogue*

One can better appreciate the psychology of conformity and obedience
by first considering examples from everyday life in relatively open societies
rather than extreme instances in extreme situations, such as conformity and
obedience in Nazi Germany, North Korea, or Iran or torture in Abu Graib.
An extraordinarily rich arena for this research project is international fashion
and the processes through which certain styles of dress and behavior become
generally recognized as "better" and widely adopted. Magazines such as *Vogue*
serve as powerful means through which fashion tastes are manufactured and
cascaded down among the wider population, with the younger generation
being more highly involved. This cascading often takes place through relatively indirect messages inserted in articles about famous personalities, as in
the case of the quoted article about the actress Carey Mulligan at the beginning of this chapter. But fashion guidelines are also given more explicitly
and directly. In the same issue of *Vogue* ("Point of View," 2010), the reader is
provided with a list of

DOI: 10.1037/14138-007
The Psychology of Dictatorship, by F. M. Moghaddam
Copyright © 2013 by the American Psychological Association. All rights reserved.

things happening in fashion this fall. Starting with:

Flared pants that flower below the knee, enfolding shoes in their tulip-like bell.

The midi length for skirts, a streamlined and sophisticated favorite that harks back to the post-Depression thirties.

A slick, strong-shouldered blazer, worn with scrunched-up sleeves for a knockout balance of professionalism and pugnacity. (p. 265)

The first thing that strikes one about this kind of list is that the guideline is completely arbitrary in the sense that it is not based on any kind of objective standard. Why flared rather than narrow pants? Why should midi length be better than mini or maxi length for skirts? Why strong-shouldered rather than soft-shouldered blazer? In the same list, readers are told that "surplus green" is the color "happening in fashion this fall." Why green? Why not blue or purple or gray? The important point is that although such fashion criteria are arbitrary, they influence behavior. This basic but powerful aspect of conformity was brilliantly demonstrated by the Turkish American psychologist Muzafer Sherif (1906–1988), whose work is discussed later in this chapter.

In March 2011, *Vogue* published an article glorifying President Assad and his family, referring to his English wife as a "rose in the desert" (Buck, 2011, p. 529), "glamorous . . . very chic" (p. 529), and to Syria as "the safest country in the Middle East" (p. 529). The article gives the impression that the Assads are ordinary Syrian people, not even needing bodyguards. The following incident was reported by Mrs. Assad about a visit by the famous Hollywood icons Angelina Jolie and Brad Pitt:

> My husband was driving us all to lunch . . . and out of the corner of my eye I could see Brad Pitt was fidgeting. I turned around and asked, "Is anything wrong?"
>
> "Where's your security?" asked Pitt.
>
> So I started to tease him—"See that old woman on the street? That's one of them! And that old guy crossing the road? That's the other one!" They both laughed. (Buck, 2011, p. 532)

The article goes on to quote the dictator Assad as saying, "Brad Pitt wanted to send his security guards here to come and get some training!"

Because Assad's regime has slaughtered tens of thousands Syrians recently, there was a huge backlash against this ill-timed public relations stunt, and *Vogue* went into damage control and even scrubbed the article from its website.

Mrs. Assad is thin, very expensively dressed, and powerful, and this makes her excellent material for *Vogue* coverage. But there is a deeper reason why it is perfectly appropriate for *Vogue* to dedicate space to Mrs. Assad, and there is a deeper link between the Assads and Hollywood icons. *Vogue* and Hollywood help shape the normative system in the fashion world, where arbitrary norms influence the masses. The influence of *Vogue* and Hollywood reflects the subtle conformity achieved in capitalist democracies. Assad's dictatorship relies on guns, tanks, tear gas, and torture; he enforces obedience and conformity through direct, brutal tactics. *Vogue*'s article on Assad, and the symbolism of bodyguards for Hollywood icons being trained by bodyguards for dictators such as Assad, is a reminder of the intertwined nature of behavior regulation in the two worlds of capitalist democracy and dictatorship, one subtle and implicit, the other direct and explicit. Common to both worlds are the psychological processes underlying conformity and obedience.

VARIETIES OF PRESSURE IN DICTATORSHIPS

During the years I lived in Iran after the 1979 revolution, there were a number of political elections, a few for important national leadership positions. The Supreme Leader of Iran at that time, Ayatollah Khomeini, made it clear that it was the duty of all Iranians to participate in the elections. Of course, I would have been very happy to participate if voters had been presented with a real choice between candidates representing genuinely competing political positions. However, like many other millions of Iranians, I felt that the candidates permitted to run in elections all represented the same extremist Islamic position; they did not represent my views. Candidates were vetted by the Council of Guardians, and besides that they had to jump through many other hoops to demonstrate their loyalty to the Supreme Leader and the fanatical clique ruling the country. Consequently, I had every motivation to not participate in elections because I could only vote in support of candidates who would continue the dictatorship.

But not voting in elections proved to be a challenge. The authorities would know who did and who did not vote because records were kept using birth certificates and ration cards. Second, those who voted had their thumbs marked with indelible ink. When I went to work after an election and did not have indelible ink on my thumb, comments were made about my un-Islamic tendencies; I had turned my back on the Supreme Leader. The pressure after one election became so intense that I actually put ink on my thumb so that people would assume I had voted. Here I was, then, forced to pretend to be like the others in obedience to the leadership. I remember that at the time two lines from Yeats's "The Scholars" came to my mind:

> All think what other people think;
> All know the man their neighbour knows.

Yeats's poem is about conformity among scholars (which is apt, because I was working in a university at the time), but of course scholars are supposed to show less *conformity*, changes in behavior that arise from real or imagined group pressure, and *obedience*, changes in behavior that arise when people follow the instructions of persons in authority. In practice, the pressures forcing individuals to conform to local norms can be as great in a university as in any other setting. Anyone who has worked in a university or any other complex organization, even in democracies, becomes keenly aware of the tremendous pressures that can be placed on individuals to force them to conform and obey, to not speak out, and to put up with the antics of *little dictators* in the work setting. But in dictatorships, this experience is magnified so that life in all of society involves absolute obedience and conformity. Parallel to the little dictators at work is the Great Dictator in the larger society. In a democracy, one can escape the little dictators at work and enjoy some freedom at the end of the working day, but in a dictatorship such as Iran there is no escape because the Great Dictator encompasses all of life. This has very important implications for inefficiency.

I discussed in earlier chapters how the closed nature of dictatorships and the intolerance for any kind of critical feedback result in greater and greater inefficiency. Conformity and obedience also have important implications for efficiency because an indispensable path for improvement of a system is through people who step out of line and provide critical feedback. In this sense, then, nonconformity and disobedience must be tolerated to some degree as a way to critically assess problem areas and improve the system.

I address two sets of questions in this chapter. First, what are the psychological processes associated with conformity and obedience? Psychologists have conducted extensive empirical research on this question and have available solid evidence that illuminates the nature of conformity and obedience in all societies, dictatorships, democracies, and otherwise. Second, how does the type of all-encompassing and absolute obedience and conformity achieved in dictatorships come about? To answer this question, I also need to examine everyday life in dictatorships.

THE PSYCHOLOGY OF CONFORMITY AND OBEDIENCE

Sherif (1935, 1936) began by exploring *spontaneous norms*, norms that evolve naturally within groups without any effort to manipulate norm formation. Participants in Sherif's study sat in a dark room and saw a pinpoint of light that appeared to move. They were asked to estimate how much the spot of light moved, for a total of 100 estimations in each of four sessions. Each participant's repeated estimates converged on a narrow range, and a personal norm emerged for that individual. Other participants also made estimates, and there were differences in the amount of movement each participant perceived. Some individuals perceived more than 6 inches of movement, others less than 1 inch. Actually, the spot of light never moved, and the perceived movement was an illusion known as the *autokinetic effect*.

After being tested in isolation, individuals were brought together in small groups. Each individual once again made estimates of the amount of movement he or she perceived, but this time in a group setting. Gradually, estimates converged around a group norm. An important finding was that when participants were tested again individually outside of the group, it was found that they continued to be influenced by the group norm. However, participants who had the opportunity to first be tested individually outside of the group were less influenced by the group norm than participants who first made estimates as part of a group and only then made estimates outside of the group. Subsequent research explored *manipulated norms*, norms explicitly brought about by design (Jacobs & Campbell, 1961). When a confederate of the experimenter was introduced into the group and made extreme estimates of the amount of perceived movement, this extreme estimate continued to influence the group norm even after the "extremist" left the group and was replaced by a naive participant. In fact, as the group membership was changed, with naive group members being replaced by new ones, several generations of naive participants continued to be influenced by the extreme estimates given by the lone confederate.

These findings demonstrate that spontaneously generated norms can influence one's behavior, even when they are arbitrary and incorrect. Moreover, extremists can influence others to conform to even more radically incorrect norms.

Groupthink

The idea that participation in groups can lead individuals to make incorrect decisions is underlined by research on *groupthink*, the tendency for people in groups to converge on unwise courses of action they would have avoided if they were making the decision individually (Janis, 1971, 1972, 1982). The early research on groupthink involved case studies of historic decision-making disasters, such as the so-called Bay of Pigs invasion. In 1961, the U.S. military and the Central Intelligence Agency provided support for an army of Cuban exiles as they invaded Cuba in an attempt to overthrow the Castro regime. The invasion had been approved by President John F. Kennedy and his highly talented band of advisers. Within 3 days, the invaders had been captured or killed or had fled. This U.S.-backed attack was a complete disaster, being condemned by many around the world and pushing Cuba into the arms of the USSR. From that time, the threat of a U.S. attack, the ever-present external threat, against Cuba was repeatedly used by the

Castro regime to repress opposition groups and stymie democratic tendencies in Cuba. How could such an intelligent president and his brilliant advisors have made such a foolish decision?

Another well-discussed case in the early research on groupthink was the escalation of the Vietnam War in the 1960s. President Lyndon B. Johnson was known as being highly intelligent, progressive, and politically astute, and in the mid 1960s he met regularly with a highly educated band of advisors known for their humanitarian outlook. Yet this same president and his advisors decided to secretly escalate the Vietnam War and try to bomb the enemy into submission. The result was that the American public became alienated from the White House, opposition to the war escalated, and the United States was forced to abandon South Vietnam, which was quickly overwhelmed by communist North Vietnam.

In recent history there seems to be no end to the instances in which people who are high in at least one type of intelligence have made disastrous decisions with enormously detrimental consequences. For example, consider the British prime minister Neville Chamberlain and his advisers who in 1938 accepted Hitler's assurances that he was not going to invade other countries despite all the evidence to the contrary. Chamberlain's declaration of "peace in our time" proved to be ridiculous. But soon after that, Hitler and his inner circle also seemed to have been victims of groupthink when they decided to invade Russia in 1941, repeating the mistake Napoleon Bonaparte and his generals made in 1812 when they invaded Russia and lost most of the French army in the long Russian winter (actually, a similar mistake was made by King Charles XII of Sweden when he attacked Russia in 1707 and his forces were destroyed by the harsh conditions; see Massie, 1980).

In the 21st century, the invasion of Iraq by U.S.-led forces in 2003 must be considered an enormous blunder by President George W. Bush's administration (2000–2008) in close collaboration with British Prime Minister Tony Blair's government (1997–2007). Despite all the evidence that Iraq did not have weapons of mass destruction, the American and British heads of state with their advisors decided to go ahead with the invasion without adequate plans for Iraqi society after the military operations were completed. The result was greater instability in the Near and Middle East, the killing of hundreds of thousands of people, and the dramatically increased influence of America's foe in the region, Iran. The war cost several trillion dollars at a time when the United States could ill afford such disastrous adventures. In addition, the invasion of Iraq and the mismanagement of the postinvasion situation resulted in a marked increase in radicalization and terrorism among Muslims (Moghaddam, 2006).

Although the concept of groupthink continues to be influential (Esser, 1998), critics have argued that evidence in support of groupthink tends to be from case studies that might be interpreted differently and that group decision-making that is open can still yield negative outcomes (Tetlock, Peterson, McGuire, Chang, & Feld, 1992). There seems to be no end of examples of groupthink when one considers events retrospectively, as Janis (1971, 1972, 1982) did, and selects cases to support the concept. However, early attempts at more tightly controlled experimental tests of the idea of groupthink have had rather mixed results (e.g., Leana, 1985). Despite this, there is general agreement that groupthink is more likely to come about when a group functions in isolation from expert opinion, is highly cohesive, has a directive leader with a preferred solution, and there is a lack of procedures for critical assessment.

Two particularly promising lines of research have explored the role of identity and identification (Packer & Chasteen, 2010) and strategies for preventing groupthink (Mok & Morris, 2010). The general assumption had been that group cohesion increases the chance of groupthink, but it is also clear that those who are highly loyal and dedicated group members are more likely to speak up when the group is in danger of making destructive decisions. Thus, identifying with the group more strongly can mean being ready to criticize group decisions and prevent groupthink. Also, it is more likely that people will speak up and prevent groupthink when there is cultural diversity among members. Indeed, a promising idea is that in creating work groups, managers should intentionally create diversity as an antidote to groupthink (Fernandez, 2007).

Conformity to Norms Established by Majorities and Minorities

Sherif's (1935, 1936) studies using the autokinetic effect demonstrated the power of arbitrary norms, such as those found in fashion, but what about situations in which the criteria are more objective? People are influenced by group norms when the issue is something like the "correct" skirt length or tie color, but what about situations in which the criteria allow for a clear-cut distinction between correct and incorrect. Would one still be influenced by a group if one could clearly recognize the correct answer to a question, but the majority of people in the group insisted on giving an incorrect answer? This research question was tackled by Solomon Asch (1951, 1955, 1956) in innovative studies focused on line estimations.

As a participant in Asch's study, individuals first underwent an eye examination to ensure that they had normal vision. Next, participants entered a laboratory and found themselves in a small group of seven people. The experimenter showed participants three lines of different lengths, and they had to assess which of these was the same length as a standard line. Actually, the correct answer was easily identified, and participants were certain of their answers. When tested individually, they gave the correct answer in almost 100% of trials. In the group setting, one participant was the last person to arrive, and so that individual was the last group member to call out his or her answers. The rest of the group all saw the lines as that person did, and for a number of trials they all agreed in their answers. But then something unexpected happened: The rest of the group, who were actually Asch's confederates and all trained to give the same answers, gave answers that seemed obviously wrong to the last participant. The question was, would that participant go against the rest of the group and give what he or she believed to be the correct answer, or would that participant conform and give the wrong answer?

Approximately one third of the participants conformed to the majority norm and gave wrong answers on most of the trials, and about 70% of participants yielded to the majority norm on some trials. This Asch study has been replicated in both Western and non-Western societies, and although there is some variation in the level of conformity, in all societies a sizable group of participants went along with the majority and gave the wrong answers (Nicholson, Cole, & Rocklin, 1985; Noriyuki, 1985). When interviewed after the experiment, participants often reported that they realized they were giving the wrong answer but that it had felt easier to go along with the group. However, more recent research using functional magnetic resonance imaging suggested that conformity in the Asch-type experimental situation can be associated with changes in perception; that is, participants actually see differently when they conform and might not be aware of their own change in perception (Berns et al., 2005).

What is the source of conformity? Undoubtedly, the major source is socialization; people are trained to conform to group norms. From birth, children are shaped to conform by and within their families and then placed in schools and other institutions for more formal training in how to think and act correctly. Such training is in line with ideas about correct ways of behaving for people in different groups, such as male and female, rich and poor, powerful and relatively powerless; as stereotypes change, so does conformity by different groups. For example, early research on conformity found that female participants conform more than male participants mainly in studies reported by men (Eagly & Carli, 1981). As gender stereotypes changed, it was found that conformity can be common to both males and females (Eagly & Wood, 1991). Indeed, when women are given greater power, they conform less (Alizadehfard, 2010).

The research on the emergence of group norms (following Sherif, 1935) and conformity to majority established norms (following Asch, 1956) provides experimental demonstrations of how in dictatorships people are forced to conform to norms that are often arbitrary in the sense that they have no objective basis. Of course, the regimes in dictatorships attempt to establish their norms as scientific. Thus, "race experts" attempted to provide objective justifications for Nazi policies toward Jews, Gypsies, the "feebleminded," and other minorities (Gellately, 2001). In Iran, I listened to so-called scientific explanations of how men are affected by the "rays of light" from women's hair as a justification for forcing women to wear the veil (for some reason, women are immune from the effects of rays of light from men's hair).

But, to look on the bright side from the perspective of prodemocracy forces, the most important finding from research on conformity is that many people, often most people, did not conform in the situations described by Sherif and Asch. Most people did not give the incorrect answer under pressure from the majority. True, in real-life situations nonconformity often has a very high cost: In Russia, North Korea, Iran, China, Saudi Arabia, and other contemporary dictatorships, nonconformists are routinely harassed, imprisoned, and even killed. Researchers cannot replicate this kind of horrendous cost—such as a women being stoned to death in Iran for behaving "improperly"—in a laboratory.

Nonconformity

Nonconformity does have a cost even in laboratory studies. In the Berns et al. (2005) study that used functional magnetic resonance imaging to track brain activities of participants who went through a conformity study similar to that of Asch (1956), it was discovered that only participants who did not conform had high levels of activity in brain regions associated with emotions (increased amygdale and caudate activity). One interpretation of this finding is that conflicting emotions are associated with, or a cost of, nonconformity. Those who conformed and gave the wrong answer had higher brain activity in areas of the brain associated with vision and spatial awareness rather than areas associated with higher level decision making and emotions.

The emotional costs of nonconformity indicate the enormous difficulties faced by those who currently campaign for sociopolitical reforms in dictatorships (e.g., Mikhail Khodorkovsky in Russia, Shirin Ebadi and Akbar Ganji in Iran, Abdelnasser al-Rabbasi in Libya, Ayman Nour in Egypt, Yusuf Jumaev in Kazakhstan, Liu Xiaobo and Gao Zhisheng in China, Aung San Suu Kyi in Burma, Arnold Tsunga in Zimbabwe, Golden Misabiko in Congo, Yoani Sánchez in Cuba, and Le Cong Dinh in Vietnam). The French researcher Serge Moscovici pointed to what is arguably a qualitative difference between majority and minority influence: Majorities have the power to force compliance (and then conversion might arise as people change their attitudes in line with their changed conformist behavior), but minorities do not have the power to force compliance and have to rely on conversion instead (Moscovici, Mucchi-Faina, & Maas, 1994).

Obedience

To obey God we must obey the Prophet;
To obey the Prophet we must obey Imam Ali;
To obey Imam Ali we must obey the clergy,
Especially Imam Khomeini;
And to obey Imam Khomeini we must obey his successor,
His Eminence Ayatollah Khamenei, the leader of the Islamic Revolution.
(Ayatollah Azari-Qomi cited in Abrahamian, 1993, p. 132)

As the cases of Iran, Saudi Arabia, and other religion-based dictatorships demonstrate, religion can provide a powerful justification for absolute obedience. Looking at the situation of Iran and other such countries from the vantage point of the West, one might ask, whether there is something wrong with people in Iran that they obey religious authority figures. Why are they not able to break away from this tradition of blind religious obedience? But one needs to be cautious in reaching judgments in this arena for a number of reasons. First, dictatorships such as North Korea clearly show that absolute obedience can be achieved without the state using a religious justification. Second, the greatest modern examples of dictatorships in which absolute obedience came about have been based on Nazi and communist (rather than religious) ideologies headed by Hitler and Stalin, respectively. Third, research evidence strongly suggests that under certain conditions human beings, irrespective of their culture, religion, gender, and other group characteristics, blindly obey authority figures in ways that result in destructive outcomes. The key task is to examine the conditions that result in such obedience.

Of course, there is a need for some types and levels of obedience for effective group functioning. For example, when a traffic accident occurs and police officers divert traffic to an alternative route, the situation would become completely chaotic if drivers decided to disobey the police. So one needs to differentiate between obedience that is necessary to ensure the smooth functioning of society and obedience that is destructive and results in harm to others. Thus, I am concerned in this discussion with obedience that has resulted in enormous wrongs (Kelman & Hamilton, 1989), the classic examples being the Holocaust and other terrible outcomes of blind obedience during World War II.

THE MILGRAM EXPERIMENTS

Indeed, it was the puzzle of obedience during World War II that led Stanley Milgram (1933–1984) to design and carry out the most important psychological studies ever conducted on obedience (discussed in Chapter 1, this volume). Milgram (1974) identified the key characteristics of obedience, as different from conformity. First, obedience regulates the behavior of individuals with unequal status (e.g., soldiers and their commander), whereas conformity regulates the behavior of individuals with equal status (e.g., soldiers in a unit). Second, obedience involves following orders, whereas conformity involves behaving the same through imitation. The leader issuing orders does not necessarily have to carry out the order— the commander who orders followers to "attack and sacrifice your blood" does not have to attack and sacrifice himself. But unlike in obedience, in conformity there is similarity in behavior. Third, obedience to authority is explicit: The leader orders "attack," and the followers explicitly know what they are supposed to do. Conformity is often implicit: People are influenced by subtle cues and change their own behavior in line with others without explicit acknowledgment. Finally, obedience is involuntary: The soldier has to follow the orders of the commander. Conformity is voluntary in the sense that people who conform at least believe they are behaving in a certain way because they want to. For example, people who follow a new fashion norm feel they do so because they want to rather than because they have been ordered to.

With these distinct features of obedience in mind, Milgram designed his famous studies on obedience to authority, carried out at Yale University. He advertised for volunteers ages 20 through 50 to participate in studies ostensibly on the psychology of learning. Participants from a broad range of backgrounds were selected after being screened to ensure that they were within the normal range in terms of personality characteristics. As in most learning situations, this one involved a teacher and a learner. Participants worked in pairs, and they drew lots to decide which of them would be in the role of teacher and which in the role of learner. In practice, the situation was arranged for Milgram's confederate, an actor who played the role of a 47-year-old accountant, to always become the learner. The naive participant always drew lots and became the teacher.

The task of the teacher was to teach the learner a series of work associations. When the learner made a mistake, the teacher's task was to inflict punishment using a shock generator consisting of 30 switches set in a horizontal line. The switches were clearly marked in 15-V increments, from 15 to 450 V. Additionally, each group of four switches was labeled from *slight shock* to *moderate shock* to *danger: severe shock* to *XXX*. The teacher was given a shock of 45 V just so that he or she understood what a mild shock felt like. The learner was then seated, and the learning task began. The authority figure in this learning situation was the scientist in the white lab coat who instructed the teacher to increase the level of punishment by 15 V each time the learner made a mistake.

Before this experiment was undertaken, Milgram described the procedures to a group of 40 psychiatrists and asked them to predict the percentage of American citizens who would obey to harm others in this situation. These experts predicted that only about 1% would keep administering shocks to the highest levels and most people would stop before 150 V. Laypeople also predicted that normal participants would avoid harming others (of course, in the real experiment the learner was a confederate of the experimenter, and the learner did not actually receive electric shocks—he simply acted as if he did). Thus, both experts and laypeople predicted (incorrectly) that the Milgram experimental situation would not result in obedience to authority to harm an innocent other.

The Shocking Results

The results of the Milgram obedience experiments were an utter shock: The majority (about 65%) of normal, healthy participants continued to increase the shocks to the highest level. Even when the learner screamed out that he had a bad heart and wanted to be set free, most teachers followed the instructions of the scientist, the authority figure, and continued to administer increasingly higher levels of shock. These results were completely unexpected. Moreover, when the Milgram obedience study was repeated with female participants, the same pattern of results was replicated. But perhaps this is a pattern peculiar to Americans? No: When the experiment was repeated in other countries, including Australia (Kilham & Mann, 1974), East Africa (Munroe, Munroe, & Whiting, 1981), Italy (Ancona & Pareyson, 1968), Jordan (Shanab & Yahya, 1977), Germany (Mantell, 1971), and the Netherlands (Meeus & Raaijmakers, 1986), the results showed obedience levels from 40% to 90%, so participants from some cultures were even more obedient than Americans. A recent partial replication of Milgram's study demonstrated only slightly lower levels of obedience among Americans (Burger, 2009; only a partial replication was attempted because new ethics rules prevented a full replication of Milgram's procedures).

Milgram's studies also suggested ways in which obedience could be decreased, for example, if the teacher is physically closer to the learner when the shock is administered and if the authority figure is in a different room from the teacher (the naive participant) and communicates by telephone. Similarly, if a second teacher (actually a confederate of the experimenter) is present who refuses to administer shocks, then obedience declines. Most important from the perspective of the main focus of this book, when there are two authority figures and they show signs of disagreement, then obedience declines significantly. This last point is vitally important because it underlines the key role of solidarity in the authority or ruling group.

Institutions and Dominant–Subordinate Relations

Conformity and obedience often take place in the context of institutions, and one of the tactics used by dictatorships is to create and expand institutional control throughout society. The most explicit example of this is through political parties, such as the Communist Party in the Soviet Union and the Nazi Party in Germany, but religious institutions have also been used, such as in Iran where the network of mosques has been used to reinforce conformity and obedience. One of the most powerful demonstrations of the power of institutions to bring about behavioral change was the prison simulation study by Zimbardo (1972, 2008).

The results of Zimbardo's (1972, 2008) study were as unexpected and surprising as those of Milgram's (1974) obedience studies in large part because people underestimated the power of the situation to influence normal participants to behave destructively (for an alternative perspective on Zimbardo's study, see Reicher & Haslam, 2006). The context of Zimbardo's study was a simulated prison at Stanford University. The participants were recruited through a newspaper announcement informing them they would receive $15 per day and the experiment would last 2 weeks. Zimbardo selected 24 participants judged to be "normal" in terms of personality characteristics, and randomly assigned them to play either the role of prison guard or prisoner. The prisoners were picked up by the Palo Alto Police Department and taken to the simulated jail. Both prisoners and prison guards wore uniforms, and the prison guards also had clubs and whistles. The guards were instructed to keep order, and the experiment began.

The surprising result was that the study had to be abandoned on Day 6 because the prisoners were being severely mistreated by the guards. The prisoners became passive accepters of degrading treatment, and the guards developed sadistic routines of behavior that resulted in the breakdown of some prisoners. Later, Zimbardo (2008) used the findings of the Stanford prison study to help interpret the mistreatment of Iraqi prisoners by American prison guards at Abu Ghraib Prison in Iraq:

> The primary simple lesson the Stanford Prison Experiment teaches is that situations matter. Social situations can have more profound effects on the behavior and mental functioning of individuals, groups, and national leaders than we might believe possible. Some situations can exert such powerful influence over us that we can be led to behave in ways we would not, could not, predict was possible in advance. (pp. 211–212)

The psychological research on conformity and obedience demonstrates how group norms become established, how arbitrary group norms can influence conformity among group members, and how under certain conditions even normal individuals can do terrible harm to others. But the brilliant studies on conformity and obedience innovated by Sherif, Asch, Milgram, Zimbardo, and others need to be supplemented by more detailed assessments of how, in practice, conformity and obedience are brought about in dictatorships.

CONFORMITY AND OBEDIENCE IN DICTATORSHIPS

Dictatorships use brute force to create conditions that maximize conformity and obedience in a population. As implied by Tyler's (2012) group value model, because people do not have voice in dictatorships, attachment to the regime can only come about through force. In response to those who refuse to conform and obey, dictatorships consistently resort to brute force to crush dissent. More specifically, the following are some of the procedures used by dictators to isolate "rebels" and to use isolation and silence to create conformity and obedience in the larger society. In the Iranian dictatorship, this isolation has been reinforced by strategies designed to minimize the capabilities of dissenters and maximize conformity to norms established by the regime. The four basic steps to this strategy are detailed next.

Maximum Control of Public Space

Through the *basij, gasht,* the Republican Guards, and other non-uniformed and uniformed security forces, which are to greater and lesser degrees under central control, the public sphere is "guarded" against un-Islamic activities. This security is ostensibly needed to guard against immorality, but in the context of the Iranian dictatorship an enormously wide-ranging set of behaviors comes under the umbrella of morality. The most obvious concerns of security forces are immoral self-presentation and gender relations in public: Women are the primary targets of morality policing, whereby they can be arrested, for example, if their hair shows from under their hejab or if they use cosmetics. However, men also often become targets for wearing the wrong kind of clothing or touching or standing too close to a woman or even looking the wrong way at a woman.

Men can also become targets by having the wrong kind of hairstyle or beard. In 2010, the government of Ahmadinejad publicly introduced a set of acceptable and unacceptable hair styles for men. Given that acceptable and unacceptable can be influenced by subjective judgments, there is always a high level of uncertainly about what the borderline is between moral and immoral. The result is continual uncertainty about safety among ordinary people. This uncertainty is exactly what the dictatorship requires. A male friend of mine attempted to circumvent the ambiguity by arranging his outward appearance as unambiguously Islamic. When his house was raided by Republican Guards, he was instructed to shave his beard: They did not want him looking like an Islamic fundamentalist.

Speedy Identification, Isolation, and Destruction of Opposition Voices

A major difference between traditional and modern dictatorships is reflected in their use of torture. As Rejali (1994, 2007) has pointed out, traditional torture was public, ritualized, and ceremonial. It took place as part of the public discourse and theatrics. Crowds would gather to watch, marvel, and even cheer as bodies were tortured and dismembered. Modern torture is secretive and takes place away from public scrutiny. In 21st-century Iran, torture continues even more prevalently than before, but out of sight, behind the locked gates of Evin (in Tehran) and other prisons. Similarly, traditional dictatorships did not feel the need to hide behind a facade of popular support; they could simply exert power and rule through the legitimacy of power. Opposition to the traditional dictatorships could be crushed openly. Modern dictatorships crush oppositional power secretly.

Typical of the routines for crushing the opposition is what happened to an acquaintance of mine in the Iranian dictatorship in the early 1980s. He disappeared, and as with all such disappearances, people suspected that he had been arrested by security forces. Family and friends started a search, going to major prisons, Republican Guard centers, and other such places. In the meantime, his wife received telephone calls from unknown persons, telling her that they could help free her husband for a fee. She was prepared to pay what she could but wanted to make sure that she made the payment to people who would actually help free her husband. She was in the city of Ghom, the home of many influential clerics, trying to gain influence by paying Islamic taxes when other family members back in Tehran discovered (one of them received a telephone call) that her husband had been executed. They were to collect his body, pay for bullet expenses, and bury him without ceremony. There would be reprisals if the family made a fuss about the execution. After all, he was an enemy of the revolution, and anyone who objected to his execution would be seen as sympathetic to his cause.

Of course, as in most such cases in Iran, the court case that decided the fate of the prisoner was secret, and his family never discovered exactly what he was accused of or what evidence was brought against him or by whom. Some prisoners of Evin have lived to tell the tale, both during the Shah's dictatorship (Baraheni, 1977) and during the postrevolution dictatorship (e.g., Ghahramani, 2009). Reports of survivors in dictatorship prisons and Gulags shows how luck, guile, resilience, and sometimes bizarre twists of fate are needed to come out alive. For example, a strategy that worked for a female prisoner in Iran's Evin prison was to marry her prison interrogator for a while (Nemat, 2008).

Social and Family Programs and the Role of Women in Dictatorships

It is impossible to overstate the role of sheer violence, actual or threatened, in forcing people to silently conform and obey as participants in social and family programs in dictatorships. At the center of this attention on the part of authorities is the shaping of the role of women, which represents the enormous depth and extent of the penetration achieved by various dictatorships in the everyday lives of ordinary people. Even in relatively inefficient dictatorships such as Mussolini's Italy, there was a serious program designed to control leisure time activities, particularly for the lower classes (de Grazia, 1981). The manufacturing of a culture of consent in Fascist Italy touched a wide range of activities, from sports to dancing to theater to local neighborhood social clubs.

Common to many dictatorships is heightened vigilance about the role of women as well as attempts to shape the ideals toward which women should strive. The traditional roles of women as wife and mother have been a priority for almost all dictatorships, with great importance being given to the ideal of fertile women. Thus, again and again one finds in dictatorships caricatures of feminist women as self-absorbed, neurotic, super thin, professionally ambitious, and infertile (de Grazia, 1992). This is contrasted with a caricature of the ideal Nazi woman in Hitler's Germany, fascist woman in Mussolini's Italy, communist woman in Stalin's Russia, Islamic woman in Iran, and so on, who is buxom, self-sacrificing, warm, and very fertile. Again and again in dictatorships, there is a return to the need for women to have large numbers of offspring. For example, leaders in Iran have strongly propagated this need.

Above all, dictatorships have manufactured an ideal of womanhood that centers on sacrifice and the unique ability of women to sacrifice for others, with special emphasis on national sacrifice. Immediately after Khomeini grabbed power in Iran in 1979, I witnessed thousands of women, most of them poor, line up to hand over their few items of jewelry, from wedding rings to gold bands, to the representative of the absent Imam. Such sacrifice on the part of women has been encouraged in all the dictatorships.

Random Terror

Of course, some individuals refuse to conform to the norms prevailing in dictatorships. In such cases, brute force is used to try to enforce conformity. The target of this naked force is not necessarily the nonconformist. In dictatorships, the general population often becomes the target in revenge reprisal attacks when authorities are unable to capture those really responsible for a misdeed. For example, under Mussolini's dictatorship, on March 24, 1944 (by this time, Mussolini was actually acting as Hitler's puppet), 335 civilian Italians were shot and left dead in the Ardeatine caves in reprisal for a partisan attack on German soldiers (Bosworth, 2006). Those killed represented a broad cross-section of Italian society:

> . . . workers and artisans, diplomats and chauffeurs, lawyers and trainmen, municipal clerks and pedlars, physicians and mechanics, professors and students, musicians and shop-keepers, generals, waiters, bankers, industrialists, shoemakers, pharmacists, sailors, farmers, butchers, landlords, postmen, boys, Jews, and a Roman Catholic priest. (Bosworth, 2006, p. 499)

This was one of many massacres in Mussolini's Italy and like the others was intended to instill mortal fear into common people and silence all dissent.

A key feature of the strategy used to maintain control in dictatorships is randomness, in the sense that anyone could become a victim at any time in any place. During the height of the terror campaign in Stalin's Russia, "So many people disappeared in 1937–8, particularly in the Party and intelligentsia circles of the major capitals, that the arrests appeared random, as if anyone could be picked up by the Black Marias that roamed the streets at night" (Figes, 2007, p. 241).

In Iran, there is a random war on the part of the so-called morality police in major urban centers where prodemocracy movements and liberals and cultural deviants are concentrated. Most important, major urban centers are where young women with their displays of cultural defiance appear. The morality police roam the streets and randomly pounce on suspects, terrorizing their victims. At any moment, young women can be grabbed, bundled into vans, disappeared, and violated—setting off a frantic search by family and friends for the disappeared. The randomness of the violation means that the general population is always uneasy and on the defensive in public urban spaces.

CONCLUDING COMMENT

Conformity and obedience, extensively studied by psychologists, take place in all societies but take on special qualities in dictatorships. Conformity and obedience are strictly enforced, particularly among the power elite in dictatorships. This cohesion at the top enables the power elite to force their will on the rest of the population, particularly through policies that involve some level of randomness. Terror in dictatorships is heightened by the unpredictability of who will become a victim and when. Rumors spread, encouraged by the regime, about the terrifying vengeance brought down on those who rebel. A consequence is that the system receives less critical feedback and becomes even more corrupt and inefficient. In Chapter 7, I explore in more detail the varieties of coercive techniques used to achieve conformity and obedience in dictatorships.

7

FROM TORTURE TO COGNITIVE DISSONANCE: VARIETIES OF COERCION IN DICTATORSHIP

Public monitoring leads institutions that favor painful coercion to use and combine clean torture techniques to evade detection, and, to the extent that public monitoring is not only greater in democracies, but that public monitoring of human rights is a core value in modern democracies, it is the case that where we find democracies torturing today, we will also be more likely to find stealthy torture.

—Rejali (2007, p. 559)

In Harold Pinter's (1998) play *The New World Order* (first performed in 1991) two torturers speak to one another while they walk around a blindfolded man in a chair. The mood they create is controlled uncertainty: The blindfolded man is completely powerless, he has only the faintest idea of what they are going to do to him and his wife, and there seem to be no limits to what they cannot or will not do. One of the torturers sobs and shakes the hand of the other because he feels so pure. They look into each other's eyes as they congratulate one another; after all, they are working to keep everything pure for democracy.

Pinter captures an essential element of how torture works: uncertainty about what might happen. This uncertainty, discussed in Chapter 6 of this volume, exists in torture chambers operated by democracies, but in dictatorships the entire society is engulfed by uncertainty about when, how, and where the authorities will pounce and disappear the ordinary citizen.

DOI: 10.1037/14138-008
The Psychology of Dictatorship, by F. M. Moghaddam

Rejali (2007), quoted at the beginning of this chapter, made a very useful distinction between clean and scarring torture. His extensive study suggested that where there is public monitoring, there tends to be a shift from scarring to clean torture. Because of the monitoring of Amnesty International and other human rights agencies, the largest dictatorships of the 21st century, China and Russia, are shifting to cleaner torture and more tolerance for public disagreements. But the brutality of torture in many smaller dictatorships is more open and public. It is important to keep in mind, however, that the smaller dictatorships also use torture sometimes on behalf of what I have termed *strategically open democracies*, such as the United States. For example, the United States and other countries have transferred a number of terrorist suspects to Egypt, with the high certainty that these prisoners were tortured while they were in the Egyptian "black hole" (as reported by Human Rights Watch, 2005). This is another reminder that one should not view societies as either dictatorships or democracies in a categorical manner but view all societies as situated on a dictatorship–democracy continuum. In some circumstances, societies closer to the democracy end of the continuum can move toward the dictatorship end.

In this chapter, I explore a variety of coercive methods used by authorities to keep control in dictatorships. I am particularly focused on coercive methods that involve psychological processes. The most powerful methods of coercion often involve mere threats, rather than actual physical force. Of course, behind mere threats are actual cases of torture, assassination, kidnapping, rape, and mutilation. The threat experienced by people in dictatorships such as Iran, North Korea, Russia, China, Syria, and the like is reinforced regularly by actual events that demonstrate that the threat is real.

I begin by examining how in dictatorships the Supreme Dictator becomes a weapon in the hands of authorities: Expressing anything negative about the Supreme Dictator is akin to sin, and he is used by *little dictators* both as a shield against criticism and a hammer with which to smash down nonconformity and disobedience. But in general dictators prefer to rule in the belief that they are loved, and they would rather not use open violence against protesters. This fallacy crumbles when mass protests take place and violence spills into the streets, as has happened in Syria, Iran, and Russia since 2009. Next, I discuss how dictatorships construct a social reality that shows the masses as happy and the leadership as united: No deviance is tolerated at the top. In the final section, I discuss cognitive dissonance, an important coercive tactic used in dictatorships. Cognitive dissonance is brought about particularly through forced repeated and public displays of loyalty to the regime and to the Supreme Dictator.

THE COERCIVE ROLE OF THE SUPREME DICTATOR

Telling an anti-Stalin joke, if detected, could not go unpunished, for Stalin stood symbolically for the ideology. In those years telling an anti-Stalin joke was always potentially lethal. Under Brezhnev it did not matter much if someone told an anti-Brezhnev joke, even if detected. As long as people marched duly in the May Day parades and offered their bodies for the mass-media representation of power to the regime and the outside world, the regime was content. (Plamper, 2009, p. 71)

Dictatorships are regimes of coercion and force, but they vary, to some degree intentionally, with respect to how much nonconformity and disobedience they allow. As the preceding quotation from Plamper (2009) makes clear, even within the same dictatorial society there can be enormous changes over time with respect to how much resistance is tolerated. That is, the situation of a society on the dictatorship–democracy continuum shifts over time. In the Soviet Union during the time of Stalin's rule, the smallest sign of disrespect toward the leader was severely punished, sometimes by death. The same zero-tolerance policy is presently found in Iran and North Korea, where disrespect toward the Supreme Dictator results in very serious punishment. But by the 1970s in the Soviet Union, jokes told in public about the leader were overlooked.

However, the zero tolerance policy in some dictatorships against the slightest disrespect toward the Supreme Dictator is not implemented only through the will of the Supreme Dictator. Other factors play a vital role in this process. First and foremost, other members of the ruling elite see it as being in their own interests to have such a zero tolerance policy, in large part because absolute submission to the will of the Supreme Dictator gives the rest of the ruling elite more room to carry out their own plans and satisfy their own interests. The ruling group recognizes their fate as being intimately tied up with that of the Supreme Dictator, and so they provide the backbone and resolve needed to crack down on any dissent.

By extension, the minor officials also support zero tolerance as a way to line their own pockets. For example, during the post-revolution era in Iran I witnessed even minor revolutionaries pressuring people to give money, jewelry, and other valuables to support various causes, such as the war effort during the 1980–1988 war against Iraq. In one incident in which a woman was "volunteering" her jewelry and her husband wanted to know what the officials were going to do with it, they responded by saying, "We all have faith in Imam Khomeini." The husband could say nothing critical in response because he might have been accused of not having faith in Imam Khomeini, with dire consequences. He was forced to watch his wife hand over her gold bracelets and rings, with the high certainty that they would enrich the minor officials taking them. Under the protection afforded by the Supreme Dictator, then, other members of the regime, from the littlest of the little dictators to the powerful members of the ruling group, can go about their self-serving tasks more freely.

Representations of the Supreme Dictator

The interests of the ruling group often tend to converge on a common strategy of supporting the Supreme Dictator and converting the Supreme Dictator into a sacred carrier (discussed in Chapters 3 and 4, this volume). The dictator, as varied in ideology as Stalin, Pinochet, Assad, Castro, and Khomeini, is transformed into something that is both sacred and a means of further propagating the values of the regime.

As sacred, the dictator becomes beyond criticism and beyond the realm of human evaluation. Anyone daring to criticize the dictator is immediately struck down, literally. The image of the dictator becomes very similar to the image of prophets and saints and is venerated the way religious believers venerate prophets and saints. This is perhaps more expected in the case of leaders such as Khomeini who directly use religious ideology as a basis of their power, but it is just as true in the cases of Napoleon, Stalin, Hitler, and other ostensibly secular leaders. Again and again, one is struck by how the Supreme Dictator is depicted in portraits and other representations as having the kinds of sacred, divine, superhuman characteristics that are usually attributed to prophets and saints. Even Stalin and Hitler, whose features and reputations were in some respects closer to characters in horror movies than to religious figures, are depicted in portraits as saintly.

The Bolsheviks who seized power in Russia in 1917 developed visual art in particular as a means to craft and propagate the image of the Great Leader (Bonnell, 1988). Rather than turn their backs on the religious imagery familiar to the Russian masses through the Russian Orthodox Church, the revolutionary Russian artists incorporated and built on this imagery:

> The ideas of Stalin as savior, as the source of supernatural power, as prophet and redeemer, were borrowed from traditions in Russian popular religion. . . . in the 1930s Stalin was sometimes presented with his arm raised in a red background, like iconographic images of Christ. (Overy, 2004, p. 121)

By the 1930s the Soviet propaganda machine had gained momentum so that "Stalin depicted as a living god, moves to center stage in visual propaganda, displacing both his predecessor Lenin and the proletariat as the core elements in Bolshevik mythology" (Bonnell, 1997, p. 9). With this holy status of Stalin in mind, one can better appreciate Plamper's (2009) comment that "telling an anti-Stalin joke, if detected, could not go unpunished" (p. 71), but it was not only because Stalin stood symbolically for the ideology but also because Stalin came to acquire superhuman, divine status. He became a holy religious figure.

Similarly, in Nazi Germany, Hitler was propagated as the savior of the German people through the use of religious imagery. Chidester (2000) noted insightfully that "in theory and practice . . . Nazism emerged as a religious movement on its own right. . . . the Nazi movement mobilized a religious politics of redemption. Through the new medium of film, Nazi propaganda used strikingly religious imagery" (p. 497). Rather than turn against Hitler, "the German Christian movement saw World War II as the fulfillment of its ideals of race, gender, and militant nationalism" (p. 500).

Teaching the Young to Revere the Supreme Dictator

This depiction goes hand in hand with the subtle but steady socialization of the young to treat the Supreme Dictator as a sacred carrier. The Nazis placed great emphasis on the socialization of the young, not just through organizations such as the Brownshirts but also through the family and the spread of Nazi norms about the correct way to bring up children. This is illustrated by autobiographical accounts of people who lived a Nazi childhood.

> Shortly after my third birthday, in the summer of 1937, my father taught me to stand straight and raise my right arm in the "Heil Hitler" greeting. We stood in front of the Führer's portrait . . . I laughed at first and thought we were playing some kind of game but quickly realized that Vati was dead serious. He insisted that I thrust my small arm forward in just the right way. This would be the greeting I would use with strangers and especially if a swastika flag was carried past. (Hunt, 2005, pp. 57–58)

I witnessed the same kind of socialization in Iran, both during and after the revolution, when the Supreme Dictator (the Shah before the revolution and Khomeini after the revolution) served as a sacred carrier. In the 1970s, I witnessed children being trained to bow and wave flags before the Shah, who despite being secular adopted religious imagery to present himself as Iran's savior. The one so-called political party he allowed during his own reign was called the Resurrection party. In the early 1980s, I witnessed the same kind of socialization for conformity and obedience, with children learning to chant prayers and slogans in praise of Khomeini.

The behavior of adults in the presence of the two sacred carriers, the Shah and Khomeini, was very similar. In both cases the Supreme Dictator was venerated, and ordinary people would show extreme signs of humility in his presence: bowing, kissing of the hand and clothes of the Great Leader, and not showing their backs as they bowed and left his presence. This served as an example that children also followed, so it was not unusual to see young children being intensely moved before the Supreme Dictator. As the representative of the absent Imam, Khomeini in particular moved people through religious associations. Adult followers of Khomeini were so moved by him that they often wept and became deeply emotional in his presence.

Continuities in behavior toward the Supreme Dictator before and after the revolution reflect continuity more broadly and are unearthed when one digs beneath the surface level changes. For example, after the revolution, furniture and decorations in homes became simpler, and some politically correct families reverted back to sitting on Persian carpets rather than imported Western-style furniture. Thus, the look and atmosphere of some homes changed dramatically. However, the norms and rules regulating behavior remained the same. Rooms continue to have a top (*ballaa*) away from the entrance and toward the center of the room and a bottom (*paa-een*) closest to the entrance. The lowest status persons sit *paa-een*, and the highest status persons sit *ballaa*, irrespective of whether Western-style furniture is used or people sit on traditional cushions and carpets.

INVESTING IN REPRESSION

The ruling group in dictatorships must decide how large an investment of resources they will make to stamp out nonconformity and disobedience in the public and private spheres and also with respect to behavior in political, economic, cultural, and other spheres. The variation in the policies adopted by dictatorships is probably greatest in the areas of economic activities and least in the area of political activity. That is, whereas some dictatorships adopt a capitalist economic model (e.g., China in 2011) and others adopt a communist economic model (e.g., North Korea in 2011), all dictatorships are the same with respect to the tight control they exert on political behavior. To adopt a Dickensian manner of speaking: Whereas there are many ways for dictatorships to deal with economic issues, all dictatorships are the same with respect to political issues, in the public sphere at least.

Dictatorships do vary in their control of political behavior in the private sphere. Whereas all dictatorships exert tight control of political behavior in the public sphere, only some dictatorships invest resources to also control political behavior in the private sphere. For example, notorious examples of dictatorships controlling the private sphere are Stalinist Russia and Nazi Germany, with North Korea and Iran particularly during the 1980s and again in 2010s as contemporary examples.

The situation in Iran before and after the 1979 revolution clearly illustrates the difference between dictatorships that do and those that do not extend their control over the private sphere. In the postrevolution era many Iranians, even those who supported the revolution, have expressed a longing for the dictatorship of the Shah before the 1979 revolution brought the Pahlavi dynasty crashing down. At least during the Shah's dictatorship, they say, the security forces did not raid people's homes to stop them from drinking alcohol, dancing, or listening to Western music. At least at that time women enjoyed basic social freedoms, and Iranians could express themselves culturally in private (of course, such longing neglects the fact that it was the corruption of the Shah's dictatorship that served as the foundation for the mullahs' dictatorship). During the government of Mohammad Khatami (1997–2005), there was a period of slightly greater freedoms for Iranians, but particularly since the imposition of tighter sanctions against Iran (from 2010) by the United States and others, the Iranian security forces have reverted to tightening control of both public and private spheres in contrast to the Shah's dictatorship, which concerned itself mainly with controlling political life and allowed greater social and cultural freedoms.

The investments made by dictatorial regimes to force conformity and obedience within the home population (and among expatriates abroad) in large part depend on the level of threat from external and internal sources perceived to be present against the regime. When external threat increases, such as through economic sanctions or direct support for opposition groups inside and outside the country, then the dictatorship typically increases its interventions in the public sphere and extends these interventions to the private sphere. Thus, stricter economic sanctions against Iran since the late 2000s have resulted in harsher security measures, so that since 2010 any gathering of a group of people in either public or private spheres becomes suspect and a likely target of attack from security forces. Under conditions in which a dictatorship feels the external and internal threats to be seriously challenging its power monopoly, brute force is used in a far more extensive manner, as in Libya and Syria in 2011–2012, when thousands of civilians were attacked and killed by security forces.

The Dictator's Fallacy

But for the most part, dictatorships would rather rule without resorting to violent crackdowns in the public sphere and even without having to invest resources in controlling the private sphere. Dictatorships far prefer to live with the illusion that the people love and support their leaders: Qaddafi of Libya, Than Shwe of Burma, Omar al-Bashir of the Sudan, Mugabe of Zimbabwe, Kim Jong Il of North Korea, and Assad of Syria; these and the other leaders of dictatorships prefer to believe that they are adored by their people. This is the *dictator's fallacy*. Violent crackdowns and violence against large numbers of people, particularly in the age of the Internet and instant communications, can ruin this illusion on the global stage. This is what happened in Iran in 2009 when enormous numbers of Iranians protested the robbed election that brought Mr. Ahmadinejad back for a second term as president and the scenes of security forces killing and injuring Iranians were flashed around the world.

So the question confronting dictatorships is how much dissent to allow without losing control and having to enforce order through a bloody and public crackdown. On the one hand, too obvious and brutal a crackdown breaks the illusion that the people love and support the leadership; on the other hand, too relaxed a security policy might allow for dissenters to grow stronger and gain the courage needed for a full-scale rebellion. When enough people lose their fear of the regime, the mass revolt becomes impossible to stop, even though the regime might recognize the danger and put its forces of repression into action. The world witnessed this in Tunisia, Egypt, and Libya in 2011. Thus, at the heart of dictatorial rule is the challenge of achieving just the right amount of repression to maintain control and successfully propagate the illusion of popular support.

But one should not make the mistake of believing that the dictator's fallacy has to be shared by all of the people. The main concern of the ruling group in a dictatorship is that the elite in society, those who hold the reins of power, should believe in this fallacy. Most important, there should be absolutely no public sign of disagreement among the elite about the legitimacy of the regime. This need for the elite to present a united front explains the draconian steps taken by dictators and the ruling clique to immediately cast out any of their members who display signs of stepping out of line. For example, when Ayatollah Ruhollah Khomeini returned to Iran after the 1979 revolution, the other major grand ayatollah on the scene was Kazem Shari'atmadari, who soon became a magnet for critics of the fanatical tendencies in the revolutionary government. All kinds of antigovernment forces, most of them liberal and prodemocracy, began to see Grand Ayatollah Shari'atmadari as a possible shield against repression.

Khomeini's response was to put Grand Ayatollah Shari'atmadari under house arrest and demote him to a mere mister. On the other hand, Khomeini promoted another cleric, Hussein Ali Montazeri, to the lofty status of grand ayatollah because he seemed to be in line with the Khomeini-led fanatics who took power. But when Montazeri also started to criticize the revolutionary government for imprisoning and torturing political opponents, he too was demoted to mere mister in 1989. Since Khomeini's death in 1989, the Iranian regime has followed the pattern of behavior reflected in the popular saying, "The revolution devours its own children." One by one, former revolutionaries have been chewed up and spat out, even sometimes when they attempted to escape death by fleeing abroad.

Devouring the Children of the Revolution

How do we explain this tendency for revolutions to devour their own children? How do we explain Stalin's repeated purges, which never seemed to end but had a number of climaxes, such as in 1937–1938? Stalin's purges involved unpredictable and seemingly irrational sweeps of the revolutionary elite, such as when on June 11, 1937, nine members of the Red Army High Command were arrested, tortured, tried on the basis of "confessions," and summarily executed (Bullock, 1993). No doubt, part of the function of such tactics was to rule by terror, keep potential opposition forces off guard, and paralyze any semblance of resistance to Stalin's absolute rule. Of course, the purges should not be viewed as arising only from Stalin because the chaotic nature of the communist apparatus at that time also contributed to the often haphazard nature of purges (Getty, 1987). In contrast, Nazi Germany experienced fewer purges, the notable ones taking place during the Night of the Long Knives or Röhm-Putsch in 1934 and again in 1944 after the assassination attempt against Hitler (Kershaw, 1993).

A key characteristic of dictatorships such as the Soviet Union and Iran that have had numerous successive purges is that the revolutions they arose out of involved a variety of groups that cooperated to achieve power. The classic example of this is the French Revolution (1789) that eventually led to the dictatorship of Napoleon Bonaparte. A wide spectrum of French society were involved in the transformations that swept away the old regime, including some who could be interpreted as being part of the old regime itself:

> Closer inspection of the new regimes in many of France's provincial towns, large and small, reveals just how strategically placed many of these holdovers from the old regime were. . . . In Paris, no less that 20 percent of the three hundred elected representatives of the municipality were ex Parlementaires. (Schama, 1989, pp. 516–517)

The communist victory in Russia after 1917 also depended on a spectrum of groups and personalities with varying ideological positions. After Lenin's death (1924), it took Stalin decades to purify the party and in one way or another dismiss those whom he regarded as deviants from the true line. Similarly, the revolution in Iran had been successful because of the wide variety of support from secular and religious groups of all kinds for the anti-Shah platform. After the revolution, Khomeini embarked on a course to eradicate all but those who strictly followed his path. Thus, purges in such dictatorships were in one sense an inevitable consequence of a purification of the leadership to strictly follow the path set by the dictator.

THE GREAT DICTATOR AND REALITY CONSTRUCTION IN IRAN AND NORTH KOREA

> The face of Big Brother swam into his mind . . . he slid a coin out of his pocket and looked at it. The face gazed up at him, heavy, calm, protecting, but what kind of smile was hidden beneath the dark moustache? Like a leaden knell the words came back to him:
>   WAR IS PEACE
>   FREEDOM IS SLAVERY
>   IGNORANCE IS STRENGTH

Perhaps the most important feature of closed societies highlighted by George Orwell in his novel *1984* (1960, p. 87) is how language is often manipulated to deceive and to fabricate alternative worlds that are actually divorced from reality but nevertheless forced on the oppressed population. People are manipulated to accept what is untruth as truth. In Orwell's novel, the fabrication of alternative realities is continuously underway through the Ministry of Truth. In 21st-century closed societies, there are many "ministries of truth," but just as important, there are many ruthless security and military forces backing such ministries. An extreme example is in the Democratic People's Republic of Korea (established 1948), otherwise known as North Korea, supposedly a communist state that is actually ruled more like a hereditary monarchic dictatorship. Three generations of males from the same family have now served as dictators in North Korea for a combined total of 63 years (1948–2011).

The founder of the dynasty, Kim Il-Sung (1912–1994), the Great Leader and President for Eternity, was a military officer who came to power through Soviet backing. His chosen successor was his son Kim Jong Il (1942–2011), the Dear Leader, who continued to rule through the backing first of the Soviets and then the Chinese as well as the North Korean military, which he greatly expanded and enriched (the military stands at a whopping 1.2 million in a country of only 24 million total population). Kim Jong Il passed away in December 2011, and now power has been inherited, in good communist fashion (!), by his son Kim Jong Eun (believed to be in his late 20s when his father died), the Great Successor, the grandson of the founder of North Korea. Despite adopting the rhetoric of communism, the grandfather, father, and grandson have lived and ruled in sheer luxury as monarchs in a feudal society. North Korea seems like a unique dictatorship, but it actually has a number of similarities to some other dictatorships, particularly Iran (the two countries have signed a number of cooperative agreements, reflecting their common interests and characteristics).

The rulers of North Korea and Iran have created and operated dictatorships that are in some important respects very similar. First, they have militarized their respective societies, building up an enormous security apparatus with multiple layers. Second, they have privileged the security apparatus, so that much of the wealth of the country is now in the hands of the military in North Korea and the Republican Guards in Iran. Members of the security apparatus have a strong material incentive to defend the regime. Young people have a material incentive to want to become part of the security apparatus in these countries, and in many cases new recruits gain entrance through family ties. Third, in both North Korea and Iran, the state invests heavily in weapons and technology to keep control of the population and maintain its power monopoly. Fourth, in both societies power is exerted through a structure that looks very much like a feudal monarchy, with the President for Eternity in North Korea and the Supreme Leader in Iran as the center of absolute power, and the feudal lords (all male) and the rest of the population owing allegiance to him. Fifth, in both North Korea and Iran the primary concern of the regime is the continuation of the regime at all costs. That is why the regimes in both countries view the nuclear bomb as an essential weapon against their external enemies, particularly the United States. Sixth, in both countries a pervasive and all-embracing personality cult has been created around the founding father, who has taken on mythical, divine characteristics. Everywhere (literally, everywhere) in North Korea portraits of the President for Eternity hang next to portraits of the Dear Leader, just as everywhere in Iran portraits of Imam Khomeini hang next to Ayatollah Khamenai. Just as the Great Successor has been titled the Supreme Leader and is modeling himself after the founder of the current North Korean dictatorship, Khamenei is referred to as the Supreme Leader and models himself after the founder of the current dictatorship in Iran. Finally, the dictatorial regimes in both North Korea and Iran rely on cultural traditions that reinforce and facilitate the continuation of dictatorship.

Illustrative of the deep-rooted cultural traditions of both North Korea and Iran that support the continuation of dictatorship is the personality cult and hero worship of the national leader in these countries. In 2011, North Koreans mourned the death of Kim Jong Il, the Dear Leader, who apparently died unexpectedly at age 69. There have been reports of mass weeping in North Korea, with people falling to their knees and sobbing uncontrollably in public. The official mourning period lasted a year. And who is this for? A leader who led his country to economic ruin and mass starvation—probably a million North Koreans died of starvation in the mid 1990s. A leader who placed loudspeaker announcers all over the country, including in people's homes, so that propaganda could be streamed out in a centrally controlled manner at all times. A leader who kept his country completely isolated from the rest of the world, with no access to the Internet or to the global media for the masses. Thousands of North Koreans managed to flee the country during this period, but the Dear Leader also arranged for a number of South Koreans and others to be kidnapped and brought to North Korea. For example, the film director Shin Sang-Ok and his actress wife, Choi Eun-Hee, were kidnapped and forced to make films in North Korea. The inevitable question arises: How is it that such mass hysteria and widespread mourning followed the death of such a despotic leader?

The scenes of mourning following the death of Kim Jong Il are similar to scenes of mourning that took place in Iran in 1989 following the death of Ayatollah Khomeini, the "Founder of the Islamic Republic of Iran." Millions publicly wept and self-flagellated when Khomeini passed away. The enormous crowd carrying Khomeini's encased dead body became so hysterical that at one stage his body fell out of its container. Also, the same deep-rooted superstitious beliefs and behavior underlie the role of both leaders. For example, although Kim Jong Il was actually born in the Soviet Union in 1941, whereas his father, Kim Il-Sung, President for Eternity, was in exile, the myth created is that he was born in 1942 in a cabin in a holy site on Mount Paektu, a place that has great significance in Korean mythology. Similar myths were created for Khomeini. During the revolution, the myth spread that Khomeini's face was visible on the image of the moon. Believers wept at the sight of this "miracle," the Imam beaming down at them from the night skies.

The regimes of both Kim Jong Il and Khomeini involved a sharp contradiction: the rhetoric and image of fatherly affection and kindness and the brutal reality of imprisonment, torture, and assassination for those who dared to oppose the Dear Leader and the Founder of the Islamic Republic. In true Orwellian style, words were used to paint pictures that completely contradicted reality. In the case of Kim Jong Il, this was not difficult because he said so very little in public. His handlers could carefully select the words he was supposed to have spoken. But for Khomeini, it did become a problem because he made so many public speeches and almost all of what he promised about the guaranteed freedom and liberty of Iranians, including women, before he gained absolute power (around the end of 1979) had to be censored in later years. Of course, by 2010 the regime in Tehran even had to round up many of those who had been on the scene in the early days of the revolution in part because they remembered what had been promised. This included Mir-Hussein Mousavi, the prime minister (1981–1989) during the last period of Khomeini's life. Thus, the contradiction between words and reality, between freedom and liberty in rhetoric and closedmindedness and despotism in practice, has continued.

In both North Korea and Iran, behind the mirage thrown up by words is the brutal reality of prisons, torture, and assassination.

COERCION AND COGNITIVE DISSONANCE

Imagine you are asked to participate in a psychological experiment, and you arrive at the psychology laboratory to find that your main task is to tear newspapers into small strips. After spending an hour on this boring task, you are thanked and given a measly 75 cents for your time. Before you depart from the laboratory, your final task is to write to prospective participants in a future session of the same experiment, persuading them to give up their valuable time for this "interesting" experience. Unbeknownst to you, a second set of participants underwent exactly the same procedure as you, with the difference that they were given $75 instead of 75 cents. Which group of participants will write the more persuasive essay telling potential future participants about the interesting study they should give up their time for? Received wisdom suggests that it will be the group who received $75, because they were more (to use behaviorist terminology) positively reinforced. But the actual results of such studies have proved to be counterintuitive: The groups who received 75 cents wrote the more persuasive message to future prospective participants.

Since its introduction by Leon Festinger (1957), cognitive dissonance theory has become highly influential because of its ability to predict counterintuitive outcomes, such as when people report enjoying tearing newspapers into small strips and other such tedious tasks (Cooper, 2007). As one group of researchers explained, "cognitive dissonance is one of the most heavily studied phenomena in the history of psychology" (Egan, Santos, & Bloom, 2007, p. 978). According to Festinger, when humans recognize contradictions between their thoughts and actions, they experience physical discomfort that they are motivated to overcome, such as when they are thirsty. For example, when participants recognize that they have spent their time and energy in an experiment for which they received only 75 cents in payment, they feel they must justify their action by interpreting the experiment as interesting and worthwhile. After all, they think, I would not have given up my valuable time for as little as 75 cents, so it must have been that the study was interesting. The participants who received $75 for their time had a justification; they could explain that they did it for the money, and therefore, they would not contradict themselves by reporting that the experiment actually is boring ("Why did I give up my time for the study? It was actually very boring, but the pay was very good!").

Because of the change-inducing potential of cognitive dissonance, researchers have explored the utility of Festinger's insights in a wide variety of applied domains, including road rage (Takaku, 2006), conservation of energy (Kantola, Syme, & Campbell, 1984) and water (Dickerson, Thibodeau, Aronson, & Miller, 1992), prejudice reduction (Son Hing, Li, & Zanna, 2002), safe sex (Dal Cin, MacDonald, Fong, Zanna, & Elton-Marshall, 2006), mental health

(Axsom, 1989), decision making (Akerlof & Dickens, 1982), and addictive behaviors (McBride, Emmons, & Lipkus, 2003; Prochaska, DiClemente, & Norcross, 1992). In most of these cases, the goal of the applied research was to create situations in which people experience cognitive dissonance, and to resolve the dissonance, they changed their behavior rather than their attitudes and/or beliefs. For example, when John experiences dissonance because of the contradiction between, on the one hand, his negative attitudes toward smoking (he accepts that smoking causes cancer) and, on the other hand, his behavior (John smokes a pack of cigarettes a day), it is better for John and for society that John change his behavior (and stops smoking) than change his attitudes to become congruent with his smoking habit.

A powerful strategy for getting people to change what they do, rather than what they say, is the *hypocrisy paradigm* (Stone & Fernandez, 2008). The way this has been used is as follows: First, participants make a public commitment to a particular (usually prosocial) action (such as water conservation); second, participants explicitly consider the factors that in the past prevented them from taking the said action. The outcome of this public commitment and failure to carry out the said action is cognitive dissonance, which becomes resolved through changed behavior (e.g., becoming more effective at conserving water; Dickerson et al., 1992).

Although the main focus of cognitive dissonance research has been at the level of individual behavior, Festinger (1957, p. 261) discussed dissonance in groups, and the implications of his theory have been extended to the collective level (Matz & Wood, 2005). Evidence suggests that people can experience dissonance not only when they perceive inconsistency within themselves but also when they experience inconsistency within their group. This includes when other ingroup members behave inconsistently (Cooper & Hogg, 2007; Norton, Monin, Cooper, & Hogg, 2003), when they recognize that their opinions are contrary to those of other ingroup members (Matz & Wood, 2005), and when other ingroup members behave in ways that contradict their personal beliefs (Glasford, Pratto, & Dovidio, 2008). Moreover, group members who identify to a greater degree with the ingroup select dissonance reduction strategies that enhance social identity (Glasford, Dovidio, & Pratto, 2009). Thus, research strongly suggests that dissonance can be experienced within groups as well as individuals and that those who most identify with the ingroup are also concerned to avoid dissonance in a way that protects group identity.

Cognitive Dissonance and Consistency in Cultural Context

Cognitive dissonance theory is part of a long and continuing tradition in Western psychology that emphasizes the normalcy and subjective desirability of consistency in behavior (Gawronski & Strack, 2011). The heyday of balance theories in psychology was in the 1950s and 1960s, when the influence of behaviorism was waning and the first cognitive revolution was being launched (Moghaddam, 2005, Chapter 1). Fritz Heider (1946, 1958) was the first and most broadly influential thinker in this movement, placing emphasis on the assumed motivation of individuals to achieve balance and consistency in behavior. Although Heider (1946), like Festinger (1957) after him, was concerned primarily with consistency in the minds of individual actors, Lewin (1951), Cartwright and Harary (1956), and Newcomb (1961) shifted the focus to balance in interpersonal relations and group dynamics. There have also been efforts to combine research lines looking at balance within minds and within groups (Hummon & Doreian, 2003).

An important question is, why should people prefer consistency and balance? Psychologically, there is a wide range of robust reasons for this preference, but the most important reasons have to do with functionality and evolutionary history. People came to prefer consistency and balance because these make their own behavior and that of others more predictable. Social relations require fewer resources and less vigilance when people get what they expect so that they can allocate their energies to dealing with possible threats and to taking advantage of unexpected new opportunities. Second, this evolutionarily rooted preference for balance and consistency has resulted in support for social norms and a liking for those who behave correctly according to accepted norms. The extensive psychological research that demonstrates the power of norms reflects this trend (Moghaddam, 2005, Chapter 15). Third, as part of people's preference for balance and consistency, people are positively inclined toward others who are more similar to them and who endorse their view of the world (Osbeck, Moghaddam, & Perreault, 1997).

In support of the idea that people's preference for balance and consistency has evolutionary roots, Egan et al. (2007) demonstrated the influence of cognitive dissonance in both preschool children and monkeys. Preschool children were asked to choose between smiley-face stickers that preliminary research had shown were equally favored by them. It was hypothesized that after a child had made a commitment to one of the stickers, the other would be reevaluated as less favorable. This hypothesis was supported: When the unchosen alternative was now presented with an Option C that had previously been equally preferred, participants preferred Option C over the option they had previously rejected. The same study was conducted with monkeys, but using M&Ms instead of smiley faces. The monkeys also preferred Option C over the unchosen option.

The Role of Cognitive Dissonance in Dictatorships

According to empirical evidence, then, under certain conditions cognitive dissonance can lead to changes in attitudes and behavior toward congruency. Dictatorial regimes adopt a number of practices that capitalize on this relationship, although of course their tactics arise from intuition rather than empirical research.

Most important, in dictatorships there is insistence on the regular and repeated public display of loyalty to the regime. The public nature of such displays ensures that everyone can be monitored, and each person can monitor his or her neighbor, coworker, fellow student, friends, and family members. Many such displays come about at work, in the shape of workers' meetings, or special days of celebration (e.g., the national liberation day, martyrs' day, the Supreme Dictator's birthday). In dictatorships such as Iran and Saudi Arabia, prayers provide a perfect opportunity for this display. Muslims are obligated to pray five times a day, and prayers have greater worth (*savaab*) when they are made in public. Every public prayer provides an opportunity for monitoring and propaganda. Hundreds of thousands of preachers are hired by the state in Iran and Saudi Arabia to accompany collective prayer meetings with speeches lauding the regime and chastising opponents as sinners.

Individuals who want to make progress in the system are forced to participate in public events that reinforce the regime. Very often this participation is incongruent with the beliefs they hold privately and the views they dare to express in private with trusted family and friends. I have known many people in dictatorships to present a proregime face in public and an antiregime face in private. Children socialized in dictatorships learn from an early age to separate the private and the public, so that certain political sentiments said in private are routinely contradicted in public.

However, this contradiction creates anxieties. One of the common features of life in dictatorships is a continuous tension experienced by many people because of a rift between their public face and their private face—they are forced to applaud the regime, or at least not criticize it in public, while their private feelings are revulsion for the regime. Thus, cognitive dissonance works in a peculiar, different way in dictatorships, with public and private spheres being compartmentalized: People are forced to display public consistency in their actions and words in support of the regime, and the same consistency is upheld in front of visitors at home. However, among trusted friends and family, the public display of support for the regime is contradicted.

The outcome of this process is a psychological malaise characteristic of life in dictatorships: Individuals develop strategies to cope with anxiety-provoking and continuous tensions associated with the contradictory selves they have to present in different public and private contexts. This juggling act involving contradictory self-presentations exists to some degree in all societies, but in dictatorships it becomes so acute that it eats away at one's basic sense of responsibility and ethics. The customary way to cope is to retreat and define one's responsibilities in bureaucratic terms, so that doing one's duty becomes simply pleasing one's boss—nothing broader. In this way, duty becomes defined in very narrow ways—as reflected in the defense put forward by successive mass killers who had gained positions of authority in dictatorships, such as Goering, Goebbels, Himmler, and other Nazis put on trial at Nuremberg at the end of World War II: "I was only following orders," they all claimed. By narrowing their duties to carrying out orders, even mass killers could interpret their own roles in dictatorships as benign and neutral. In this way, many members of the Shah's security apparatus in Iran continued to work the same jobs after the 1979 revolution, as did members of the security apparatus in Russia after the collapse of the USSR in 1991, conducting persecution and torture in a neutral manner across regimes.

CONCLUDING COMMENT

The most important finding from psychological research on conformity and obedience is that some people always refuse to conform and obey, and heroic examples of this exist in everyday life. For example, consider the situation before the dictatorship of Hosni Mubarak and the case of Khaled Said, the 28-year old Egyptian man bludgeoned to death by Egyptian government security forces in June 2010. Mr. Said drew attention to himself for the wrong reasons, probably by posting a video on the Internet showing police corruption. Two officers brutally beat him in the lobby of a building, in public and in front of witnesses. What is unusual about Mr. Said's case is that his family did not accept the police explanation that he had choked on marijuana. A cell phone picture of the victim's bloodied and battered corpse helped to spread the word about the killing on the Internet, and the family's continued protests drew national and international attention to human rights abuses in the Egyptian dictatorship (Fahim, 2010). As in all dictatorships, the Egyptian security forces aimed to instill feelings of terror in the population, so that people were gripped by collective helplessness and were unable to react to institutional violence by government sanctioned forces.

Governments vary considerably with respect to how openly they use torture and other tactics to achieve behavior control. In dictatorships such as Egypt before the fall of Mubarak and Iran at present, government-sanctioned security forces have little to fear from oversight and correction procedures. Consequently, in such blatant dictatorships government-sanctioned security forces routinely terrorize members of their own populations in public and even in broad daylight. The cases of Iran in 2009 and Syria in 2012 demonstrate that human rights monitoring and the global media have little impact on limiting the violence inflicted by dictatorships that are determined to survive.

The springboard model leads one to consider coercion with an emphasis on both the situation and the leader, and this is in line with the earlier (but broader) mixed or interactional or integrative models of leadership developed by Fiedler (1967) and others (Avolio, 2005; House & Mitchell, 1974; Vroom, 2000)—a topic discussed in Chapter 8. But no matter how strong the coercion, how enthusiastic the followers, and how motivated the dictator, there is always the probability that people will become nonconformist and disobedient.

8

LEADERSHIP AND DICTATORSHIP

Glendower: I can call spirits from the vasty deep.
Hotspur: Why, so can I, or so can any man;
But will they come when you do call for them?"
                                    —Shakespeare, *Henry IV*

It only requires the good follower to do nothing for leadership to fail.
                                    —Grint (2005, p. 133)

All leadership involves a mystery: How do leaders exert influence on followers? The psychological literature attempting to address such questions about leadership has grown considerably (Goethals, Sorenson, & Burns, 2004), with a particular focus on leadership in organizations (Hogg, 2010). The *American Psychologist* ("Diversity and Leadership," 2010; "Leadership," 2007) had special issues devoted to leadership in 2007 and 2010, and there has been some attention to bad leadership (Kellerman, 2004; Lipman-Blumen, 2006). However, far less attention has been given to dictators as leaders. Dictatorial leadership involves an even greater mystery: How do dictators influence followers to obey them unquestioningly, sometimes to the point of doing terrible harm to others as well as to themselves? How did Mao in China in the late 1960s and Khomeini in Iran in the early 1980s inspire and guide millions of young followers to take radical positions in the so-called Cultural Revolutions in their respective countries; to verbally and physically attack intellectuals and academics; to force the closing of all universities and throw

DOI: 10.1037/14138-009
The Psychology of Dictatorship, by F. M. Moghaddam

out the faculty to be reeducated; and to attack in particular highly trained experts and professionals such as medical doctors, lawyers, and the educated class in general? What accounts for the total dedication to Hitler, even in the jaws of defeat, among young and senior "volunteers" who stood as the last line of defense in shattered Berlin during the final days of the Third Reich in 1945?

The easy way out is to claim that dictators force followers to do what they do, but as previous authors (e.g., Lipman-Blumen, 2006) have pointed out, this is too simplistic. Often the force is not physical, nor is it immediately present; rather, the force is created through a combination of powerful and complex situational factors and the personality of the dictator. The combination of magnetism, cunning, and pure evil encapsulated in some dictators, such as Hitler, seems unfathomable. This is captured by Shakespeare's most compressed representation of dictatorship, *Richard III*. After killing two young princes who might have been a threat to his reign, Richard III persuades Elizabeth, the mother of the same two princes, to convince her own daughter to marry him. That Richard would even have the nerve to conceive of and to propose such a marriage is abhorrent, but such audacity and wild twists of thinking are part of what makes him magnetic and powerful. He tells Elizabeth:

> Look, what is done cannot be now amended:
> Men shall deal unadvisedly sometimes.
> Which after-hours give leisure to repent.
> If I did take the kingdom from your sons,
> To make amends I'll give it to your daughter.
> If I have kill'd the issue of your womb,
> To quicken your increase I will beget
> Mine issue of your blood upon your daughter

(Shakespeare, *Richard III*, Act IV, Scene iv, Lines 294–301)

Through tortured reasoning, Richard III persuades Elizabeth that it would be best if her daughter did marry him, so that their son would become king and Elizabeth the grandmother of a king. After Elizabeth seems to be persuaded and leaves to argue to her daughter on his behalf, Richard contemptuously dismisses her as a "relenting fool" and "shallow changing woman." But the saying "Life is stranger than fiction" has to be kept in mind here because there are numerous real-life dictators who have proven to be even more manipulative and ruthless then Shakespeare's Richard III, for example, the political purges Stalin undertook in the late 1930s using torture and other brutal means to extract "confessions" from victims:

> Stalin and his magnates often laughed about the NKVD's ability to get
> people to confess. Stalin told this joke to someone who had actually

been tortured: "They arrested a boy and accused him of writing *Eugene Onegin,*" Stalin joked [about a novel in verse written by the great Russian poet Alexander Pushkin, 1799–1837]. "The boy tried to deny it . . . A few days later, the NKVD interrogator bumped into the boy's parents: "Congratulations!" he said. "Your son wrote *Eugene Onegin.*" (Montefiore, 2003, p. 246)

But what was the purpose of the bloody political purges of this era? Stalin's justification was that the purges were necessary to prevent a huge conspiracy to overthrow the communist regime, but no evidence of an actual conspiracy was ever produced. The real reason for the slaughter that took place was Stalin's need to eliminate everyone who had helped to create the Soviet Union so that only his influence and legacy would remain. The purge resulted in "the liquidation of virtually the whole of Lenin's original party, not only in the party organization, but also of the same generation, both party and non-party" (Bullock, 1993, pp. 508–509). The purge eventually wiped out many who were silent rather than in opposition but who showed some trace of independent thinking. However, one should not assume that Stalin was more ruthless than Lenin, who was cunning in hiding his own ruthlessness during the Red Terror:

> Although Lenin all along provided the main driving force for the Red Terror and often had to cajole his more humane colleagues, he went to extraordinary lengths to dissociate his name from the terror. He who insisted on affixing his signature to all laws and decrees omitted to do so whenever acts of state violence were involved. (Pipes, 1990, p. 795)

I witnessed the same trend in Iran after the revolution, where purge after purge sent the children of the revolution to their graves or to hiding abroad. The purges continued until only those considered completely subservient and in line with Khomeini's thinking survived. The same mixture of egocentric and manipulative behavior can be witnessed in the lives of President for Life Idi Amin (1925–2003) of Uganda, Nicolae Ceausescu (1918–1989) of Rumania, and numerous other modern dictators.

DICTATORIAL LEADERSHIP

Toxic leaders often come to power through (misplaced) popular support. The list of toxic leaders is very long, from Hitler and Stalin to the more recent ones, including Chavez of Venezuela, Than Shwe of Burma, Omar Al-Bashir of Sudan, Qaddafi of Libya, Mugabe of Zimbabwe, Niyazov of Turkemenistan, Nguema of Equatorial Guinea, Saddam Hussein of Iraq, Mubarak of Egypt, Khomeini of Iran, and many others. In this chapter, I examine the nature of dictatorial leadership, with reference to psychological research on leadership.

My contention is that dictatorial leadership involves particular intelligences and skills: the ability to perceive the potential for dictatorial power, the skills to manipulate followers and situations to help create the springboard to dictatorship, and the decisiveness to spring to power when the conditions are ripe.

The complexity of understanding dictatorial leadership becomes clearer when one considers Burns's (1978) highly useful distinction between two leadership styles. *Transactional leadership* focuses on exchanges between leaders and followers, with the leader using rewards and punishments to reach particular goals, for example, the political leader who promises, "If you vote for me, I will bring new building projects to your neighborhood." In contrast, *transformative leadership* involves both leaders and followers influencing one another to bring about change at individual and collective levels. Transformative leadership is inspirational and constructive, for example, the company chief executive officer who inspires the employees to successfully expand the market for their goods and increase income for everyone involved in the company. However, transformational leadership can also be highly destructive, as when Supreme Dictators order torture, assassination, and other coercive techniques to try to remold people toward their vision of the human ideal (as discussed in Chapter 1, this volume). Dictatorial leadership is often a mixture of transactional and transformative leadership; for example, a leader such as Hitler used both rewards and punishments to move people toward his desired goals and inspired change—albeit destructive change—at micro and macro levels.

The Multiple Factors Influencing Leadership

> In the bad old days, leadership was taught mainly by means of the biographies of great men . . . one quality of a genuine discipline of leadership studies—once such an animal exists—will be its inclusiveness. No matter how many mathematical models the discipline produces, it should always have room for inspirational stories about wonderful leaders as well as grim cautionary tales about bad ones. (Bennis, 2007, p. 2)

The study of leadership faces a number of dilemmas. The most influential leaders, whether positive (e.g., Gandhi) or negative (e.g., Hitler) in their influence, are exceptional, perhaps unique, cases. But to go beyond the case study approach, involving in-depth assessment of individual leaders, researchers have found it necessary to include in their studies large samples, which necessarily means that they include many unexceptional leaders, and to try to reach generalizations from their results, which means that they overlook unique characteristics of exceptional leaders. This dilemma confronts all students of human behavior as they struggle between approaches that are *idiographic*, involving a focus on individual cases and their special characteristics, and *nomothetic,* involving studies of population samples and the general trends that such studies can yield.

In addition to the idiographic–nomothetic debate, an important continuing controversy surrounds the contributions of heredity and environment in shaping leadership. The argument for the role of hereditary factors in leadership is in part based on the research on *temperament,* a style of reacting to the environment as well as a characteristics level of energy. Temperament is assumed to be inborn and a key component of personality (M. K. Rothbart & Bates, 2006). Given that leaders are assumed to be characterized by certain personality traits (Zaccaro, 2007), a natural next step is to hypothesize that heredity plays a role in shaping leadership.

Genetics and Leadership

> You are, all of you in this community, brothers. But when god fashioned you, he added gold in the composition of those of you who are qualified to be rulers . . . silver in the Auxiliaries, and iron and bronze in the farmers and other workers. (Plato, trans. 1987, 415b)

> Most behavioral geneticists today understand that genetics and the environment interact in a dynamic way to shape individual development. (Avolio, Rotundo, & Walumbwa, 2009, p. 330)

The roots of contemporary debates about the nature of leadership go back at least 2,500 years to Plato's *Republic* (Plato, trans. 1987), when rulers stood out because of both their inborn characteristics and their special training particularly designed to achieve morally disciplined leadership. More recently, the debate has sharpened between those who argue that leaders are born and those who propose that situations create leaders. Early psychological research was strongly influenced by the *great man* view of history, reflected by works such as *On Heroes, Hero Worship, and the Heroic in History* (1841/1993) by Thomas Carlyle (1795–1881) and *Hereditary Genius: An Inquiry Into Its Laws and Consequences* (1869) by Francis Galton (1822–1911). Both of these works were influenced by ideas about evolution permeating British society even before the publication (1859/1993) of the monumental book *The Origin of Species by Natural Selection or the Preservation of Favored Races in the Struggle for Life* by Charles Darwin (1809–1882), and both tried to explain and justify the extraordinary global power of the British (and also Western) elite in the 19th century. This perspective led to a trait-based explanation of leadership: Leaders are born with special psychological characteristics, and it is the task of psychological science to discover what they are.

The ideology underlying the great man view of history that emerged out of 19th-century scholarship was characterized by two basic assumptions: first, the collective superiority of White Europeans and, second, the individual superiority of certain persons born to lead within European societies. Both assumptions involved a particular elitist interpretation of evolution theory, the social and political implications of which continue to be debated (Orr, 2009). The collective superiority of White Europeans was taken to be both a justification for, and reflected in, the colonization of large parts of the world by Western European powers, particularly Britain ("The sun never sets on the British Empire" was the standard phrase). As Kiernan (1972/1996) stated, White Europeans regarded themselves to be the "lords of humankind." But not everyone was equal in European societies; even among the "lords of humankind" there were superiors and inferiors, leaders and followers.

Eugenics in Dictatorships and Democracies

One finds in the work of Galton (1869) and those who came to be known as *social Darwinists* an attempt to use scientific research to justify a particular hierarchical sociopolitical arrangement in society. Certain aspects of this "scientific effort" were truly horrifying, such as the launching of *eugenics*, the selective breeding of humans to improve the human stock. At one level, the logic of eugenics seems straightforward enough: Humans selectively breed animals for certain characteristics (e.g., faster horses, cows that give more milk, dogs with a keener sense of smell), so why not breed humans to get people who are smarter, better looking, and so on? Of course, this "logic" leads to the idea that some people should breed more and some should not breed at all, and then one arrives at the kinds of terrifying "solutions" attempted by the Nazis.

In discussing eugenics in democratic societies, a complacency and even smugness often set in because many people assume "this could never happen here." After all, eugenics is such a horrific policy, and like dictatorship, it is foreign to the democratic way of life. Unfortunately, even in the 20th century, eugenics had supporters in the United States, and selective breeding programs were implemented in parts of America, with the idea that certain people simply should not breed (Selden, 1999). Eugenics programs in America were integral to racist policies more broadly and were based on the idea that certain races are intellectually and morally inferior. This shameful aspect of American history suggests that it would be a grave error to be complacent and assume that such an attitude could not arise here when considering larger dangers, such as that of dictatorship. A more critical and questioning approach is needed; if eugenics can be accepted in parts of America, as Selden (1999) documented, then people need to be on their guard to better safeguard against worst outcomes, such as dictatorship in all of America.

The Twins Research Method and Leadership

There were some aspects of Galton's (1869) research, other than eugenics, that were far more constructive. First, he undertook pioneering research to measure human intelligence under standardized conditions using tests designed to be objective. The idea of conducting psychological testing under standard conditions was particularly important and influenced later attempts to measure personality traits, including traits of leaders. Second, Galton was the first researcher to systematically use twins in an effort to identify the contributions of environmental and inherited factors in human behavior; Galton was specifically interested in human intelligence, but once he established the basic *twins method,* it was used in many different domains of psychological research. Although Galton did not understand the genetic differences between monozygotic (genetically identical) and dizygotic (genetically different) twins (an understanding that came after the research of Gregor Mendel, 1922–1884, became well known in the early 20th century), he did differentiate between fraternal and identical twins. He reasoned that if he could find twins separated early in life and brought up in different environments and then compare their performance as adults on objective tests in standardized conditions, he would be able to identify the contributions of inherited and environmental factors to their performance.

In recent years, a number of studies have used Galton's twins methods to examine a possible genetic basis of leadership. In a study involving 183 monozygotic and 64 dizygotic twin pairs, genetic factors were found to be associated with transactional and transformative leadership styles (Johnson et al., 1998). In a follow-up study with the same samples, it was found that particular personality traits associated with leadership were also associated with genetic factors (Johnson, Vernon, Harris, & Jang, 2004). In probably the most rigorous study conducted so far on the genetic basis of leadership, Arvey, Rotundo, Johnson, Zhang, and McGue (2006) included 213 twin pairs, 119 monozygotic twins and 94 dizygotic twins (total of 426 participants). Leadership role occupancy was measured using a *biohistory* approach in terms of various leadership roles achieved by an individual in work settings. For example, respondents answered questions about the types of leadership roles or positions they had held in the past. The authors reported that 30% of the variance in leadership role occupancy was explained by genetic factors. Even if one accepts this level of influence of genetic factors in leadership, however, Arvey et al. (2006) pointed out that

> the large amount of variance [70%] explained by environmental factors suggests malleability among individuals with regard to external factors in developing . . . leaders . . . to some extent individuals might be predisposed to engage in leadership behaviors that would propel them into

leadership roles based on their genetic influences. However, individuals who are not so predisposed may still move into leadership roles if exposed to environmental factors that help develop leadership. (p. 16)

Personality Traits and Leadership

The most well-established tradition in leadership research, influenced by the great man theory of history, is the *trait approach*, which assumes that leaders have special stable personality characteristics (Zaccaro, 2007). The assumption of stability of leadership personality characteristics is important because it implies that such characteristics are consistent across situations and that a leader is a leader at all times in all situations. An additional assumption has been that, in line with the research on temperament (M. K. Rothbart & Bates, 2006), important personality traits that characterize leadership are inborn.

Over time, a number of different personality traits have been put forward as characterizing leadership (Judge, Bono, Ilies, & Gerhart, 2002; Zaccaro, 2007). The so-called Big Five personality traits (discussed in Chapter 2, this volume) have been proposed as being universal (Marsella, Dubanoski, Hamada, & Morse, 2000), and not surprisingly, these have been a research focus in the search for special leadership personality traits. However, the claim that such traits characterize leadership independent of context, or even that such traits are universal across males and females and across contexts, is on very shaky ground (Ayman & Korabik, 2010).

Perhaps one of the most promising concepts put forward as characterizing leadership is *self-monitoring*, the extent to which individuals control and change the public self to achieve a desired public image. If this concept is interpreted positively, self-monitoring is a way for leaders to better adapt to local conditions and communicate more effectively with local voters High self-monitors, those who regulate their behavior to be more in line with local demands, are more likely to get ahead as leaders (Day, Schleicher, Unckless, & Hiller, 2002). I return to this topic later in discussing dictatorial leadership because self-monitoring in some respects can be associated with a Machiavellian style of behavior (as examined by Christie & Geis, 1970), central to which are manipulation, deceit, and distrust.

Clearly, the traditional trait-based approach to leadership is inadequate because it fails to take into consideration the important role of context as well as factors such as group membership. For example, Cheung and Halpern (2010) referred to a "culture of gender" (p. 190) to explain the cross-cultural consistencies in female–male differences in leadership behavior. They argued that in all cultures there are certain restrictions in the roles of women, particularly with respect to the responsibilities they are ascribed regarding children, the family, and the home. These restrictions make it more difficult for women to successfully take on leadership roles.

Women (and men) tend to be more successful as leaders in situations that are more congruent with their gender roles (Eagly & Carli, 2007). For example, women are more successful as leaders in educational settings, in line with the caring and nurturing aspects of their traditional role. Ayman and Korabik (2010) summarized the research on leadership behaviors and gender in this way: "Leadership is not a gender-neutral phenomenon. When women leaders adopt stereotypically masculine leadership behaviors, are in male-dominated settings, or are evaluated by men, they are particularly susceptible to being rated negatively" (p. 165).

UNDERSTANDING LEADERSHIP AS CONTEXTUAL AND RELATIONAL

> Intuition and some theories lead one to see stability and consistency in leader behavior and its outcomes, despite compelling evidence for the role of situation and context. Similarly, intuition and theories lead one to see stability and consistency in leader performance across diverse situations and to drastically overestimate leaders' control over organizational outcomes . . . the perceptual distortions have resulted from a failure to recognize the important role that situation or context plays in leadership. (Vroom & Jago, 2007, p. 23)

In recent years, it has become clear that in addition to the dispositional characteristics of the leader, an accurate explanation of leadership will also need to take into consideration the characteristics of the situation and the larger context. Imagine a national political leader who has to campaign and make speeches across the country in support of a new policy initiative. The audience and locations for such speeches could vary widely, from culturally and ethnically diverse populations in urban centers to highly educated groups in university towns to dispersed economically deprived groups in rural communities. To be effective, the politician would need to vary his campaigning style as he moved from location to location. The context-dependent nature of leadership has even been highlighted by one type of trait-focused research, which explores the adaptability of leaders (Ployhart & Bliese, 2006). More effective leaders have been seen as being able to adapt better to changing situations. The focus here is no longer solely on stability of traits across situations but rather on flexibility in response to situational changes. Thus, the constant here is change and being able to alter behavior as situational demands change (this brings us back to the topic of self-monitoring, the ability of a leader to regulate his or her behavior to meet the demands of changing situations).

Some researchers (e.g., Cohen & March, 1974) have conceptualized the role of the situation in leadership as being complete or total. In support of the argument that the situation is all powerful, researchers have studied organizations over time and found that leadership changes made very little difference to the functioning and direction of the organization. For example, institutions of higher education were found to change very little as their presidents changed (Cohen & March, 1974). A variety of factors, including situational demands, the history and traditions of the institutions, and the screening process for selecting leaders, resulted in university presidents who were influenced to behave in particular ways that were predictable from the behavioral mold of past presidents.

Interactional or contingency approaches, rather than strictly trait- or situation-based approaches, dominate 21st-century research on leadership (e.g., Vroom & Jago, 2007). The assumption underlying the interactionist approach is that both the characteristics of the leader and those of the situation are important and interdependent. For example, leader effectiveness is dependent on organizational effectiveness, and the characteristics of the situation influence both how leaders behave and the consequences of leader behavior (Vroom & Jago, 2007). In other words, leadership is situation- and context dependent.

Beyond this, leadership is relational in the sense that understanding leadership also requires examining the normative system (which includes norms, rules, and values) that regulates relations between leaders and followers. This normative system is not to be understood by examining the dispositional characteristics of the leader or those of followers but rather by examining what takes place between leaders and followers in the larger cultural context. For example, the normative system regulating leader–follower relations in Khomeini's Iran has to be understood in the larger context of Shi'a Islam, with its emphasis on the duty of Muslims to select and obey a spiritual leader as a source of emulation (Moghaddam, 2006).

The relational perspective on leadership is in important respects in line with the social identity theory of leadership (Hogg, 2001). A major proposition from social identity theory is that leaders who construct an image that is more *prototypical* (i.e., is in the ideal image of the group) will be particularly successful in gaining support: "the longer a particular individual occupies the most prototypical position, the stronger and more entrenched will be the appearance that he or she has actively exercised influence over others" (Hogg, 2001, p. 189). But in dictatorships, I have argued, this influence is actually strongest over the elites rather than the masses.

Before I end this discussion on the more traditional approaches to the study of leadership, I consider another important question that has been addressed through traditional methods: Is dictatorial leadership more efficient?

EFFICIENCY, SATISFACTION, AND DICTATORIAL LEADERSHIP

> The most common justification for dictatorship is that a strong leader (usually a military man) has taken power for the sake of the nation, in order to save a weak state from corrupt politicians and squabbling factions. (Canovan, 2004, p. 249)

Since the economic decline of 2008, many Americans have been concerned about the continuing slump in the United States economy. Unemployment stubbornly hovers around 8% to 9%, and consumer confidence is low. My academic home, Georgetown University, is intimately connected with politics inside Washington, DC, and I hear a lot of talk inside and outside campus about the gridlock in American government and the corruption of politics by money and special interest groups. The White House and the Senate are at present in the hands of the Democratic Party, but the House of Representatives is currently controlled by the Republican Party. The different governing bodies controlled by different parties cannot seem to come to an agreement as to how the federal government should tackle the enormous United States budget deficit. I have heard some Americans question the ability of the American government system to overcome the enormous challenges that lie ahead, including the challenge of competing with Communist China, which is now predicted to overtake the United States as the largest economy in the world before 2030.

In this atmosphere of national uncertainty and unease, some have criticized President Obama for leading from behind and not demonstrating strong leadership. In everyday conversations and in the media, I sense a desire for strong leadership to get Americans out of this mess. My point is not that the country is presently in danger of slipping into a dictatorship but rather that even in the United States, with its fairly robust democratic traditions of public participation in politics and decision making, at least at some levels, there has been a tendency on the part of some segments of the population to seek a solution in strong leadership. Indeed, in a recent lecture I gave to the lay public in Washington, DC, several businesspeople specifically suggested that the United States in 2012 is suffering political gridlock and should consider changing to the Chinese style of leadership!

As Canovan (quoted at the beginning of this section) pointed out, and as Arendt (2004) before her showed, a move from more open, democratic society to dictatorship most commonly arises out of a desire for stability, order, and efficiency in a situation in which democratic processes seem to be bankrupt. This desire is often on the part of diverse groups in society. Not surprisingly, potential and actual dictators position themselves as leaders capable of moving society in the right direction, toward stability and efficiency. For example, here is Stalin's story line in 1929 about how the Soviet Union (under his direction) was moving ahead of the capitalist world:

> We are advancing full speed ahead along the path of industrialization—
> to socialism, leaving behind the age-long "Russian" backwardness. We
> are becoming a country of metal, a country of automobiles, a country of
> tractors. And when we have put the USSR on an automobile, and the
> muzhik on a tractor, let the worthy capitalists, who boast loudly of their
> "civilization," try to overtake us. We shall see which countries may then
> be "classified" as backward and which as advanced. (Stalin quoted in
> Bullock, 1993, p. 259)

Hitler made similar claims and was seen by many Germans as having brought about an economic recovery:

> Above all, Hitler had ended unemployment. This was far and away the
> most important fact for the millions of working-class families who had
> known what it meant to be out of work, and without hope of it, only a
> few years before. (Bullock, 1993, p. 449)

This "economic miracle" was in large part motored by the enormous "re-armament boom" (Bullock, 1993, p. 449) launched by the Nazis. However, I argue that, first, dictatorships are not more efficient in the long term, and, second, in some dictatorships there is an explicit rejection of efficiency and such material criteria.

The Efficiency Question

The question of efficiency raises its head repeatedly: Is dictatorship more efficient than democracy? Are people more satisfied with dictatorial leadership? These questions have been addressed by researchers, starting with the pioneering studies of Kurt Lewin and his associates (Lewin & Lippitt, 1938; Lewin, Lippitt, & White, 1939; Lippitt, 1940). Lewin launched this research program at a very challenging time for Western democracies, confronted as they were in the 1930s with internal economic stagnation and also robust and growing dictatorial ideologies: the Nazi ideology of Hitler, the fascist ideology of Mussolini, and the particularly murderous version of Marxism developed by Stalin. Since this initial research program, numerous studies have explored the relative efficiency of democratic and dictatorial leadership styles as well as the satisfaction that group members have with these different styles. This literature has also been extensively reviewed over the years (e.g., Foels, Driskell, Mullen, & Salas, 2000; Gastil, 1994; K. Miller & Monge, 1986; Wagner, 1994). Looking over this body of literature and the various reviews, can one come to any general conclusions?

A first conclusion is that there is disagreement among researchers about the impact of dictatorial and democratic leadership on both performance and satisfaction among group members. For example, reviews by Locke and Schweiger (1979) and K. Miller and Monge (1986) supported the view that a more participatory leadership style results in greater efficiency and satisfaction among group members. Cotton and his colleagues reached the same conclusions (Cotton, Vollrath, Froggatt, Lengnick-Hall, & Jennings, 1988; Cotton, Vollrath, Lengnick-Hall, & Froggatt, 1990). On the other hand, Wagner (1994) reassessed this research literature and concluded that the relationship between leadership style and both satisfaction and efficiency is not strong or large. Gastil (1994) and some other reviewers (e.g., Foels et al., 2000) came to a similar but more nuanced conclusion: The relationship between leadership style and both satisfaction and efficiency can vary depending on other factors.

On the question of which other factors, perhaps the most important one is the characteristics of the group members. Style of leadership does not evolve in a vacuum but is intimately related to the behavior of followers as well as the broader culture in which leaders and followers exist (Moghaddam, 2002). In experimental studies of the relationship between leadership style and satisfaction and efficiency among group members, the participants have typically been students who were socialized to live in a democratic society (typically the United States). When this relationship was examined with participants from less democratic cultural backgrounds (e.g., Meade, 1967, 1970, 1985), a different pattern was found

> when the culture itself stressed many facets of human interaction which are authoritarian and when children grow up with that kind of interaction mode, then the response to authoritarian leadership is more positive than to democratic leadership. (Meade, 1985, p. 295)

The point Meade made is very important and pertinent to understanding why it is so difficult to change leadership style and leader–follower relationships after an antidictatorship revolution. Changing the psychological citizen (Moghaddam, 2008c) from one evolved to function in a dictatorship to one more suitable for functioning in a democracy requires a great deal more than simply providing information. The changes required tend to be subtle and involve skills in both thinking and acting. I use an example of my experiences in postrevolution Iran to clarify this point.

It is helpful to consider the case of Khomeini and think back to the contrast with Mandela I wrote about at the start of this book. One can imagine the situation if Khomeini had wanted to change himself into a democratic leader like Mandela. He would have had to reorganize certain aspects of his behavior and to acquire new values, skills, and attitudes required to enable democratic leadership. This would have required effort and time. However, it would not have been enough to change only himself, it would also have been necessary to change the Iranian population to become psychological citizens capable of full participation in a democracy. New skills would have to be acquired, such as social behavior that upholds the free speech rights of others, tolerance for differences, openness toward dissimilar others. Such changes would be difficult and require time so that a collective culture supportive of these changes could develop. Both leaders and followers would need to experience change in the same direction within a collective culture supportive of openness. The transitionary period moving from a collective culture supportive of dictatorship to one more supportive of democracy would be difficult, and from the perspective of supporters of dictatorship, it would also be inefficient.

Despite the difficulties of moving to democracy, I must examine the case for dictatorship being more efficient more critically; the example of Nazi Germany provides an excellent opportunity.

Efficiency: The Case of Nazi Germany

I now examine more seriously the claim that dictatorships have provided efficiency. The often-cited example is efficiency in Hitler's Germany and the power of the German economy more broadly:

> It is hardly an exaggeration to say that historians of twentieth-century Germany share at least one common starting point: the assumption of the peculiar strength of the German economy. Obviously, when Hitler took power Germany was in the midst of a deep economic crisis. But the common sense of twentieth-century European history is that Germany was an economic superpower in waiting . . . the assumption of Germany's peculiar economic modernity has gone largely unquestioned. (Tooze, 2006, p. xxii)

In critically examining assumptions about the "German economic miracle" under Hitler, Tooze (2006) revealed how Nazi propaganda was responsible for creating and spreading a number of myths about the economy under Hitler. Tooze's discussion of Albert Speer (1905–1981), "Hitler's architect" and also armaments minister from 1942 to 1945, is particularly enlightening (see Tooze, 2006). After the war, Speer was put on trial at Nuremberg together with the other members of the Nazi leadership who had been captured alive. He served a prison term and was released in 1966, following which he published several volumes of notes and memoirs and, despite his critics, became an international best-selling author and celebrity.

Speer's autobiographical accounts reflect his talent for the same kind of propaganda and self-aggrandizement that created the myth of the armaments miracle in Nazi Germany (as Tooze, 2006, reported in Chapter 18 of his exhaustively researched book, there was a huge gulf between propaganda and reality in the realm of German armaments production under Speer). Throughout the pages of Speer's best-selling books, one comes across numerous instances of his self-reported grand actions and gestures, including "That night I came to the decision to eliminate Hitler" (Speer, 1970, p. 429) and telling Hitler face-to-face that "the war is lost" (p. 452).

But despite the self-presentations designed to improve his own image, Speer did provide important information that helps to clarify why dictatorships are ultimately inefficient. In dictatorships, all decisions are made top-down, and there is little or no opportunity for open discussion and critical exchange—processes that are absolutely essential to arrive at the best solutions. In Nazi Germany, all important decisions were made by Hitler, and no one dared to critically question Hitler's decisions. This meant that only those who were able to practice indirect and subtle manipulations (e.g., *Machiavellian intelligence*, involving strategies for getting others to do what one wants without the other recognizing the manipulation; Gavrilets & Vose, 2006) were able to gain influence. Speer (1970) provided this explanation of how certain officials became influential:

> I often ask myself whether Hitler was open to influence. He surely could be swayed by those who knew how to manage him. Hitler was mistrustful, to be sure. But he was so in a cruder sense, it often seemed to me; for he did not see through clever chess moves or subtle manipulation of his opinions. He had apparently no sense for methodological deceit. Among the masters of that art were Goering, Goebbels, Bormann, and, within limits, Himmler. (p. 126)

The absolute and all-embracing role of the Great Dictator resulted in even greater dangers for efficiency.

The All-Embracing Supreme Leader and Efficiency

An important characteristic of most Supreme Dictators is their all-embracing style of leadership; it seems there is absolutely no aspect of life that the Supreme Dictator cannot and should not decide on. The only limitation on this in the case of leaders such as Hitler is time: Even the Supreme Dictator does not have more than 24 hours in a day (fortunately for the rest of us!).

The opening of the former Soviet Union archives has provided scholars better opportunities to examine the extent to which Stalin was ultimately behind different decisions prior to his death in 1953, and it is clear that he used his available time to exert as much control as possible. Pollock (2006) used newly available archival material to show how the campaigns launched by the Communist Party to "correct" thinking in the domains of philosophy, biology, physics, linguistics, physiology and psychology, and political economy were traced back to Stalin. Indeed, Stalin (who saw himself as the "choirmaster of science"; Montefiore, 2003, p. 577) had a direct hand in vetting and creating ideas about science and research and helping to craft attacks on what he considered slavish modeling of the West. Given Stalin's lack of research training and scholarship, his interference was equivalent to the sabotaging of Soviet research efforts in many different domains.

Perhaps the biggest disaster arising from Stalin's interference in scientific research arose in the domain of genetics because this had a direct impact on farming practices and agricultural production. After the destructive years of World War II and the major famine of 1946 in the Soviet Union, there was an urgent need for the adoption of new farming practices to increase agricultural production. But Stalin insisted on turning his back on the West, on the grounds that the Soviet Union had all the human and material resource necessary to make progress independently. He was all too ready to back the schemes of indigenous so-called researchers who claimed to have discovered revolutionary solutions based on local talent. Perhaps the most ultimately destructive of these was Trofim Lysenko (1898–1976), who propagated the so-called scientific doctrine of *Michurinism*, named after Ivan Michurin (1855–1935), a self-taught breeder who became the poster child for the proletariat scientist (Soyfer, 1994). Mendelian genetics was dismissed as bourgeois and reactionary, and thousands of scientists were expelled from their posts to open the way for new scientific developments based on indigenous talents. The brilliant plant biologist Nikolai Vavilov (1887–1943), a world pioneer in seed bank development, was arrested on trumped-up charges, tortured, tried, found guilty, and killed in jail through starvation (Pringle, 2008). His real crime was that he did not fit the profile of the proletariat scientist, like Lysenko or Michurin. Not surprisingly, these developments failed to increase agricultural production in the Soviet Union.

The All-Embracing Supreme Dictator in Iran

It is difficult to exaggerate the importance of the role played by this all-embracing feature of the dictator personality: Again and again, the dictator is assumed to know best in areas in which he clearly knows nothing of value. I witnessed this firsthand after the revolution in Iran, when absolute power was wielded by Ayatollah Khomeini (and continues to be wielded, although with less authority, by his successor, Ayatollah Khamenei). In this case, the particular cultural traditions of Shi'a Islam in Iran enhanced the Supreme Leader's tendency to have a say in everything, even the most routine matters of everyday life for the general public (Moghaddam, 2006). As discussed in Chapter 5, when an ayatollah becomes an important *mara-i-taqlid* (source of emulation), he is expected to write a *risala*, a detailed guide for behavior, for his followers. Such guides cover just about every conceivable aspect of life, from bathing to wedding, from conducting business to social relationships; almost nothing is left out. In this sense, these guides cover a great deal more ground that Mao's Red Book and Qaddafi's Green Book, which do not go into as much detail about the rules of everyday living. In addition, when followers find they have to make a decision that is not set out in the risala of their chosen mara-i-taqlid, they often directly contact the leader and ask for advice—so they are guided every step of the way in their lives. In addition to writing a risala, Khomeini explained the nature of Islamic government in a separate book (Khomeini, 1979) in which he tried to make clear his views on both a macro government level and on micro everyday level issues.

In addition to his writing, Khomeini regularly made lengthy speeches in which he provided advice as to how things should be done in a wide array of domains. For example, with respect to universities and research, he repeatedly declared that the "rotten brains" of Western-trained experts are not needed—echoing a theme well-known to anti-Western dictators from Stalin to Castro. I was in Iran in the early 1980s when, through the influence of Khomeini's tirades against rotten Western-trained brains, hundreds of thousands of the leading professionals in Iran were expelled from government institutions, including the major universities. Most of Iran's specialists with advanced degrees from the West were forced to leave Iran and start new lives abroad, as was my fate. The real damage done by Khomeini's attacks against rotten Western-trained brains became clear in the following decades as the standard of professional work and education fell in Iran and the efficiency of even the centrally important oil sector dramatically declined.

Enormous Mistakes Committed by the All-Knowing, All-Embracing Dictators

Because "all-knowing, all-embracing" dictators do not allow any kind of critical discussion, there is little possibility for propaganda and myths to be separated from reality. In the cases of Hitler and Stalin, a frank reassessment was possible only after the death of the dictator. In Hitler's case, the military defeat of Germany and the thrust of postwar Soviet and American propaganda eased the way for the German people to turn their backs on the dead dictator. In Stalin's case, by 1956, three years after Stalin's death, Nikita Khrushchev (1894–1971) had gained control of the reins of power and in a so-called secret speech denounced Stalinism and maneuvered the Soviet Union toward a slightly more tolerant political system. In China also, only a month after Mao's death in 1976, there was a sharp turn away from Mao's policies. This is symbolized by the show trial of the so-called Gang of Four, which included Mao's last wife, who were accused of counterrevolutionary activities, particularly during the Cultural Revolution. In her defense, Mao's last wife argued that she had carried out Mao's orders, which may have been accurate but was not sufficient to prevent her persecution.

Thus, in the cases of Hitler, Stalin, and Mao, the death of the dictator led to a period of critical reassessment and a turning away from the dead dictator's policies. This did not result in an end to dictatorship, but at least it resulted in the adoption of slightly more benign policies politically and changes in the economic sphere–dramatic changes in the case of China and the former East Germany.

Iran and North Korea represent examples in which the death of the dictator did not result in reassessment and questioning; rather, the regime vowed to follow the path of the dead dictator. This is highly unfortunate for the people of North Korea and Iran because it has meant repeating the same mistakes and remaining inefficient and poor economically. This stagnation is a direct outgrowth of the all-knowing, all-embracing behavior of the Supreme Dictator in North Korea and Iran. Many different experiences in everyday life would endorse this view; my own experiences during the so-called Cultural Revolution in Iran serve as an example. I recite this example not because it is important in itself but because together with the hundreds of thousands of other incidents experienced by hundreds of thousands of other people—particularly people who Khomeini described as rotten Western-trained brains—it reflects a trend showing the long reach of the never-to-be-questioned Supreme Leader and the inefficiencies it resulted in.

Before the Cultural Revolution in Iran resulted in the closing of all universities, I was a faculty member at the University of Tehran, where I had the opportunity to put forward research and publication projects, which would occupy me while there were no university classes. I put forward a proposal to write a social psychology text in Farsi, with a focus on the practical needs of Iranian society. I have always been interested in psychology for the Third World and was eager to help launch social psychological research that would address issues faced by Iranians in the postrevolution era (I actually did manage to follow up this line of work in North America; see Moghaddam, 1987, 1990, 1996, 1997; Moghaddam & Lee, 2006; Moghaddam & Taylor, 1985, 1986). However, I soon found that the revolutionaries who had gained control of higher education in postrevolution Iran and were following the line of the Imam looked on me with suspicion—I had not changed my outward appearance to look like an Islamic fundamentalist, I was Western trained, and they would not trust me to write a social psychology or any other text. The Supreme Dictator had declared that I, as well as hundreds of thousands of others like me, was not to be given responsibility.

After many years, when I had reestablished myself in the West, I went back to Iran and was curious to see what kinds of progress had been made in my specialty area. The revolutionaries had rejected my plan for a social psychology text addressing the issues of postrevolution Iran, so what had they produced? What was being taught in the leading Iranian universities? To my dismay, I discovered that the texts used in Iranian classrooms were translations of out-of-date traditional American (!) social psychology texts. To add to the irony, I was later asked if I would be interested in having my social psychology text, published by a New York publisher (Moghaddam, 1998), translated into Farsi. It was a deeply sad occasion for me when my book was put on display in an international book fair in Iran because I could have produced a far more effective book for the Iranian context in Farsi. Through my travels and meetings with Iranian exiles, I realized that hundreds of thousands of other Western-trained professionals have shared my experience of being prevented from contributing to Iranian society by the "all-knowing, all-embracing" talent of the Supreme Dictator, who decides everything for all Iranians.

The Supreme Dictator sacrifices everything to achieve absolute obedience. Thus, efficiency is secondary for the Supreme Dictator, and expertise, education, and professional skills are all expendable: The obedient person is always preferred, even if he or she is illiterate and unskilled.

DICTATORIAL LEADERSHIP, SOCIAL LIFE, AND GENDER RELATIONS

Perhaps nowhere is the impact of the all-knowing, all-embracing Supreme Dictator felt more than in social life and the arts. This is because the goal of dictators, from Hitler to Khomeini, has been the transformation of the citizen, and changes in social relationships and in the arts are seen as essential for achieving this goal. Consequently, Supreme Dictators focus a great deal of resources on controlling social life and all activities in the arts; this includes the details of how people dress, how they speak, and gender relations.

The particular focus of total dictatorships is on women because of the centrally important role of women in reproduction, the family, and the socialization of the next generation. In total dictatorships, women are permitted to take only low-status positions in the workforce; they are prohibited, sometimes by explicit legislation, from reaching the top positions in political and economic arenas. Also, the liberation of women is opposed by total dictatorships because it interferes with reproduction and having large families. For example, in Mussolini's Italy, there was a systematic campaign in support of traditional women and against modern women:

> Fascist newspapers often excoriated the vices of the modern *donna crisi* (twitchy woman), thin, neurotic, and very likely sterile, as distinct from the virtues of the traditional *donna madre* (woman and mother), stocky, large-hipped, big-bosomed and, above all, fertile. . . . From 1934 Mussolini in annual homage received a couple from each of the nation's ninety-two provinces and handed over a purse of five thousand lire to those chosen to meet their *Duce*. By 1937, a special party organization was created to provide increased welfare for large families. (Bosworth, 2006, pp. 267–268)

The Supreme Dictator and Women

The psychological study of Supreme Dictators is incomplete if it does not include a discussion of the relationship between the dictator and women. I do not mean this only in the interpersonal sense, for example, the relationship between Hitler and his mistress, Eva Braun. As Albert Speer (1970) recounted, Eva Braun was treated as an inferior and banished to her room when dignitaries arrived. Hitler is quoted as saying about male–female relations in general, "A highly intelligent man should take a primitive and stupid woman. Imagine if on top of everything else I had a woman who interfered with my work! In my leisure time I want to have peace" (p. 92). Speer reported Hitler as saying that "he certainly did not want witty and intelligent women about him. In making such remarks he was apparently not aware of how offensive they must have been to the ladies present" (p. 92).

But beyond the personal relationship between the total dictator and women, there is the more important societal treatment of women as inspired and guided by the Supreme Dictator. In the cases of Iran, Saudi Arabia, and other Islamic societies, the Supreme Dictator works within religious traditions that treat women as second-class citizens. In every important sphere of life, women are at a huge disadvantage, starting with religion itself. The fact that women are not able to join the clergy in these societies where the voice of religion is so powerful is one of many factors that work against them. In the justice system, women are not permitted to become judges, and their voice as witnesses has less weight than that of a man. When women want to travel, they need the permission of their husband or father or some other male guardian. Women are barred from most important positions in both the public and private spheres.

Legal restrictions on the activities of women in the public sphere have resulted in a strange situation in Iran, where prior to the 1978–1979 revolution women were permitted to compete openly for entrance to universities. Despite the fact that a large number of university places are now reserved for those affiliated with the regime, and despite efforts by the regime to restrict the numbers of women in universities, the majority of undergraduates in Iranian universities are women. Unfortunately, these talented women find that after graduation, there are few employment options open to them. Men with lower qualifications and lower aptitudes soon overtake them. But the most visible signs of the treatment of women in Iran, Saudi Arabia, and other Muslim dictatorships is in their treatment at the hands of the so-called morality police.

The enforcement of the Islamic *hejab* (veil) by the morality policy is symbolic of the treatment of women in the wider society. The Islamic hejab is an example of a sacred carrier, a means by which social status relations (among other things, including values) are publicly displayed and reinforced. The defenders of the hejab claim that it protects women and prevents them from being treated as sex objects. However, from the perspective of liberated women, or women who are motivated to become liberated, the hejab is symbolic of the control of women in the public sphere. This control function becomes clear when one witnesses the morality police, or anyone taking up the role of morality police, enforcing the hejab in public. I have witnessed highly cultured women with advanced degrees being attacked in the street by fundamentalist men who could barely read or write but who used their male position to bludgeon women down on the pretext that they were not wearing the hejab properly. The shame and anger experienced by the women is enormous because they have to remain passive and accept their humiliation. They know that if they react in anger, they and any men accompanying them will be attacked more savagely. This pattern of using low-status and poorly educated men to attack "uppity" women is repeated by different Supreme Dictators.

Just as dictatorial regimes are centrally concerned about the family and the role of women, even those very different in espoused ideology also focus on education as a tool for remolding the citizen. For example, East Germany was unfortunate enough to experience from the 1930s to the 1980s two different dictatorships one after another, under the ideological banner of Nazism and communism. "The National Socialists and Communists both saw teachers as a professional group that was to play a crucial role in the transformation of German society, creating via education Nazis in the Third Reich and 'antifascists' in the post-war era" (Lansing, 2010, p. 221). Thus, there was continuity across Nazi and communist dictatorships in East Germany, both using education to try to subjugate the masses.

The Supreme Dictator and the Arts

In "Dancing Toward Dictatorship: Political Songs and Popular Culture in Malawi," Chirwa (2001) described how President for Life Hastings Banda (1898–1997) harnessed the power of popular songs and dances to gain complete control in Malawi.

> By the 1970s, he [Hastings Banda] had become *Ngwazi*, the conqueror and the hero, the Lion of Malawi, the government and the law . . . the members of the Women's League sang of him as 'the government':
> When we see the *Ngwazi*, we are happy
> We are happy, happy indeed.
> The *Ngwazi* is government, now!
> The *Ngwazi* is government, he is government,
> We are happy indeed. (p. 9)

Next to the control of women, Supreme Dictators are focused on controlling the arts. This is in large part because the very nature of the arts, requiring free expression and exploration, makes them contradictory to the goals of the Supreme Dictator, whose goal is total control of all activities in society. The Supreme Dictator strives to harness all artistic efforts to help him maintain complete control, and of course artists find this stifling and against their own instincts and urges.

Russia and Iran are examples of societies that experienced a brief period of artistic growth in the postrevolution period between two dictatorships before the lid was placed back on and censorship was reimposed. This pattern also took place after the French Revolution, when for a few years there was artistic experimentation before Napoleon reimposed absolute control. Around the time of the Russian revolution, avant-garde art flourished for a short period before Soviet realism was imposed and experimentation was thwarted (Sitsky, 1994). Composers and musicians, including the greats such as Shostakovich, Prokofiev, and Khachaturian, were kept on a short leash by Stalin and his cronies. Art was made subservient to the personality cult of the Supreme Dictator, Stalin (Dobrenko & Naiman, 2003).

Stalin gave considerable power to Andrei Zhdanov (1896–1948) in controlling the arts, and both men were determined not to allow Soviet artists freedom to experiment. The two men were "obsessed with the greatness of nineteenth-century culture and repulsed by the degeneracy of modern art and morals." They devised "a savage attack on modernism . . . and foreign influence on Russian culture" (Montefiore, 2003, p. 541). The alcoholic Zhdanov was given the power to attack and shut down entire art forms, particularly those (e.g., jazz) that seemed to him to combine the bad elements of foreign influence and modern morality. Stalin sought to rediscover Russian authenticity through and in art forms, and he was particularly obsessed with achieving a good and pure art. The same obsession was evident in Hitler's attitudes toward art, although he was far more effective at harnessing art for his personality cult and ideology. For example, Hitler used art and architecture very effectively at the outdoor Nazi party rallies. The Nuremberg party rally used light so dramatically that it was described as "a cathedral of ice" (see an illustration in Speer, 1970, pp. 166–167).

CONCLUDING COMMENT

Dictators tend to be all embracing, to dictate what is to be enforced as correct behavior in every domain of life. This tendency arises, on the one hand, because the mechanisms of coercion (from torture to cognitive dissonance) mean that people do not dare to oppose the dictator and, on the other hand, because the dictator attempts to control every thought and action in the population as a zero tolerance policy intended to prevent rebellion. The outcome of this process is that even the most minute aspects of life, including in the cultural, social, economic, and, of course, political domains come under the dictates of the Supreme Dictator. The family and the role of women become particularly important because of the role of families and women in shaping citizens of the future. The Supreme Dictator's ultimate goal is the strengthening and continuation of certain styles of thinking and acting that perpetuate the dictatorship, a topic I explore in Chapter 9.

9

COGNITION AND ACTION SUPPORTIVE OF DICTATORSHIP

The Party told you to reject the evidence of your eyes and ears. It was their final, most essential command. His heart sank as he thought of the enormous power arrayed against him.

—George Orwell, *1984*

Early on the morning of December 17, 2011, Mohammed Bouazizi, a 26-year-old street vendor, set out to take fruit to sell in the market of Sidi Bouzid, a small rural town in Tunisia where he and his mother and siblings lived (M. Fisher, 2011). Like the rest of Tunisian society, the town of Sidi Bouzid was rife with injustice and corruption. Since gaining independence from France in 1956, Tunisia had first been ruled for 30 years (1957–1987) by Habib Bourguiba (1903–2000) and then by Zine al-Abidine Ben Ali. Like many other despots, these two "elected" leaders in what I have termed *democratic dictatorships* enjoyed some popular support at the start of their reign, but corruption and nepotism corroded their regimes over time. I had visited Tunisia during Ben Ali's rule and found it to be a society suffering from extreme corruption: The locals seemed to have to pay bribes for just about everything, from getting driving licenses to landing places for their children in better schools.

DOI: 10.1037/14138-010
The Psychology of Dictatorship, by F. M. Moghaddam
Copyright © 2013 by the American Psychological Association. All rights reserved.

When Mohammed Bouazizi pushed his fruit-laden cart toward the market early that December morning, he was accosted by several male and female police officers; this was not unusual because the police regularly harassed the market vendors and stole from them. That day, the police officers beat and humiliated Bouazizi, and stole fruit from him. His mistreatment at the hands of a female police officer might have been particularly galling for him in a society in which people honor traditional masculine and feminine roles. When the young man complained to the town authorities, he was dismissed and told to go home. His next move was completely unexpected, as was the outcome of what he did. In protest against his humiliating treatment, Bouazizi stood in front of the town municipal building, doused his entire body with paint thinner, and set himself on fire. He died 3 weeks later; but by the time of his death he had sparked a revolution and helped to launch the Arab Spring.

The dictator, President Ben Ali, and the Tunisian authorities attempted to display concern by visiting Mohammed Bouazizi in hospital and promising to help his family, but their expressions of sympathy rang hollow, and it proved to be too late for the Ben Ali regime to change its spots. Demonstrations and riots swept Tunisia, and Ben Ali and his family and close associates were forced to flee the country (he now lives in Saudi Arabia, a dictatorship that has become the refuge of a number of other dictators and their families, including the late Idi Amin). But that was just the beginning: Over the next few months, large-scale protests also broke out in Algeria, Egypt, Jordan, Yemen, Bahrain, Libya, Morocco, Kuwait, Iraq, and even Iran. This popular unrest across the Near and Middle East led to actual regime changes in Tunisia, Egypt, and Libya. The president of Yemen has also stepped aside (in March 2012), and popular pressure is increasing for changes in some other countries in the region. It is only by massive military assault on the civilian population as well as the direct military backing of Iran and the support of China and Russia in the United Nations Security Council that Bashar al-Assad's dictatorship has survived so far in Syria.

The action taken by Mohammed Bouazizi and the powerful explosion of social unrest and revolution represent a clear demonstration of social change triggered by an event that disrupted the normative system established by the ruling elite. I argue that it was this rupturing of the normative system that enabled the Tunisian masses to perceive the possibility of social change. This change in perceptions is at the collective level, involving a shift in norms as to how society should be construed. However, there are differences in the propensity of individuals to experience this perceptual shift and to continue to support dictatorship. Psychological research on authoritarianism (Adorno, Frenkel-Brunswik, Levinson, & Sanford, 1950; Altemeyer, 1988), social dominance orientation (Pratto, Sidanius, Stallworth, & Malle, 1994), the need for certainty (Kruglanski, 2004), and Machiavellianism (Christie

& Geis, 1970) can provide insights on tendencies to support dictatorship. However, in line with my discussion of causal and normative interpretations of psychology in Chapter 2, I must take great care in how I incorporate the results of research using such individual difference measures in my analyses.

Psychological measures such as authoritarianism, social dominance orientation, the need for certainty, and Machiavellianism require participants to express their level of agreement or disagreement with a number of statements. For example, the Right-Wing Authoritarianism scale (Altemeyer, 1981), one of the most psychometrically sophisticated scales in this topic area, asks participants to rate their level of agreement, from *disagree strongly* (1) to *agree strongly* (6), with statements such as "The facts on crime, sexual immorality, and the recent public disorders all show we have to crack down harder on deviant groups and troublemakers if we are going to save our moral standards and preserve law and order" and "Obedience and respect for authority are the most important virtues children should learn." The ratings made by participants are taken as indications of underlying personality characteristics.

In interpreting the results of this research, one must keep a number of potential limitations in mind. First, a major shortcoming has been the heavy reliance on students (most commonly, psychology undergraduates attending universities in Western countries) as participants in studies that helped to develop these scales. This shortcoming dogged the research from earlier times; for example, in the pioneering study of Adorno et al. (1950) on the authoritarian personality, the majority of participants were students. Indeed, in a survey of leading psychology journals, researchers found that the percentage of psychological studies using student samples as participants had increased, even in cross-cultural journals (Moghaddam & Lee, 2006). This overreliance on students, mostly from Western countries, is obviously problematic because Western undergraduates are not an accurate representative of seven billion humans around the world.

Of course, the claim could be made that the psychological processes or mental mechanisms of interest are universal, and, therefore, it does not matter what the sample is as long as it is human. But this is an assumption that has to be empirically demonstrated. Moreover, this claim runs against the view that although there are some universals, social cognition and social actions are largely cultural constructions (Cole, 1996; Harré & Moghaddam, 2012; Sampson, 1981; Stigler, Shweder, & Herdt, 1990; Valsiner, 2000).

Second, one must take care not to assume that the individual is the source of the ratings made on the authoritarianism scale and other such measures. From the discussion of the topic of embryonic fallacy (see Chapter 2, this volume), it is wrong to treat individuals as self-contained and as having within themselves certain fixed levels of authoritarianism, for example, that arise independent of the context in which they live. The type of thinking found by psychological measures at the level of the individual is a product of larger cultural processes and has as its source societal characteristics. When an individual uses a rating scale to indicate 5 or some other number in response to a question (item) on Altemeyer's (1981) Right-Wing Authoritarianism scale, this rating does not arise in an isolated mind. Rather, such ratings arise out of socialization processes and training as to what is a correct response to such a question. Of course, there are variations across individuals in how they respond, but the general trend shown by a sample population is indicative of the characteristics of the population from which the sample is selected. The primacy of context has been noted in the pioneering research on authoritarianism (e.g., Adorno et al., 1950), and I return to this topic again in this chapter.

INDIVIDUAL DIFFERENCE MEASURES

Individual difference measures such as the Authoritarian Personality, Social Dominance Orientation, and the Need for Closure scales, can provide insights into psychological factors that make it possible for dictatorship to come into being and be sustained. However, my focus is on the question of how pervasive thinking styles such as authoritarianism are in a particular population rather than what particular individual scores are on such measures. The societal score on such thinking styles will be related to socialization processes and educational systems nurtured by regimes in power.

The Authoritarian Personality

> It is a well-known hypothesis that susceptibility to fascism is most characteristically a middle-class phenomenon, that it is "in the culture" and, hence, that those who conform the most to this culture will be most prejudiced. (Adorno et al., 1950, p. 229)

The study of the thinking styles of profascist individuals gained momentum from the 1930s (e.g., Edwards, 1941; Stagner, 1936) in large part as a result of the rise of extremist right-wing movements in Europe, culminating in dictatorships in Germany and Italy. This research trend on authoritarianism came to fruition after World War II, with the publication of the seminal study on the authoritarian personality by Adorno et al. (1950). These authors began their work by looking back at the horrors of World War II and raising questions that the social sciences should be committed to address: How could genocide and the terrible horrors of the war have been perpetrated by people representing the most "advanced" societies on earth? Although Adorno et al. adopted a psychodynamic approach, the manner in which they raised questions made it clear that they saw the individual responding to certain characteristics of the cultural context, "what within the individual organism responds to certain stimuli in our culture with attitudes and acts of destructive aggression." (p. v).

This tradition of giving importance to the cultural context to explain authoritarian attitudes continues in some important contemporary works dealing with the same themes. For example, in Staub's (2011) insightful analysis of how people can best strive to overcome evil, there is a strong emphasis on socialization practices:

> In societies that promote strong respect for authority, children are usually raised by adults who set rules with little or no explanation, demand and enforce unquestioning obedience, and punish deviation from rules or disobedience. This can happen in the home, as well as in schools. (p. 225)

I am most interested in the role of culture in nurturing the authoritarian personality because culture also plays a central role in bringing into being the authoritarian state.

Adorno et al. (1950) concluded that the authoritarian personality has a number of clearly identifiable characteristics that are interrelated, so that attitudes toward authority, minorities, religion, and the opposite sex, among other things, come as an integral package. However, at the root of this is socialization processes, starting with the culture of the family:

> a basically hierarchical, authoritarian, exploitative parent–child relationship is apt to carry over into a power-oriented, exploitively dependent attitudes toward one's sex partner and one's God and may well culminate in a political philosophy and social outlook which has no room for anything but a desperate clinging to what appears to be strong and disdainful rejection of whatever is relegated to the bottom. (Adorno et al., 1950, p. 971)

There is no doubt that the family can play a central part in socializing children to become psychological citizens capable of functioning in and upholding dictatorship. This makes the role of women particularly important because the traditional role of women is the foundation for the traditional family. The supporters and opponents of dictatorship seem to be instinctively aware of this because (as discussed in Chapter 8, this volume) they have fought fiercely to define the "correct" role for women. For example, in Iran, Saudi Arabia, and other Islamic dictatorships, the governments enforce a version of Sharia law that tries to ensure that women are kept limited to a highly backward, traditional gender role.

Right-Wing Authoritarianism

Research on authoritarianism made advances through the work of the Canadian researcher Bob Altemeyer (1981, 1988) with his measure of Right-Wing Authoritarianism. Altemeyer's measure was developed with a great deal of care in terms of its reliability and validity (at least for the mostly student samples used). Altemeyer made more explicit a long-established tradition in this research area of conceiving authoritarianism as being associated with the political right, rather than the political left (see discussions in Christie & Jahoda, 1954). This focus on dangers from the right seemed appropriate in the post–World War II era because of threats from Hitler, Mussolini, and the international fascism movement. However, it seems inconceivable that one can look at cases such as Stalin and Mao and not conclude that there is an equally great danger of authoritarianism from the political left (for arguments opposed to this view, see Stone & Smith, 1993). The left-wing authoritarianism of Stalin and Mao and that of despots in some smaller dictatorships, such as Pol Pot in Cambodia, inflicted terrible injuries on entire populations, resulting in tens of millions of deaths.

According to the research following the tradition of Adorno et al. (1950), the hallmark of the high authoritarian is a number of what I term *attitudinal styles*. (In Adorno et al., 1950, they were termed *sub-syndromes*, and nine of these were identified. However, I interpret authoritarianism in terms of attitude rather than personality; see also Roiser & Willig, 2002.) In this discussion, I focus particularly on those attitudinal styles that have continued to be important in current research. The first are submissiveness to authority and the acceptance of group-based differences as part of the natural order. A second is a punitive orientation toward minorities; high authoritarians tend to show prejudice against all minorities rather than just a particular group. Thus, high authoritarians have a "double kick" quality: extreme submissiveness and obedience to those with power and authority and extreme prejudice against those unfortunate enough to be below them and to suffer low status.

Another important attitudinal style identified in the original study by Adorno et al. (1950) and continuing in current research is intolerance of ambiguity, a version of which has recently been termed *need for closure* or *need for certainty* (Kruglanski & Orehek, 2012). In the original research, "intolerance for emotional and cognitive ambiguity" (Adorno et al., 1950, p. 464) was found to be associated with certain attitudes toward science and knowledge in general:

> The inability to "question" matters and the need for definite and dogmatic answers, as frequently found in high scorers (on authoritarianism), leads either to an easy acceptance of stereotyped, *pseudoscientific* answers, of which escape into ready made hereditarian explanations is but one manifestation, or else to an explicitly *antiscientific* attitude. (Adorno et al., 1950, p. 464)

I found this intolerance toward science a very strong theme among fundamentalist Muslims in Iran as well as fundamentalist Christians in the United States.

Historical experience shows that, psychologically, all religious fundamentalists, such as in Iran and America, are in important respects similar, including in their (actual or potential) support for dictatorship that upholds their particular view of God and science.

Social Dominance Theory

> The evolutionary perspective suggests . . . that humans will tend to live in group-based and hierarchically organized social systems. (Sidanius & Pratto, 1999, p. 54)

Social dominance theory comes from a long line of theories, from Plato (trans. 1987) in ancient Greece to Pareto (1935) in 20th-century Europe, that view group-based inequalities as arising out of human nature or temperament in modern terminology. By couching their theory in the terminology of sociobiology (Sidanius & Pratto, 1999), the proponents of this theory have opened themselves up to attacks from those who are particularly alert to issues of feminism and racism. The implication of social dominance theory seems to be that humans are condemned to live with group-based inequalities, and some authors have even attacked this theory for depicting inequalities as "genetically mandated" (Jost, Banaji, & Nosek, 2004, p. 912).

Social dominance theory asserts that hierarchies based on sex and age are universal. Hierarchies on other bases, such as religion and race, are malleable, can vary across cultures, and are made possible by the production of a surplus. Second, the predisposition to form group-based hierarchies results in various forms of aggression, such as sexism, racism, classism, and so on. Since the development of this theory in the early 1990s, a measure was also developed to find support for the theory in the form of the Social Dominance Orientation scale, which attempts to get at individual differences "expressing the value that people place on nonegalitarian and hierarchically structured relationships among social groups" (Sidanius & Pratto, 1999, p. 61). Research using this scale has yielded evidence in line with social dominance theory by, for example, demonstrating that majority group members endorse group-based inequalities more than do minority group members, and certain institutions, such as the police force, attract more people who particularly endorse group-based inequalities (see Pratto & Stewart, 2012, and Sidanius & Pratto, 1999, for broad discussions of this theory and its implications; see J. C. Turner & Reynolds, 2003, for a critique).

A central research question has concerned the extent to which social dominance orientation measures prejudice against minorities independent of context. Identity-based theories such as self-categorization theory (J. C. Turner & Reynolds, 2012) give importance to the particular identity of the individual that is made salient in a particular context: For example, does Joe give priority to his personal or to his group identity in a particular context? From this perspective, racist attitudes would be high when ethnic identity is evoked but less so when personal identity is evoked independent of ethnicity. Studies assessing this question found that although context did impact the level of racism, social dominance orientation predicted racist attitudes to some degree independent of the identity evoked in a context (Perry & Sibley, 2011; Sibley & Liu, 2010). Research is showing that context does have an important impact on social dominance orientation (Jetten & Iyer, 2010), but a more foundational impact of context remains neglected—the impact of the larger culture.

Just as there are differences across individuals with respect to social dominance orientation, there are differences across cultures, a topic I return to later in this chapter.

The Need for Closure

Following the attention given to intolerance for emotional and cognitive ambiguity by Adorno et al. (1950), Webster and Kruglanski (1994) developed a measure of *need for closure*, the preference for a firm, clear answer, any answer, to a question rather than to have ambiguity and questions left unanswered. Individuals who are high on the need for cognitive closure endorse statements such as, "I enjoy having a clear and structured mode of life"; "I don't like situations that are uncertain"; and "I dislike questions that can be answered in many different ways." The Need for Cognitive Closure scale has now been tested and used in an impressive set of studies, and a clear pattern of thinking style has been identified among those high on this need (Kruglanski, 2004; Kruglanski, Pierro, Mannetti, & De Granda, 2006).

I am particularly focused on the implications of the need for cognitive closure for dictatorship, and there is evidence that those high on this need are more likely to support autocratic leadership. For example, in a study on the need basis of values, it was found that those high on the need for cognitive closure give high priority to conformity, tradition, and security and low priority to making decisions for themselves (Calogero, Bardi, & Sutton, 2009). In a study conducted in organizations in Italy, it was found that supervisors high on need for cognitive closure preferred hard power tactics (e.g., reminding the worker that the supervisor could make it difficult for him or her to get a promotion and that as a subordinate he or she has no choice but to comply), implying that high need for closure is more likely to be found among autocratic leaders (Pierro, Kruglanski, & Raven, 2012). Thus, high need for cognitive closure is associated with support for autocratic leadership and autocratic leaders.

COGNITIVE ALTERNATIVES: RECOGNIZING THAT
A DIFFERENT WORLD IS POSSIBLE

I began this chapter with the case of Mohammed Bouazizi in Tunisia, the fruit vendor who set himself on fire to protest the injustices he suffered at the hands of the Tunisian authorities. Obviously, he was one of millions of Tunisians suffering such injustices. Was it his sense of humiliation from the treatment he received at the hands of the police, including female police, that resulted in his rebellious action? We do not have enough information on Bouazizi to make this judgment. The research literature on dispositional characteristics such as authoritarianism would be misleading if it only led researchers to look for personality traits within individuals to explain this kind of societal conformity and obedience. Rather, researchers have to look at the larger shared and collectively upheld culture. Mohammed Bouazizi could not appeal to other Tunisians in socially acceptable ways because the normal way to behave in Tunisian culture was to go along with the directives of the dictator Ben Ali and his thousands of *little dictators* around the country. It was only by breaking out of the normal style of behavior that Bouazizi could ignite the imaginations of the rest of Tunisia to help them recognize what Tajfel and Turner (1979) referred to as a *cognitive alternative*, the vision that things could be different, that a more just sociopolitical order could exist in Tunisia.

Social identity theory gives considerable importance to the conditions under which people will give priority to two main strategies for changing their situation. The first strategy is *social mobility*, whereby individuals see the system as permeable and give priority to attempting to move up the social hierarchy by themselves, independent of groups. This fits in with the American Dream narrative, the idea that anyone with drive and hard work and talent can make it in America and that there is a meritocracy in place: Where individuals end up in the social hierarchy depends on their own individual characteristics and not on the groups they are born into (e.g., in terms of ethnicity, gender, social class).

The second strategy is *social change*, whereby individuals attempt to improve their own situation by collaborating with others to change the intergroup situation. This group-oriented action arises because of the

> belief that he is enclosed within the walls of the social group of which he is a member, that he cannot move out of his own into another group in order to improve or change his position or his conditions of life; and that therefore the only way for him to change these conditions (or for that matter, to resist the change of these conditions if he is satisfied with them) is together with his group as a whole, as a member of it rather than someone who leaves it. (Tajfel, 1974, pp. 5–6)

The strategy of social change necessarily involves increased intergroup competition and, potentially, intergroup conflict because one group is attempting to bring about or prevent change against the interests of other group(s).

Subsequent theory and research identified a preference among individuals, at least students in Western societies, for social mobility over social change (Moghaddam, 2008b; Taylor & McKirnan, 1984). That is, people have a preference for trying to move up as individuals first, and only if that fails will they resort to collective action. In one study, participants began as members of a disadvantaged group and had the opportunity to try to work their way up into an advantaged group, which had more resources and power (Taylor, Moghaddam, Gamble, & Zellerer, 1987; Wright, Taylor, & Moghaddam, 1990). Even when participants received unfair treatment, they preferred to continue to try to improve their situations as individuals rather than to join other disadvantaged group members to take collective action. It was only when there was no possibility of succeeding through individual effort and mobility that they turned to collective action. Even a 2% chance of success dramatically diminished their zeal for collective action; "I can do it by myself!" seemed to be their motto.

Social Loafing and Human Nature

This preference for individual action seems to reflect a me-first attitude, which is also demonstrated in the research literature on *social loafing,* the tendency for people to put in less effort when they are working as part of a group compared with when they are working on the same task by themselves (Karau & Williams, 1993). Most people have probably had the experience of working in a group toward the task of completing a joint group project and sensing that some of the group members are coasting and not pulling their weight. Received wisdom indicates that this is a main reason why the Soviet Union and the Communist Bloc failed: Apparently, collectivization does not motivate individuals to work hard because in collectivist systems individuals do not get rewarded for personal effort. So why should Ivan work hard if he is going to receive the same reward as all the other group members, no matter how little or how much he works?

But social loafing arises out of the psychological characteristics of the group members, such as the extent to which they adhere to the Protestant ethic of self-help, individual effort, and personal responsibility (Smrt & Karau, 2011). Not surprisingly, the members of more traditional societies have been found to show less social loafing; for example, in one study (Gabrenya, Wang, & Latané, 1985) carried out in the early 1980s, Chinese and American participants were compared, and Americans had a greater tendency to show social loafing. (During my travel in China more recently, I sensed that the urban Chinese are now as capitalistic as Americans and just as likely to show social loafing. Indeed, it seems like "Wild West capitalism" out there!) Thus, the motivation of individuals can to some degree be changed in the social loafing situation.

The literature on social loafing raises foundational questions about human nature. Supporters of the free market system would argue that humans are naturally inclined to be motivated by personal incentives rather than collective incentives. That is why, they argue, capitalism is inherently a more successful system than communism because capitalism is more in tune with human nature. Individuals like Bill Gates need to be given the freedom to work for personal incentives and the accumulation of personal capital, and through their efforts all of society will benefit because they create wealth and jobs on a large scale. On the other hand, supporters of communism argue that humans can be socialized to be motivated by collective rather than individual rewards, and collective rewards are more beneficial for all of society.

In their study of social identity theory, Tajfel and Turner (1979) argued that people will only recognize the possibility of social change, involving collective mobilization and attempts to transform the intergroup situation, when two conditions are met. First, people must see the present intergroup situation as unstable enough to bring about change in intergroup relations. For example, people in Tunisia had to see the overthrow of the dictator Ben Ali as realistically possible. Second, people must see the present intergroup situation as illegitimate. For example, people in Tunisia had to view the rule of the dictator Ben Ali and his cronies as unfair and unjust. These two conditions were clearly met in the case of Tunisia in 2011.

My contention is that in the vast majority of cases in dictatorships, the illegitimacy condition is met well before the instability condition. That is, people in dictatorships come to see the sociopolitical system as unjust and unfair well before they perceive the possibility of realistically overthrowing the dictatorship. Indeed, there are many cases in which the majority of people see the dictatorship as illegitimate but face death, imprisonment, and torture if they resist and therefore are forced to continue life under dictatorship—the situation in North Korea, Syria, Iran, and many other dictatorships illustrates this point in 2012.

Threats "in the Air"

> If cues in a setting that point to an unsettling direction mount up, a sense of identity threat is likely to emerge. But if cues are sparse in a setting and/or point in a benign direction, then a sense of identity threat should not arise or should subside. (Steele, 2010, p. 140)

When one considers the style of thinking that helps sustain dictatorship, authoritarianism and some other traits are highly relevant, but it is important to treat authoritarianism as more than just part of personality inside independent individuals. Rather, one needs to conceptualize authoritarianism as part of the culture and integral to the dominant narrative of the larger society. Certainly it is reflected in the attitudes of individual persons, but it is the collectively shared and collaboratively upheld nature of authoritarianism that makes it so difficult to change. To further illustrate this point, it is useful to consider the example of how stereotypes function.

In an age in which Barack Obama is president of the United States and African Americans, women, and other power minorities have equal rights on the basis of formal black letter law, it could be argued that prejudice against minorities is a thing of the past and should not be a topic for research. However, this assumption is negated by research on stereotype threat, which shows that people perform poorly when the cues in a situation remind them that according to prevailing stereotypes, they should perform poorly. Since the early 1990s an impressive body of research has developed on stereotype threat, showing that, for example, when women take tests in mathematics, they perform less well in a condition in which they are, even very indirectly, reminded of the stereotype that women are not good at mathematics. The basic stereotype threat effect has now been demonstrated in a wide range of situations and with different minority and majority groups (Inzlicht & Schmader, 2012; Schmader, 2010).

The power of stereotype threat is that it is in the air and not in private, individual minds. As Steele (2010; quoted at the beginning of this section) noted, subtle cues in the environment—on billboards and posters, in songs and jingles, in newspapers, in popular phrases, in television advertising—can have a powerful impact on individual performance. For example, in a study on television commercials, a first group of women watched commercials that included a woman who conformed to an "empty-headed, party-girl" stereotype, and a second group watched commercials with no gender content (P. G. Davies, Spencer, Quinn, & Gerhardstein, 2002). Both groups then went to another location to participate in what was ostensibly a different study in which they had the opportunity to work on many different verbal and math problems. The group of women who saw the gender content commercials tried fewer math problems, succeeded on fewer math problems, and showed less interest in studies and careers related to mathematics. But, "it's not just a women's issue" (J. L. Smith & White, 2002, p. 179): In another study, women did less well on math when they were made aware that they would be compared with men, and White men did less well when they were told they would be compared with Asian men.

There is no doubt that some women and men are affected more by stereotype threat than are others, but the presence of stereotype threat in the air impacts the entire group to some degree. Similarly, authoritarianism as part of a culture impacts some men and women more than it does others, but the key point is that authoritarianism is powerful in contexts such as Hitler's Germany and Stalin's Russia because it is in the air—beyond the control of any one individual but integral to the dominant narratives of society. In a similar manner, social dominance orientation, need for closure, and Machiavellianism are all among measures that reflect collective as well as individual processes.

CONCLUDING COMMENT

> Subtly, skillfully, Alexander Alexandrovich proposed that I "help the internal security organs" by keeping them informed about the reactions of my colleagues and coworkers to the issues of the day. Nothing special— I was just to report my impressions on a regular basis. I protested that I knew my duty . . . and did not have to be monitored. He increased the pressure: Surely, you are willing to help the Party and the government in its struggle against enemies of the people and to consolidate socialism. We need this information to help us shape policy. (Leder, 2001, pp.153–154)

In the account of her life in Stalinist Russia, Leder (2001) described the pervasive value system endorsing the dictatorship under Stalin. There is no doubt that some individuals in Stalinist Russia conformed and obeyed more than did others, that some would score higher on right-wing authoritarianism (Altemeyer, 1988), social dominance orientation (Pratto et al., 1994) need for cognitive closure (Webster & Kruglanski, 1994), but such individual differences need to be understood in the larger context of a societal system endorsing dictatorship. In a North Korean context in which several hundred thousand political prisoners struggle to survive in camps that are as bad as the Gulags in Stalin's dictatorship (Harden, 2012), and in an Iranian society in which systematic murder, torture, and rape of women and men have been used to subjugate the population, the role of individual differences is less powerful. Even individuals low on authoritarianism, social dominance, and need for cognitive closure in other contexts find themselves reshaped by the power of the larger context in which security, conformity, and obedience is given highest priority. Individuals low on authoritarianism in a democracy would probably be higher on authoritarianism in a dictatorship, where the collective culture is and strongly supports authoritarianism.

The recognition of the collective, shared character of psychological processes underlying dictatorship is a useful point of departure to consider the future of dictatorship and democracy in Chapter 10.

10

THE FUTURE OF DICTATORSHIP AND DEMOCRACY

The falcon cannot hear the falconer;
Things fall apart; the centre cannot hold.
 —William Butler Yeats (1921/1962), "The Second Coming"

The dawn of the third millennium is a time of momentous global trans-formations, with the rise of China, the resurgence of Russia, the Arab Spring, disunity in the European Union, and America's loss of moral authority and its weakened position as the "policeman of the world." A new world order seems to be emerging, although the unpredictability of technological and economic transformations means that it is impossible to foretell what shape the new order will take. The old "centre cannot hold," but new centers have yet to take control.

Accelerating fractured globalization is associated with uncertainties and anxieties about the future, and a new global insecurity characterizes human experiences at the dawn of the third millennium (Moghaddam, 2010). The combination of economic and political uncertainties in Europe and elsewhere has strengthened radical political factions and placed European democracy under pressure. The experiences of the 1930s, which culminated in dictator-ships and dictatorial movements in important parts of the world, including

DOI: 10.1037/14138-011
The Psychology of Dictatorship, by F. M. Moghaddam

197

almost all of Europe, must make us particularly cautious in preparing for the future. People displaying neo-Nazi salutes are still a small minority in Europe, but they tend to thrive in a climate of economic and political instability—as have Islamic extremism and support for Islamic dictatorships.

In this final chapter, I tackle major issues that arise directly from my analysis in earlier chapters and are based on the springboard model of dictatorship. My point of departure is the proposition that societies are dynamic and fluid and political systems continually change over time: Under certain conditions, dictatorships can become more open and democratic, and democracies can become closed and dictatorial. No society is destined to remain frozen in time, and change is continually taking place in political systems and the level of openness in societies.

But change in dictatorships and democracies is potentially skewed because of the ever-present and sometimes very strong pull of history. All societies started as dictatorships and have within them elements, notably the military and the church, that could pull them back to dictatorship once again. Supporters of democracy must continually struggle to maintain the open society. Without a conscious push for openness, there will be a shift back to dictatorship—the dominant form of political system in human societies throughout history.

With this real and always imminent threat in mind, in this final chapter I examine issues central to the struggle to end dictatorship. I begin by assessing two related issues from the perspective of the springboard model: how to topple dictatorships and what to expect after a dictatorship has collapsed. The springboard model has direct implications for the kind of help that should be offered to the power elite and to the masses toward ending dictatorship.

Next, I discuss three issues related to democracies and the challenges they face. First, I consider threats associated with globalization and the danger posed by the new global insecurity experienced by people in many parts of the world. Second, I discuss the new dangers faced by democracies, including those in North America, Western Europe, India, and Brazil. Economic, environmental, and political challenges threaten contemporary democracies, so that they might experience decline and even collapse. Third, I examine the interactions of fear, trust, engagement, and apathy in dictatorship and democracy. In conclusion, I contrast a dictatorship of ideas with a democracy of ideas, the latter being an ideal model for the open society.

ENDING DICTATORSHIP

A number of guides are already available for ending dictatorship, notably Sharp's (2010) very well-known contribution, widely available in numerous languages. There are also arguments from demographers (e.g., Cincotta,

2008–2009) about the role of population structure on the transition from dictatorship to democracy and the fact that societies characterized by *youth bulges*, or high percentages of young people in the population, are less likely to achieve a stable democracy. Intriguing as these arguments are, my focus is far narrower and is a response to the following question: What does the springboard model imply for action to end dictatorship?

The Springboard Model's Implications for Ending Dictatorships

The springboard model of dictatorship proposes that the power elite and the nonelite masses in dictatorships are kept in their places by two very different mechanisms. Understanding these mechanisms allows one to intervene more effectively to end dictatorship.

The power elite, who include the dictator himself (or the clique who serve as dictators in cases such as contemporary China), achieve cohesion through a uniform, shared ideology. The nature of this ideology varies considerably across dictatorships, and it also changes within each dictatorship over time. Thus, for example, the Chinese and North Korean power elites achieve cohesion through particular interpretations of Marxism–Leninism, whereas the Iranian and Saudi power elites achieve cohesion through particular interpretations of Islam. However, within these dictatorships, interpretations of Marxism–Leninism and Islam change over time. The acceptable ideology in dictatorships continually changes, and power elite members have to hustle to "keep in line"—some of them fail to catch up with the latest changes and are ousted, so there is continual jostling as power elite members come and go and compete for power positions.

Strict ideological cohesion enables the power elite to justify the subjugation of the nonelite masses in dictatorships, using varieties of direct and indirect means of coercion. Of course, the rudimentary features of the ideology that keeps the power elite cohesive are also propagated throughout society, and the nonelite masses are expected to pay lip service to the broad features of this ideology. Thus, agents of oppression in the shape of morality police force conformity with Islamic law in public spaces in Iran and Saudi Arabia, just as security forces pressure people to conform with Marxist–Leninist ideology in North Korea and other communist dictatorships. However, the key enforcers of mass conformity and obedience in dictatorships are the gun and the torture chamber and only indirectly ideology. It is not belief in Islam that keeps the masses from revolting in Iran and Saudi Arabia or belief in Marxism–Leninism that keeps the masses from revolting in North Korea, China, and other communist dictatorships; rather, it is the gun held to their heads that forces them to conform and obey. These guns are held in place by power elites solidified through ideological cohesion.

This does not mean that the power elite do not preach ideology to the masses. On the contrary, the power elite make it their highest priority to preach ideology to the masses, but it is important to think more deeply and critically about the real purpose of this preaching. When the power elite preach ideology, they are preaching first and foremost to the other members of the power elite and to themselves; they are reinforcing their own solidarity.

The dictator is very closely listened to when he preaches because the rest of the power elite need to know the latest adaptation of the accepted ideology and how they have to change to keep in line. Often the masses are not even aware of the latest nuances of change in the ruling ideology, but the members of the power elite are held to a higher standard when it comes to ideological conformity in public. Publicly, power elite members have to move in step with every minute movement of the leader, like a tightrope walker who will fall to his death if he does not follow exactly what the leader is doing on the tightrope further ahead.

These realities have important implications for how to most effectively end dictatorships. The most important potential weakness of the power elite in dictatorships is their fabricated ideological cohesion, achieved through sheer force, and this is where critics must attack. There are always factions within the power elite that have beliefs and values different from those of the Supreme Dictator. The specific goal must be to peel away factions of the power elite who actually or potentially think differently and to help these factions achieve a platform and voice. In Pareto's (1935) terms, the idea is to help create counterelites, ones that could lead a new revolution.

Regime change in dictatorships is typically initiated by disgruntled members of the ruling power elite moving in a new direction. This top-down initiative can inspire mass involvement, as happened in the former Soviet Union when Mikhail Gorbachev, the last head of the USSR until its collapse in 1991, led the Soviet regime through *perestroika* (reconstruction) toward *glasnost* (openness). The Soviet masses were always ready for a change, but they needed this spark from above to ignite their movement. In Iran, the best recent chance of regime change came when members of the ruling power elite, such as Hussein Mousavi, former prime minister, and Akbar Hashemi Rafsanjani, former president, initiated top-down change and created space for hundreds of thousands of people to pour out into the streets in protest against the regime. Thus, in combating dictatorship, the goal with respect to the power elite must be to challenge, weaken, and splinter its ideological base and support counterelites.

Unlike the power elite, the nonelite masses in dictatorships do not have a cohesive ideology; they are overwhelmed not by a dominant ideology but by the grinding daily battle of putting bread on the table and paying their bills. The masses are actually or at least potentially highly dissatisfied with their lives and mismanagement by the regime. They live in a closed system, a dictatorship, which by its very nature nurtures corruption and inefficiency. The nonelite masses are well aware of this unfortunate reality; they do not need to be awakened, but they do need to be organized. The nonelite masses lack time—the heavy weight of everyday work to pay the bills ensures that—and effective organization and leadership, which can help channel their dissatisfaction. In certain exceptional circumstances (e.g., Libya and Syria during the Arab Spring), for a dictatorship to be toppled, the organization of the masses needs to go hand in hand with the supply of weapons from the outside.

The most important mistake made by opponents of dictatorship has been to assume that they have achieved their goal when a dictatorship is toppled. On the contrary, the toppling of a dictatorship often turns out to be the start of a new dictatorship: Witness the resurgence of dictatorship after the fall of the Shah in Iran in 1979 and after the fall of communism in Russia in 1991. Both Iran and Russia are firmly back in the hands of dictators, after a brief period of freedom in 1979 and 1991, respectively. Supporters of democracy must attend more closely to the enormous challenges in the immediate postdictatorship era.

Challenges That Remain After a Dictator Is Toppled

The most important limitation confronting supporters of democracy in the postdictatorship period is captured by the *micro–macro rule of change* (Moghaddam, 2008b): The maximum speed of change at the micro level of psychological processes and social skills is generally much slower than at the macro level of economic and political systems. A revolution can topple a dictatorship overnight and change the political and economic system—a democracy can be set up quickly, on paper at least—but changes in actual behavior are far slower. It can take a long time for people used to living in a dictatorship to change their thinking and for actions to fall in line with the demands of democracy. Everyday social skills and thinking styles have to change to become supportive of democracy. This lag in the speed of change between small-scale and large-scale levels, between micro psychological processes and macro economic and political systems, explains the paradox of revolution and the repeated return of dictatorship after a revolution has toppled a dictator. To further clarify this point, I discuss an example from my experiences in the immediate postrevolution era in Iran.

In 1979 and early 1980, the Islamic fundamentalists had not yet achieved a power monopoly in Iran. Women were still able to be fairly active in the public sphere, religious minorities were anxious but still not targets of state repression, there was still some press freedom, a few political groups that stood against Islamic fundamentalism and for democracy were still active, and it was still possible for individuals other than those vetted by Islamic fundamentalists to contest some elections. The clouds of repression and dictatorship were gathering, but there were still glimmers of sunshine and hope for supporters of human rights and democracy. In this atmosphere, I systematically observed how people behaved during elections, the first held after the fall of the Shah.

My research involved visiting voting stations in Tehran and making observations in three phases during political elections. Phase 1 involved situating myself within about 30 to 50 meters from the entrance to the voting station and observing what took place as people approach the entrance. Most of the time I was seated in a car, but in several cases I could not park the car in a suitable location and had to stand or sit on a sidewalk or a street corner. In Phase 2, I observed what happened at the entrance as people entered the voting station. This was often the shortest phase because I could not "hang around" the entrance for long, sometimes for no more than a few minutes, without drawing suspicion (the people guarding the entrance were typically hypervigilant because there was still sporadic violence in Tehran). In Phase 3, I entered the voting station and observed social interactions as people filled out their ballots.

Before explaining what I observed in the three phases, a note of clarification is required about the voting stations. In the ideal, voting stations used in democratic elections should be politically neutral buildings, and there should not be political campaigns going on using the building. In Iran, most of the voting stations were mosques, which by their very nature offer endorsement of Islamic parties. Moreover, there was a heavy presence of people and literature associated with the mosque during the time it served as a voting station, and this obviously worked against neutrality (since then, the Islamic fundamentalists in Iran have made it clear they are not interested in neutral and democratic elections; their goal is the implementation of Islamic rules as they interpret them).

Phase 1

In Iran at that time, and to a large degree today, it was possible to fairly accurately tell the political positions of people by their dress and behavior. For example, a man with a full beard and traditional dark clothes and a woman wearing a black *chador* (full veil) would in all probability support traditional or fundamentalist Muslim politicians. On the other hand, a man with a cleanly shaved face and wearing Western clothes and a woman with either no *hejab* (veil) or scanty hejab and signs of cosmetics and perfume (in the months when I first started my observations, the enforcement of the veil had not come into effect, and in some parts of some urban centers women could get away with wearing no veil or a scanty veil) would in all probability support more liberal, antifundamentalist politicians (during the time of this research, I had not shaved for about a week, and I wore dark clothing to escape the label *liberal*). Thus, it was possible to profile people approaching a voting station and, on the basis of their external characteristics, predict how they would vote in the election. I observed that the informal group of men guarding the entrance to the voting station acted very differently toward voters, depending on their outward appearances. On several occasions, they harassed liberal voters, telling women that they could not enter the voting station because they did not have proper hejab. I witnessed several scuffles in which voters attempted to push past the guards. This situation led some voters to adopt a new tactic: to first coordinate with like-minded others by telephone, to agree to meet to vote at a certain time, and then to approach and rush a voting station in a larger group so as to intimidate and push past the guards.

Phase 2

On the occasions when I managed to position myself close to the entrance of the voting station for more than a few minutes so I could observe and listen to social interactions at the entrance, it became very clear that the guards believed they should serve as a screen to try to filter out un-Islamic voters. On several occasions representatives from liberal candidates attempted to position themselves at the entrance to the voting station, but fighting ensued and they were pushed out. The simple fact was that, compared with liberals, the fundamentalists were more willing to use violence to get their way (interestingly, the label *liberal* took on negative connotations in postrevolution Iran, just as it has taken on negative connotations in the United States in 2012).

Phase 3

I attempted to enter voting stations when they were busiest so that I would be less noticeable in the chaos. Of course, democratic elections require that voters have the opportunity to cast their votes anonymously. This happened in some cases, but in other cases people were "helped" in the voting process by "officials" who basically told them how to vote. But it was not only the officials who disregarded the need for anonymity; in some cases voters themselves talked with others, exchanged ideas, showed their ballots, looked over the shoulders of other voters, and generally acted in inappropriate ways. In one instance I witnessed a debate in the voting station, with voters loudly exchanging views about candidates. This was not because the individuals involved intended harm or mischief; rather, they had no experience of what behavior should be like in a voting station.

Thus, even in the period immediately following the revolution in Iran, when the fundamentalists had not yet established dictatorial power and there still was an opportunity to cast votes for some prodemocracy candidates in some elections, a key challenge was that at least some—perhaps most—voters had not had time to develop the micro-level social skills needed to think and act in line with the requirements of democracy. Of course, the situation in Iran is dramatically different now because only hard-line fundamentalists are permitted to compete in elections (see the lively account by Secor, 2012, of a recent election in Iran). Despite the severe political crackdown, the facade of elections is still maintained and the people continue to be strongly encouraged to vote as a means of implicating them in the selection process. This encouragement is very strong in smaller towns and rural areas, where there is little possibility of being sheltered from the wrath of the Supreme Dictator and the many local dictators who serve as his representatives.

The social skills, attitudes, values, and entire behavioral repertoire of people brought up in dictatorships evolved for survival in a dictatorial sociopolitical order; all these characteristics have to be changed to become suitable for democratic contexts. Such a change is not a matter of a few months or a few years; it can require change across much longer time periods. A consequence is that the transition period from democracy to dictatorship is full of grave dangers, with a gravitational pull back toward dictatorship a real possibility. To overcome this pull, people need to be given enough time and support, perhaps through international efforts, to develop the micro-level skills needed to make democracy work for their own societies.

CHALLENGES FACED BY DEMOCRACIES

Democracies continually face the danger of slipping back to dictatorship, a danger that is particularly relevant during times of economic and political instability, such as the world is experiencing in the second decade of the 21st century. Earlier, in Chapter 3, I discussed the role of external threat in bringing about the springboard to dictatorship. In this section, I expand on the theme of perceived threat, starting with a discussion of globalization.

Threats Associated With Globalization

> People . . . try to escape from freedom. . . . The principal social avenues
> of escape in our time are the submission to a leader, as has happened to
> fascist countries, and the compulsive conforming as is prevalent in our
> own democracy." (Fromm, 1941, p. 134)

The research of Fromm (1941), Adorno, Frenkel-Brunswik, Levinson, and Sanford (1950), and others provides reminders of the popular appeal of fascist movements in Western Europe and North America, which has been largely forgotten. Students today are often very surprised when they are told that fascism had mass appeal in the 1930s, even in the homeland of Winston Churchill (1874–1965), and that many among the British aristocracy were openly pro-Nazi in the 1930s. The British Union of Fascists was established by Sir Oswald Mosely (1896–1980), a member of the British aristocracy who led large marches of fascists through London in the 1930s (discussed in Chapter 3, this volume). Mosely organized the Blackshirts, fascist zealots equivalent to Hitler's Brownshirts. King Edward VIII (1984–1972) of Britain, who abdicated and became Duke of Windsor, publicly supported fascism. He visited Nazi Germany with his wife, met with Hitler, and was even actively pro-Nazi early in World War II before being packed off to the Bahamas by the British government to keep him out of harm's way (more can be found about the support the Nazis received from unexpected quarters in *Who Financed Hitler: The Secret Funding of Hitler's Rise to Power 1919–1933*, Pool & Pool, 1979).

The appeal of fascism, according to Fromm (1941), is explained by the anxieties associated with the modern world with its increased uncertainty and unpredictability. The medieval system was characterized more by certainty and stability. People knew their places in the social hierarchy, and they mostly lived, worked, and died where they were born with basically the same people surrounding them throughout their lives. The main source of wealth was land, and the main activity was farming. The medieval system was based on duties, the duties of peasants to lords and lords to kings. Of course, as the barons reminded the king of England when they forced him to sign the Magna Carta in 1215, the monarch also had duties to his subjects. Medieval society involved people in stable, interlocking relationships of duties.

Industrialization and the transition from feudalism to capitalism accelerated from the 18th century and created new living conditions and social relations. The mechanization of agriculture forced millions of peasants to move from rural to urban areas to find work in the newly emerging industries. The focus of wealth changed from land and rural activities to industry and urban activities. The landed aristocracy lost power, and the new capitalist class emerged as dominant. Whereas the landed aristocracy was fixed in place, the new capitalist class could move their wealth within and across national borders to take advantage of cheaper labor and more lucrative investment opportunities. In line with the mobility of capital, working- and middle-class people were forced to become geographically mobile to sell their labor in the most profitable markets. Traditional relationships and the extended family faded away as labor was forced to migrate.

These changing relationships are brilliantly portrayed in *Middlemarch* (Eliot, 1872/2011), a novel set in the early 19th-century England. George

Eliot (1819–1880) depicted a fictional town where life was characterized by change, with the rise of the new middle-class professionals—the banker, Mr. Bulstrode; the medical man, Dr. Lydgate; and the mayor, Mr. Vincy—and the decline in influence of the traditional landed gentry, represented by Sir James Chettam, Mrs. Cadwallader, and Mr. Brooke. This was a time of political agitation and change, and the future belonged to Will Ladislaw, a self-made man who rebelled against conventions and traditional duty-based relations.

The emergence of industrial capitalism involved a gradual shift of priorities from duties to rights, from the collective to the individual, and of the highest importance for my discussion, from stability and predictability as the norm to change and uncertainty as the norm. Part of this change involved popular agitation for expanded individual rights. The shift to individual rights is reflected in changing ideas about the social contract and the rights of individuals (Moghaddam, 2008c). This is best illustrated by a series of declarations from the English Bill of Rights (1688) to those associated with the French and American revolutions, such as *The Social Contract* by Jean-Jacques Rousseau and *The Federalist Papers* by James Madison and other American revolutionaries.

The shift to individual rights was also associated with a change of focus from the collective to the individual, culminating in the self-contained individualism of modern American culture (Sampson, 1977). Underlying this self-contained individualism is the assumption that American society is an open meritocracy, a place where individuals rise and fall in the status hierarchy depending on their own personal merits and efforts; as Cawelti (1965) stated in his examination of the self-made man,

> If you tell an American that he has no more chance to get ahead than a Frenchman, he will probably not believe you, for Americans are fiercely proud of the opportunities which they believe their uniquely open society offers the average man. (p. 2)

It does not matter that the empirical evidence shows social mobility in the United States to be about the same as in the "class-ridden" United Kingdom (Devine, 1997) and that there seems to have been a decline rather than a rise in social mobility since the 1970s (Acs & Zimmerman, 2008; Beller & Hout, 2006, reported no change in intergenerational economic mobility in America since 1984). In the minds of many Americans, the election of Barack Obama as the president of the United States confirmed the belief that anyone can make it in America—the path is wide open for talent to show itself. Of course, this idea of an open society in which people, including ethnic minorities, can rise to the top is unsettling for those who enjoy privileges or imagine that they do so (e.g., working-class Whites clinging to White supremacy).

The exaggerated individualism and assumptions about social mobility found among Americans are extreme indicators of a more widespread trend sweeping across capitalist societies over the past few centuries. The American and French revolutions of the late 18th century launched a cascade of changes culminating in popular uprisings across Europe in 1848, the year of the publication of *The Communist Manifesto* (Marx & Engels, 1967). These vast political changes were overshadowed by even greater economic transformations whereby enormous business empires stretching across many nations determined the lives of individuals. Even in Britain, where from the 18th century radical revolutions were avoided through a step-by-step policy of "a little change in a time of change," technological innovations and economic forces pushed forward social and political changes, thwarting attempts to conserve the social hierarchy and limit change. In the case of Britain, mobility and uncertainty were even greater because of the vastness of the empire and the continual need to send more British people to maintain the empire on which "the sun never set." Fromm (1941) argued that, paradoxically, the promise of geographical and social mobility and greater freedoms generally left the individual in a more precarious situation; because of these "new freedoms which capitalism brought . . . The individual became more alone, isolated . . . an instrument in the hands of the overwhelmingly strong forces outside of himself; he became . . . bewildered and insecure" (p. 120). The thrust of Wilson's (1973) argument is similar: Fear of uncertainty results in an authoritarian form of conservatism, which includes intolerance toward the "other." Individuals high on Machiavellianism share this distrust of the threatening world and a tendency to believe that we should get them before they have a chance to attack us (Christie & Geis, 1970).

The proposition that threat and anxiety result in an escape from freedom has received some empirical examination. In these studies, escape from freedom has been operationalized, albeit simplistically, as a turn to conservatism and support for authoritarian organizations and policies. One set of studies looked at past trends through aggregated data on the impact of threats. For example, during the Great Depression of the 1930s, more authoritarian church denominations attracted more followers (Sales, 1972). During the high-threat years of the 1960s and 1978–1982, there was an increase in indicators of authoritarianism, such as the length of prison sentences for sex offenses and the size of police budgets (Doty, Peterson, & Winter, 1991; Sales, 1973; see also discussions in Hogg & Blaylock, 2012, on the relationship between uncertainty and freedom).

A number of studies have also examined the relationship between threat and authoritarianism at the individual level. Failure on a task in an experimental context was found to increase authoritarianism (Sales & Friend, 2007), presumably because being seen as a failure feels threatening.

Available evidence underlines the complexity of the relationship between perceived economic threat and authoritarianism (Feldman & Stenner, 1997); there is not a direct causal link, but a complex interaction. Although Fromm's (1941) analysis seems simplistic in places, he does place this complexity at the heart of his efforts to show that "certain factors in the modern industrial system in general and in its monopolistic phase in particular make for the development of a personality which feels powerless and alone, anxious and insecure" (p. 240).

The most coherent recent body of research exploring the association between perceived threat and authoritarian tendencies has evolved from terror management theory (Pyszczynski, Solomon, & Greenberg, 2004). This theory assumes that human awareness of mortality is potentially anxiety provoking. If Joe, a member of Community Z, continually thinks about the fact that he is going to die, he could become traumatized and unable to function. To overcome this difficulty, Joe and his community members use a narrative that is self-protective. They all share the belief that when they die, they will be carried to heaven on the back of a great white turtle, and they will live forever in tranquility and bliss. This is fine as long as they interact with other members of Community Z, who share their beliefs. However, when Joe comes across members of Community P, they ridicule his beliefs, claiming that the great white turtle is a myth and that only members of Community P will be taken to heaven, not by a mythical white turtle but by a giant green fish. The claims of each group serve as a rude reminder to individual members that they could be wrong: Death becomes terrifying again because of the presence of the other. Accumulated evidence provides some at least indirect support for the idea that mortality salience is associated with behaviors indicative of authoritarianism (Burke, Martens, & Faucher, 2010).

Sudden Contact and Catastrophic Evolution

The acceleration of globalization in the 21st century has added a new dimension to the theme raised by Fromm and others: Large-scale movements of people are resulting in sudden contact (touched on in Chapter 3, this volume) and raising the threat of *catastrophic evolution*, the rapid decline and possible extinction of cultures and languages (Moghaddam, 2008a, 2010). Historical evidence points to the strength of this trend: About 9,000 languages (out of a total of about 15,000) have become extinct over the past 500 years, and most of the languages alive today will be dead by the end of the 21st century (Crystal, 2000). Parallel to the decline in language diversity is a decline in cultural diversity.

From the perspective of the non-Western world, globalization means Westernization and, more specifically, Americanization and the spread of

Hollywood culture. This is highly threatening to non-Western traditionalists and fundamentalists because they feel that their values and ways of life are under attack. As a result, fundamentalists and traditionalists are "up in arms," sometimes literally, to defend themselves against what they see to be a direct attack against them.

It is not only Islamic extremists who feel threatened by globalization and massive population movements. The arrival of millions of Asians and Africans in Western Europe has helped to invigorate right-wing fundamentalism in a number of Western societies. In July 2011, acting to wake up his nation to the threat of the ongoing "Islamic invasion," a 32-year-old Norwegian right-wing extremist detonated a car bomb near the office of Norway's prime minister and then went on a shooting rampage at a youth summer camp. By the time he had finished, he had killed well over 70 people and seriously injured hundreds more. Less violent, but just as dangerous, are the extremist political factions that have sprung up in Europe as a reaction against the "threat of invasion" by Muslims and other outsiders. Such extremist movements always weaken democracy and strengthen prodictatorship tendencies in societies.

Democracies in Danger of Sliding Into Dictatorship

> The framers lived under autocratic rule and understood this danger better than we do. James Madison famously warned that we need a system that did not depend on the good intentions or motivations of our rulers. . . . Since 9/11 we have created the very government the framers feared: a government with sweeping and largely unchecked powers resting on the hope that they will be used wisely. (Turley, 2012, p. B4)

Throughout this book, I have maintained a focus on the long-term prospects of human societies to resist dictatorships: For societies such as China, Russia, and Iran, already existing under dictatorship, the challenge is to move to greater openness, and for societies such as the United States and the members of the European Union, currently enjoying some level of democracy, the challenge is to maintain and extend democracy. In all cases, the challenge to resist dictatorship is enormously difficult.

The transition from dictatorship to democracy has proved to be very slow and hazardous, in large part because the psychological changes needed in citizens and leaders and in citizen–leader relations come about very, very slowly and not always in a manner supportive of democracy. Even massive and violent revolutions do not achieve this change, as evident from the revolutions in France in 1776 (where Napoleon became emperor/dictator), Russia in 1917 (where Stalin eventually became dictator), and Iran in 1978–1979 (where Khomeini became dictator). But the challenge to maintain democracy is equally great, with Germany proving the most important example of movement back from democracy to dictatorship in the 1930s. The combined forces of external and internal threat impacting on the United States in the past 2 decades and particularly since 9/11, among other factors, have resulted in a serious set of limitations on civil liberties and a massive expansion of federal government power. Unger (2012) argued persuasively that a succession of U.S. presidents have interpreted events through the prism of "permanent emergency" and have used various national threats to expand executive power and government influence in the larger American society.

The legal scholar Jonathan Turley (2012) examined the 10 most important of these expanded powers claimed by the U.S. federal government. These expanded powers pertain to the right of the U.S. president to (a) order the assassination of U.S. citizens, (b) order the indefinite detention of terrorist suspects, (c) decide whether an individual will be tried in a military tribunal or a federal court, (d) order warrantless surveillance, (e) use global positioning system devices for continuous monitoring of citizens, (f) use secret evidence and (g) secret courts, (h) refuse to allow U.S. government employees to be investigated for war crimes, (i) give immunity from judicial review to companies that undertake the warrantless surveillance of citizens, and (j) transfer both citizens and noncitizens to other countries, under *extraordinary rendition*. These expanded federal government powers are, of course, justified as necessary to fight the war on terror, a war with no end! As Turley (quoted at the beginning of this section) pointed out, the result is a situation in which citizens can only hope that the government will use these sweeping powers wisely. A democracy that depends on the good will of its leaders is a seriously weakened and flawed democracy.

Can Democracy Coexist With Enormous and Increasing Group-Based Resource Inequalities?

> In America: productivity rose by 83% between 1973 and 2007, but male median real wages rose by just 5%. (Buttonwood, 2011, p. 85)

Despite the rise in worker productivity, the income of American workers has stagnated since the 1970s. In contrast, the share of the nation's income taken by the top 1% of earners more than doubled over the past 3 decades. There is solid evidence demonstrating that income inequality has been increasing in the United States and many other countries (Noah, 2012). Despite some variation across countries over the past few decades—for example, in Sweden the income of the richest 10% is 5 times higher than that of the poorest 10%; in the United States it is 14 times higher—the trend of increasing income inequality is common to many countries.

Given this resource inequality, democracies are faced with a dilemma: Is there a relationship between resource inequality and the quality of democracy? Responses to this question relate to one's political ideology. Those to the political right, believers in smaller government and free market, tend to argue that resource inequality has no serious implications for the quality of democracy achieved. As long as elections for political office are free and fair, all citizens have the right to vote and to compete for political office, and free speech is guaranteed, then resource inequality is irrelevant. In support of this argument, people on the right point to very rich individuals who have attempted but failed to win political office using their great wealth, an example being the billionaire Ross Perot, who ran for president of the United States as an independent candidate in 1992 and as the candidate of the Reform Party (which he helped to establish) in 2006. The fact that such billionaires fail to win political office using their enormous wealth, people on the right argue, means that you cannot buy the government in democracies such as America.

Critics argue that greater resource inequality does have serious implications for the quality of democracy and can even mean the end of democracy. First, because of a variety of factors, the voter participation rate of citizens in elections is low in many democracies, particularly the United States (see Leighley, 2010). Even in presidential elections, the percentage of voters in the United States has rarely reached 60% of eligible voters in recent decades, and in many local elections only about 20% to 30% percent of eligible voters participate. A variety of factors account for the so-called disappearing American voter, including the various restrictions placed on potential voters (e.g., millions of citizens lose the right to vote while in prison) as well as a general feeling among voters that their vote does not make a difference. The general trend is that voter participation is lower among ethnic minorities, the young, and the economically poor.

Critics also point to a second factor showing that resource inequalities have serious implications for democracy: the interpretation by the U.S. Supreme Court of monetary spending in political campaigns as a form of protected free speech (Sullivan, 2010). According to (mainly left-leaning) critics, this interpretation of free speech has opened the floodgates to corporate spending in political campaigns. It has meant that lobbyists and corporate interests, rather than the voices of citizens, reach elected officials (there is a feeling that the Supreme Court under Chief Justice John Roberts has leaned broadly in favor of the powerful rather than the powerless: "Under Chief Justice Roberts, the high court has grown less attentive to the precious rights of the small and the weak, more eager to strengthen the already strong"; Shipler, 2011, p. 305). The question of how to limit the corrupting influence of money in American politics has been taken up by numerous thinkers and activists throughout American history (McCormick, 2006), and a number of solutions have been proposed.

One solution already adopted in a number of democracies, such as Australia, is to interpret voting in elections as a *duty*, what a person owes others, as well as a *right*, what is owed by others to oneself. A citizen who did not carry out this duty would be punished (just as, for example, a citizen who failed to pay taxes is punished). I agree with authors (e.g., Hill, 2006) who argue for this strategy, but in discussions with Americans I have found it an uphill battle to convince them. Even when I have discussed voting as a right and/or duty with liberal-minded young American students, I have found that about 40% of them raise objections to changing the present system. Their objections include ideas such as "People who do not make the effort should not be forced to vote," and "Voting as a duty would mean that more voters who have little knowledge of the issues would have a say." However, even if Americans could be persuaded to make voting compulsory, some research casts doubt on the idea that compulsory voting lowers resource inequality in society and leads to a more complex picture of the impact of compulsory voting (Quintelier, Hooghe, & Marien, 2011).

In response to the challenge of how to prevent wealthy citizens from dominating political life, McCormick (2011) critically reviewed strategies used at various times over approximately the last 2,500 years and put forward some intriguing possibilities. A first is to exclude the wealthiest citizens from certain offices or assemblies. For example, a rule might be that no member of the top 1% income group could be a member of certain assemblies, such as the U.S. Senate or the U.S. House of Representatives. A second strategy he considered is to combine both election and lottery procedures for filling some posts. Lotteries would obviously give members of the 99% less resourced group a greater opportunity to win political office. A third proposal McCormick considered is to have all citizens as ultimate deciders in some political trials. This idea is rooted in ancient Greece, where

> most cases came before panels (*dikasteria*) of the court of appeal, whose juries could range from 200 to more than 1000 members. The jurors were selected by lot, and this, combined with the large number of individuals sitting on even the smallest panels and the random assignment of cases, made juries truly representative and precluded bribery or corruption. (American School of Classical Studies at Athens, 1994, p. 2)

Such a strategy for the large-scale participation of citizens in courts is made more feasible by 21st-century electronic communications systems.

Technological innovations can only help us move toward greater openness and democracy if we have an ideal goal in mind.

Fear, Trust, Apathy, and Engagement in Dictatorship and Democracy

I have described dictatorship and democracy as constituting the end poles of a continuum, with societies situated on different locations on this continuum. The exact location of each society on the continuum varies over time, so that with the passage of time some societies become more democratic and some become more dictatorial. The movement of societies on the dictatorship–democracy continuum, and how stable and how vulnerable to political change a society becomes, is associated with the experiences that citizens have with fear, trust, apathy, and engagement.

Traditionally, one thinks of fear and trust as the key requirements for the survival of dictatorship and democracy, respectively. That is, it is assumed that a high level of fear among citizens is necessary for the stability and survival of dictatorship, and a high level of trust is necessary for the stability and survival of democracy. However, in combination with fear and trust, apathy and engagement also play a vitally important role in the stability and survival of dictatorships and democracies. A high level of apathy toward political processes poses a danger for the survival of democracy, and a high level of engagement in political processes poses a danger for the survival of dictatorship. The interactions of fear, trust, apathy, and engagement provide different possibilities for stability and survival for dictatorships and democracies. The various alternatives can be conceived of as lying at some point in a space delimited by two vectors (see Figure 10.1). The first vector has as its polar opposites Trust and Fear, and the extreme poles of the second vector are Apathy and Engagement. The resultant four possibilities are democracy vulnerable, democracy stable, dictatorship stable, and dictatorship vulnerable.

Dictatorship is more stable when apathy and fear are both high, a condition in which citizens have become apathetic to political processes and are too fearful of repercussions to attempt to oppose the regime. However, when citizens become highly engaged in the political process, they can even overcome fear of the regime, and dictatorship becomes unstable.

Democracy is more stable when citizens have a high level of trust and are more fully engaged in the political process. This is the democratic ideal in which (for justifiable reasons) citizen participation in political processes is high and trust in government institutions and representatives is also high. In this situation, government representatives have earned the trust of citizens. On the other hand, democracy is most vulnerable when trust in government representatives and institutions falls to low levels and apathy among citizens increases to high levels. In this situation, citizens are disengaged from political processes, and they do not trust the government officials and institutions that supposedly represent their interests. Some critics would contend that the situation in the United States is moving in this direction, leading to an

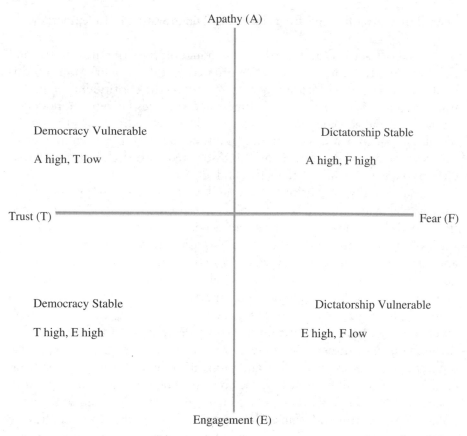

Apathy (A)

Democracy Vulnerable

A high, T low

Dictatorship Stable

A high, F high

Trust (T) ———————————————————————————— Fear (F)

Democracy Stable

T high, E high

Dictatorship Vulnerable

E high, F low

Engagement (E)

Figure 10.1. Diagrammatical representation of vulnerability and stability in dictatorships and democracies.

American citizenship that is to a high degree distrustful of government and disengaged from political processes, making American democracy vulnerable to shifts more toward the dictatorship end of the dictatorship–democracy continuum (a topic beyond the scope of this book).

Finally, I consider a democratic ideal that all societies should strive toward: a democracy of ideas.

CONCLUDING COMMENT

A neighbor came to Nasrudin for an interpretation on a point of law.
"My cow was gored by your bull. Do I get any compensation?"
"Certainly not. How can a man be held responsible for what an animal does?"

"Just a moment," said the crafty villager. "I am afraid I got the question back to front. What actually happened was that *my* bull gored *your* cow."

"Ah," said Nasrudin, "this is more involved. I shall have to look up the book of precedents, for there may be other factors involved which are relevant and which could alter the case." (Shah, 1993, p. 64)

I grew up listening to Sufi stories like this one about Nasrudin, who serves in the role of wise fool, something akin to the jester in Shakespeare's plays. One interpretation of this Sufi story is that people take positions on right and wrong on the basis of their own interests. Of course, this is very familiar to observers of the contemporary political scene in the United States, where partisanship has reached a destructively high level. Ideas are assessed not on their own merit but on the basis of the source (Mann & Ornstein, 2012). The new dictum is, "Ask not the merit of the idea, but who proposed it."

The extreme of this situation is the dictatorship in which whatever the dictator says on whatever subject is treated as sacred truth. To question the word of the Supreme Leader in Iran or North Korea and dozens of other large and small dictatorships is to risk death or imprisonment. This is the *dictatorship of ideas* in which one man decides for everyone. But there is an alternative ideal, a *democracy of ideas* in which speaking opportunity is given to every voice. Fortunately, there are examples of democracies of ideas in action, such as in academic research.

The peer review procedure practiced today in academic research is the crowning glory of 2,500 years of research culture that began with classical Greek scholarship and Plato's Academy. Peer review is recognized as democracy in action (Rennie, 1999). The basic principle of peer review is that the contents of a piece of work, rather than the characteristics of the reviewer(s) and author(s) and their relationships, determine the outcome of the review. In this way, ideas and research products are evaluated completely independent of the source. This is the opposite of the dictatorship of ideas in which whatever the Supreme Dictator says is treated as truth because *he* said it.

Historical progress away from a dictatorship of ideas and toward democracy has been tortuously slow, uneven, and painful. In many parts of the world, a dictatorship of ideas is still the norm. No large society is as yet a democracy of ideas. Plans for a more open, democratic world must move forward on the basis of a better understanding of dictatorship so that people's optimism remains realistic and their policy goals remain feasible. The psychological study of dictatorship is a vital part of this effort.

REFERENCES

Abercrombie, N., Hill, S., & Turner, B. S. (1990). *Dominant ideologies*. London, England: Unwin Hyman.

Abercrombie, N., & Turner, B. S. (1978). The dominant ideology thesis. *The British Journal of Sociology, 29*, 149–170.

Abrahamian, E. (1993). *Khomeinism: Essays on the Islamic republic*. Berkeley: University of California Press.

Abrams, D., & Hogg, M. A. (2010). Social identity and self-categorization. In J. F. Dovidio, M. Hewstone, P. Glick, & V. M. Esses (Eds.), *The SAGE handbook of prejudice, stereotyping and discrimination* (pp. 179–193). London, England: Sage. doi:10.4135/9781446200919.n11

Acemoglu, D., & Robinson, A. (2001). A theory of political transitions. *The American Economic Review, 91*, 938–963. doi:10.1257/aer.91.4.938

Acemoglu, D., & Robinson, J. A. (2006). *Economic origins of dictatorship and democracy*. New York, NY: Cambridge University Press.

Acs, G., & Zimmerman, S. (2008). *U.S. economic mobility from 1984 to 2004*. Washington, DC: Pew Charitable Trusts, Economic Mobility Project.

Adorno, T. W., Frenkel-Brunswik, E., Levinson, D. J., & Sanford, B. W. (1950). *The authoritarian personality*. New York, NY: Harper & Row.

Akerlof, G. A., & Dickens, W. T. (1982). The economic consequences of cognitive dissonance. *The American Economic Review, 72*, 307–319.

Alizadehfard, S. (2010). Effect of gender and social status on conformity. *Psychological Research, 13*, 30–50.

Allport, G. W., & Postman, L. (1947). *The psychology of rumor*. Oxford, England: Holt.

Altemeyer, B. (1981). *Right-wing authoritarianism*. Winnipeg, Canada: University of Manitoba Press.

Altemeyer, B. (1988). *Enemies of freedom: Understanding right-wing authoritarianism*. San Francisco, CA: Jossey-Bass.

Altemeyer, B. (2004). Highly dominating, high authoritarian personalities. *The Journal of Social Psychology, 144*, 421–448. doi:10.3200/SOCP.144.4.421-448

American School of Classical Studies at Athens. (1994). *Life, death and litigation in the Athenian agora*. Athens, Greece: Author.

Ancona, L., & Pareyson, R. (1968). Contributo allo studie della aggressione: La dinamica della obbedienza distruttiva. [Contribution to the study of aggression: The dynamics of destructive obedience]. *Archivadi psicologia, neurologia e psichiatria, 29*, 340–372.

Andrews, E. (Ed.). (2011). *Legacies of totalitarian language in the discourse culture of the post-totalitarian era*. New York, NY: Lexington Books.

Arditti, R. (1999). *Searching for life: The grand-mothers of the Plaza de Maya and the disappeared children of Argentina*. Berkeley: University of California Press.

Arendt, H. (2004). *The origins of totalitarianism* (Rev. ed.). New York, NY: Schocken. (Original work published 1951)

Arian, A., Shamir, M., & Ventura, R. (1992). Public opinion and political change: Israel and the intifada. *Comparative Politics, 24*, 317–334. doi:10.2307/422135

Arjomand, S. A. (1988). *The turban for the crown: The Islamic revolution in Iran*. New York, NY: Oxford University Press.

Armstrong, K. (2000). *The battle for God: A history of fundamentalism*. New York, NY: Ballantine Books.

Aronson, E. (2007). *The social animal* (10th ed.). New York, NY: Worth.

Arvey, R. D., Rotundo, M., Johnson, W., Zhang, Z., & McGue, M. (2006). The determinants of leadership role occupancy: Genetic and personality factors. *The Leadership Quarterly, 17*, 1–20. doi:10.1016/j.leaqua.2005.10.009

Asch, S. E. (1951). Effects of group pressure upon the modification and distortion of judgments. In H. Guetzkow (Ed.), *Groups, leadership, and men* (pp. 177–190). Pittsburgh, PA: Carnegie Press.

Asch, S. E. (1955). Opinions and social pressure. *Scientific American, 193*, 31–35. doi:10.1038/scientificamerican1155-31

Asch, S. E. (1956). Studies of independence and conformity: A minority of one against a unanimous majority. *Psychological Monographs, 70* (9, Whole No. 416).

Avolio, B. J. (2005). *Leadership development in balance*. Mahwah, NJ: Erlbaum.

Avolio, B. J., Rotundo, M., & Walumbwa, F. O. (2009). Early life experiences as determinants of leadership role occupancy: The importance of parental influence and rule breaking behavior. *The Leadership Quarterly, 20*, 329–342. doi:10.1016/j.leaqua.2009.03.015

Axsom, D. (1989). Cognitive dissonance and behavior change in psychotherapy. *Journal of Experimental Social Psychology, 25*, 234–252. doi:10.1016/0022-1031(89)90021-8

Ayman, R., & Korabik, K. (2010). Leadership: Why gender and culture matter. *American Psychologist, 65*, 157–170. doi:10.1037/a0018806

Baraheni, R. (1977). *The crowned cannibals: Writings on repression in Iran*. New York, NY: Vintage Books.

Barbu, Z. (1956). *Democracy and dictatorship: Their psychology and patterns of life*. New York, NY: Grove Press.

Baron, R. S., Crawley, K., & Paulina, D. (2003). Aberrations of power: Leadership in totalist groups. In D. van Knippenberg & M. A. Hogg (Eds.), *Leadership and power: Identity processes in groups and organizations* (pp. 169–183). London, England: Sage. doi:10.4135/9781446216170.n13

Bechtel, R., & Churchman, A. (2002). *Handbook of environmental psychology*. New York, NY: Wiley.

Beller, E., & Hout, M. (2006). Intergenerational social mobility: The United States in comparative perspective. *The Future of Children, 16*, 19–36. doi:10.1353/foc.2006.0012

Bennett, M. R., & Hacker, P. M. S. (2003). *Philosophical foundations of neuroscience.* Oxford, England: Blackwell.

Bennis, W. (2007). The challenge of leadership in the modern world. *American Psychologist, 62*, 2–5. doi:10.1037/0003-066X.62.1.2

Benton, G., & Chun, L. (2010). *Was Mao really a monster?* London, England: Routledge.

Bernazzoli, R. M. (2010). Embodying the garrison state? Everyday geographies of militarization in American society. *Political Geography, 29*, 157–166. doi:10.1016/j.polgeo.2010.02.014

Berns, G. S., Chappelow, J., Zin, C. F., Pagnoni, G., Martin-Skurski, M. E., & Richard, J. (2005). Neurobiological correlates of social conformity and independence during mental rotation. *Biological Psychiatry, 58*, 245–253. doi:10.1016/j.biopsych.2005.04.012

Berry, J. W., Poortinga, Y. H., Segall, M. H. & Dasen, P. R. (2002). *Cross-cultural psychology: Research and applications.* New York, NY: Cambridge University Press.

Billig, M. (1982). *Ideology and social psychology: Extremism, moderation, and contradiction.* London, England: Sage.

Billig, M. (1991). *Ideology and opinions: Studies in rhetorical psychology.* London, England: Sage.

Blank, S. (2006). The 18th brumaire of Vladimir Putin. In U. Ra'anan (Ed.), *Flawed succession: Russia's power transfer crisis* (pp. 133–166). New York, NY: Lexington Books.

Blum, G. P. (1998). *The rise of fascism in Europe.* Westport, CT: Greenwood Press.

Bonnell, V. E. (1988). The representation of politics and the politics of representation. *The Russian Review, 47*, 315–422. doi:10.2307/130593

Bonnell, V. E. (1997). *Iconography of power: Soviet political posters under Lenin and Stalin.* Berkeley: University of California Press.

Boswell, J. (1980). *Life of Johnson.* Oxford, England: Oxford University Press. (Original work published 1791)

Bosworth, R. J. B. (2006). *Mussolini's Italy: Life under the fascist dictator 1915–1945.* New York, NY: Penguin Books.

Bratton, M., & Van de Walle, N. (1994). Neopatrimonial regimes and political transitions in Africa. *World Politics, 46*, 453–489. doi:10.2307/2950715

Breakwell, G. (1986). *Coping with threatened identities.* London, England: Methuen.

Brooker, P. (2000). *Non-democratic regimes: Theory, government and politics.* New York, NY: St. Martin's Press.

Brown, G. D. A., Gardner, J., Oswald, A., & Qian, J. (2008). Does wage rank affect employees' wellbeing? *Industrial Relations: A Journal of Economy and Society, 47*, 355–389.

Bruner, J. S. (1990). *Acts of meaning*. Cambridge, MA: Harvard University Press.

Buck, J. J. (2010, October). The talented Miss Mulligan. *Vogue*, 266–279.

Buck, J. J. (2011, March). A rose in the desert. *Vogue*, 529–533, 571.

Bullock, A. (1993). *Hitler and Stalin: Parallel lives*. New York, NY: Vintage Books.

Burger, J. M. (2009). Replicating Milgram: Would people still obey today? *American Psychologist, 64*, 1–11. doi:10.1037/a0010932

Burke, B. L., Martens, A., & Faucher, E. H. (2010). Two decades of terror management theory: A meta-analysis of mortality salience research. *Personality and Social Psychology Review, 14*, 155–195. doi:10.1177/1088868309352321

Burns, J. M. (1978). *Leadership*. New York, NY: HarperCollins.

Burton, M. (2010). The Black Sash story: Protest and service recorded in the archives. *English Academic Review, 27*, 129–133.

Buttonwood. (2011, March 24). *Marx, Mervyn or Mario? What is behind the decline in living standards?* [Web log post]. Retrieved from http://www.economist.com/node/18443402

Byman, D., & Pollack, K. (2001). Let us now praise great men: Bringing the statesman back in. *International Security, 25*, 107–146. doi:10.1162/01622880151091916

Calogero, R. M., Bardi, A., & Sutton, R. M. (2009). A need basis for values: Associations between the need for cognitive closure and value priorities. *Personality and Individual Differences, 46*, 154–159. doi:10.1016/j.paid.2008.09.019

Canovan, M. (2004). The leader and the masses: Hannah Arendt on totalitarianism and dictatorship. In P. Baehr & M. Richter (Eds.), *Dictatorship in history and theory* (pp. 241–260). New York, NY: Cambridge University Press. doi:10.1017/CCOL0521825636.XML.012

Carlyle, T. (1993), *On heroes, hero worship, and the heroic in history*. Berkeley and Los Angeles: University of California Press. (Original work published 1841)

Cartwright, D., & Harary, F. (1956). A generalization of Heider's theory. *Psychological Review, 63*, 277–293. doi:10.1037/h0046049

Cawelti, J. G. (1965). *Apostles of the self-made man: Changing concepts of success in America*. Chicago, IL: The University of Chicago Press.

Chang, J., & Halliday, J. (2005). *Mao: The unknown story*. New York, NY: Knopf.

Cheung, F. M., & Halpern, D. F. (2010). Women at the top: Powerful leaders define success as work and family in a culture. *American Psychologist, 65*, 182–193.

Chidester, D. (2000). *Christianity: A global history*. New York, NY: HarperCollins.

Chirwa, W. C. (2001). Dancing toward dictatorship: Political songs and popular culture in Malawi. *Nordic Journal of African Studies, 10*, 1–27.

Chomsky, N. (1965). *Aspects of the theory of syntax*. Cambridge, MA: MIT Press.

Christie, R., & Geis, F. L. (1970). *Studies in Machiavellianism*. New York, NY: Academic Press.

Christie, R., & Jahoda, M. (1954). *Studies in the scope and method of "the authoritarian personality."* Glencoe, IL: Free Press.

Cincotta, R. P. (2008–2009). Half a chance: Youth bulges and transitions to liberal democracy. *ECSP Report, 13,* 10–18.

Cohen, M. D., & March, J. G. (1974). *Leadership and ambiguity: The American college president.* New York, NY: McGraw Hill.

Cole, M. (1996). *Cultural psychology: A once and future science.* Cambridge, MA: Belknap Press.

Cooper, J., & Hogg, M. A. (2007). Feeling the anguish of others: A theory of vicarious dissonance. In M. P. Zanna (Ed.), *Advances in experimental social psychology* (Vol. 39, pp. 359–403). San Diego, CA: Academic Press.

Cooper, J. M. (2007). *Cognitive dissonance: 50 years of classic theory.* Thousand Oaks, CA: Sage.

Corach, D., Sala, A., Penacino, G., Iannucci, N., Bernardi, P., Doretti, M. . . . Hagelberg, E. (1997). Additional approaches to DNA typing of skeletal remains: The search for "missing" persons killed during the last dictatorship in Argentina. *Electrophoresis, 18,* 1608–1612. doi:10.1002/elps.1150180921

Corcoran, K., Crusius, J., & Mussweiler, T. (2011). Social comparison: Motives, standards, and mechanisms. In D. Chadee (Ed.), *Theories in social psychology* (pp. 119–139). Oxford, England: Wiley-Blackwell.

Corner, P. (2009). Fascist Italy in the 1930s: Popular opinion in the provinces. In P. Corner (Ed.), *Popular opinion in totalitarian regimes: Fascism, Nazism, and communism* (pp. 122–146). New York, NY: Oxford University Press.

Coser, L. (1956). *The functions of social conflict.* New York, NY: Free Press.

Cotton, J. L., Vollrath, D. A., Froggatt, K. L., Lengnick-Hall, M. L., & Jennings, K. R. (1988). Employee participation: Diverse forms and different outcomes. *The Academy of Management Review, 13,* 8–22.

Cotton, J. L., Vollrath, D. A., Lengnick-Hall, M. L., & Froggatt, K. L. (1990). Fact: The form of participation does matter—A rebuttal to Leana, Locke, and Schweiger. *The Academy of Management Review, 15,* 147–153.

Crystal, D. (2000). *Language death.* Cambridge, England: Cambridge University Press. doi:10.1017/CBO9781139106856

Dahl, R. A. (1971). *Polyarchy: Participation and opposition.* New Haven, CT: Yale University Press.

Dal Cin, S., MacDonald, T. K., Fong, G. T., Zanna, M. P., & Elton-Marshall, T. E. (2006). Remembering the message: Using a reminder cue to increase condom use following a safer sex intervention. *Health Psychology, 25,* 438–443. doi:10.1037/0278-6133.25.3.438

Darwin, C. (1993). *The origin of species by natural selection or the preservation of favored races in the struggle for life.* New York, NY: Modern Library. (Original work published 1859)

Davies, J. C. (1974). The J-curve and power struggle theories of collective violence. *American Sociological Review, 39*, 607–619. doi:10.2307/2094425

Davies, P. G., Spencer, S., Quinn, D. M., & Gerhardstein, R. (2002). Consuming images: How television commercials that elicit stereotype threat can restrain women academically and professionally. *Personality and Social Psychology Bulletin, 28*, 1615–1628. doi:10.1177/014616702237644

Day, D. V., Schleicher, D. J., Unckless, A. L., & Hiller, N. J. (2002). Self-monitoring personality at work: A meta-analytic investigation of construct validity. *Journal of Applied Psychology, 87*, 390–401. doi:10.1037/0021-9010.87.2.390

de Bellaigue, C. (2012). *Patriot of Persia: Muhammad Mossadegh and a very British coup*. London, England: Bodley Head.

de Grazia, V. (1981). *The culture of consent: Mass organization of leisure in fascist Italy*. New York, NY: Cambridge University Press. doi:10.1017/CBO9780511528972

de Grazia, V. (1992). *How fascism ruled women: Italy, 1922-1945*. Berkeley and Los Angeles: University of California Press.

Devine, F. (1997). *Social class in America and Britain*. Edinburgh, Scotland: University of Edinburgh Press.

Diamond, L. (2002). Thinking about hybrid regimes. *Journal of Democracy, 13*, 21–35. doi:10.1353/jod.2002.0025

Dickerson, C. A., Thibodeau, R., Aronson, E., & Miller, D. (1992). Using cognitive dissonance to encourage water conservation. *Journal of Applied Social Psychology, 22*, 841–854. doi:10.1111/j.1559-1816.1992.tb00928.x

Diversity and leadership. (2010). [Special issue]. *American Psychologist, 65*(3).

Dobrenko, E., & Naiman, E. (Eds.). (2003). *The landscape of Stalinism: The art and ideology of Soviet space*. St. Louis, MO: University of Washington Press.

Doise, W. (1986). *Levels of explanations in social psychology*. Cambridge, England: Cambridge University Press.

Doise, W. (2012). The homecoming of society in social psychology. In J. P. Valentim (Ed.), *Societal approaches in social psychology* (pp. 9–34). Bern, Switzerland: Peter Lang AG.

Dollard, J., Bood, L., Miller, N., Mowrer, O., & Sears, R. (1939). *Frustration and aggression*. New Haven, CT: Yale University Press. doi:10.1037/10022-000

Doty, R. M., Peterson, B. E., & Winter, D. G. (1991). Threat and authoritarianism in the United States, 1978–1987. *Journal of Personality and Social Psychology, 61*, 629–640. doi:10.1037/0022-3514.61.4.629

Duckitt, J., Wagner, C., du Plessis, I., & Birum, I. (2002). The psychological basis of ideology and prejudice: Testing a dual process model. *Journal of Personality and Social Psychology, 83*, 75–93. doi:10.1037/0022-3514.83.1.75

Duhigg, C. (2012). *The power of habit*. New York, NY: Random House.

Eagly, A. H., & Carli, L. L. (1981). Sex of researchers and sextyped communications as determinants of sex differences in influenceability: A meta-analysis of social influence studies. *Psychological Bulletin, 90*, 1–20. doi:10.1037/0033-2909.90.1.1

Eagly, A. H., & Carli, L. L. (2007). *Through the labyrinth: The truth about how women become leaders*. Boston, MA: Harvard Business School Press.

Eagly, A. H., & Wood, W. (1991). Explaining sex differences in social behavior: A meta-analytic perspective. *Personality and Social Psychology Bulletin, 17,* 306–315. doi:10.1177/0146167291173011

Earle, B. H., & Madek, G. A. (2007). The mirage of whistleblower protection under Sarbanes-Oxley: A proposal for change. *American Business Law Journal, 44,* 1–54. doi:10.1111/j.1744-1714.2007.00030.x

Edwards, A. L. (1941). Unlabeled fascist attitudes. *The Journal of Abnormal and Social Psychology, 36,* 575–582. doi:10.1037/h0062075

Egan, L. C., Santos, L. R., & Bloom, P. (2007). The origins of cognitive dissonance: Evidence from children and monkeys. *Psychological Science, 18,* 978–983. doi:10.1111/j.1467-9280.2007.02012.x

Eliot, G. (1872/2011). *Middlemarch* (Reprint ed.). New York, NY: Penguin Group (USA).

Ellickson, R. C. (1991). *Order without law: How neighbors settle disputes*. Cambridge, MA: Harvard University Press.

Erdbrink, T. (2012, February 10). Iran increasingly controlling online content, access. *The Washington Post*, p. A10.

Esser, J. K. (1998). Alive and well after 25 years: A review of groupthink research. *Organizational Behavior and Human Decision Processes, 73,* 116–141. doi:10.1006/obhd.1998.2758

Ezrow, N., & Frantz, E. (2011). *Dictators and dictatorships: Understanding authoritarian regimes and their leaders*. New York, NY: Continuum.

Fahim, K. (2010, July 18). Death in police encounter stirs calls for change in Egypt. *The New York Times*. Retrieved from http://www.nytimes.com/2010/07/19/world/middleea

Feldman, S., & Stenner, K. (1997). Perceived threat and authoritarianism. *Political Psychology, 18,* 741–770. doi:10.1111/0162-895X.00077

Fernandez, C. P. (2007). Creating thought diversity: The antidote to groupthink. *Journal of Public Health Management and Practice, 13,* 670–671.

Festinger, L. (1957). *A theory of cognitive dissonance*. Stanford, CA: Stanford University Press.

Fiedler, F. (1967). *A theory of leadership effectiveness*. New York, NY: McGraw-Hill.

Figes, O. (2007). *The whisperers: Private life in Stalin's Russia*. New York, NY: Picador.

Figes, O., & Kolonitskii, B. (1999). *Interpreting the Russian revolution: The language and symbols of 1917*. New Haven, CT: Yale University Press.

Finkel, N., & Moghaddam, F. M. (Eds.). (2005). *The psychology of rights and duties: Empirical contributions and normative commentaries*. Washington, DC: American Psychological Association. doi:10.1037/10872-000

Fisher, M. (2011, March 27). The spark that ignited a revolution. *The Washington Post*, pp. A1, A10–11.

Fisher, R. A. (1915). The evolution of sexual preference. *The Eugenics Review, 7,* 184–192.

Fisher, R. A. (1930). *The genetical theory of natural selection.* Oxford, England: Clarendon Press.

Foels, R., Driskell, J. E., Mullen, B., & Salas, E. (2000). The effects of democratic leadership on group member satisfaction: An integration. *Small Group Research, 31,* 676–701. doi:10.1177/104649640003100603

Foucault, M. (1995). *Discipline and punish: The birth of the prison* (A. Sheridan, Trans.). New York, NY: Vintage Books.

Frank, T. (2005). *What's the matter with Kansas? How conservatives won the heart of America.* New York, NY: Holt.

Freeman, M. (2003). *The consequences of democracies using emergency powers.* Westport, CT: Praeger.

Freud, S. (1955). Group psychology and the analysis of the ego. In J. Strachey (Ed. & Trans.), *The standard edition of the complete psychological works* (Vol. 18, pp. 67–143). London, England: Hogarth Press. (Original work published 1922)

Freud, S. (1961). Civilization and its discontents. In J. Strachey (Ed. & Trans.), *The standard edition of the complete psychological works* (Vol. 21, 64–145). London, England: Hogarth Press. (Original work published 1930)

Friedrich, C., & Brzezinski, Z. (1956). *Totalitarian dictatorship and autocracy.* Cambridge, MA: Harvard University Press.

Fromm, E. (1941). *Escape from freedom.* New York, NY: Holt, Rinehart, & Winston.

Fukuyama, F. (1992). *The end of history and the last man.* New York, NY: Free Press.

Fulbrook, M. (1995). *Anatomy of a dictatorship: Inside the GDR 1949–1989.* New York, NY: Oxford University Press.

Gabrenya, W. K., Jr., Wang, Y. E., & Latané, B. (1985). Social loafing on an optimizing task: Cross-cultural differences among Chinese and Americans. *Journal of Cross-Cultural Psychology, 16,* 223–242. doi:10.1177/0022002185016002006

Galton, F. (1869). *Hereditary genius: An inquiry into its laws and consequences.* London, England: Macmillan. doi:10.1037/13474-000

Gandhi, J., & Przeworski, A. (2006). Cooperation, cooption, and rebellion under dictatorship. *Economics and Politics, 18,* 1–26. doi:10.1111/j.1468-0343.2006.00160.x

Garrett, R. K. (2009). Echo chambers online? Politically motivated selective exposure among Internet news users. *Journal of Computer-Mediated Communication, 14,* 265–285. doi:10.1111/j.1083-6101.2009.01440.x

Gastil, J. (1994). A meta-analytic review of the productivity and satisfaction of democratic and autocratic leadership. *Small Group Research, 25,* 384–410. doi:10.1177/1046496494253003

Gavrilets, S., & Vose, E. (2006). The dynamics of Machiavellian intelligence. *PNAS: Proceedings of the National Academy of Sciences of the United States of America, 103,* 16823–16828. doi:10.1073/pnas.0601428103

Gawronski, B., & Strack, F. (Eds.). (2011). *Cognitive consistency: A fundamental principle in social cognition*. New York, NY: Guilford Press.

Gazzaniga, M. S. (2011). *Who's in charge? Free will and the science of the brain*. New York, NY: HarperCollins.

Geddes, B. (1999). What do we know about democratization after twenty years? *Annual Review of Political Science, 2,* 115–144. doi:10.1146/annurev.polisci.2.1.115

Gellar, S. (2005). *Democracy in Senegal: Tocquevillian analytics in Africa*. New York, NY: Palgrave Macmillan. doi:10.1057/9781403982162

Gellately, R. (2001). *Backing Hitler: Consent and coercion in Nazi Germany*. New York, NY: Oxford University Press.

Gentry, C. (2001). *J. Edgar Hoover: The man and the secrets*. New York, NY: Norton.

Gessen, M. (2012). *The man without a face: The unlikely rise of Vladimir Putin*. New York, NY: Riverhead Books.

Getty, A. A. (1987). *Origin of the great purges*. Cambridge, England: Cambridge University Press.

Ghahramani, Z. (2009). *My life as a traitor*. New York, NY: Farrar, Straus & Giroux.

Gibler, D. M. (2010). Outside-in: The effects of external threat to state centralization. *The Journal of Conflict Resolution, 54,* 519–542. doi:10.1177/0022002710370135

Gilbert, G. M. (1950). *The psychology of dictatorship*. New York, NY: Ronald Press.

Gilbert, G. M. (1995). *Nuremberg diary*. New York, NY: Da Capo Press. (Original work published 1947)

Gillmor, D. (2006). *We the media: Grassroots journalism by the people, for the people*. Sebatopol, CA: O'Reilly Media.

Glasford, D. E., Dovidio, J. F., & Pratto, F. (2009). I continue to feel so good about us: In-group identification and the use of social identity-enhancing strategies to reduce intragroup dissonance. *Personality and Social Psychology Bulletin, 35,* 415–427. doi:10.1177/0146167208329216

Glasford, D. E., Pratto, F., & Dovidio, J. F. (2008). Intragroup dissonance: Responses to in-group violation of personal values. *Journal of Experimental Social Psychology, 44,* 1057–1064. doi:10.1016/j.jesp.2007.10.004

Godwin, P. (2010). *The fear: The last days of Robert Mugabe*. New York, NY: Picador.

Goethals, G. R., Sorenson, G. J., & Burns, J. M. (Eds.). (2004). *Encyclopedia of leadership*. Thousand Oaks, CA: Sage.

Goffman, E. (1967/2005). *Interaction ritual*. New Brunswick, NJ: Transaction Publishers. First published 1967.

Golding, W. (1997). *Lord of the flies*. New York, NY: Riverhead. (Original work published 1954)

Gopnik, A., Meltzoff, A. N., & Kuhl, P. K. (2000). *The scientist in the crib: What early learning tells us about the mind*. New York, NY: Morrow.

Grafton, R. Q., & Rowlands, D. (1996). Development impending institutions: The political economy of Haiti. *Canadian Journal of Development Studies, 17,* 261–277. doi:10.1080/02255189.1996.9669654

Greenstein, F. I. (1975). *Personality and politics: Problems of evidence, inference, and conceptualization*. New York, NY: Norton. (Original work published 1965)

Greenstein, F. I. (2002).The qualitative study of presidential personality. In L. O. Valenty & O. Feldman (Eds.), *Political leadership for the new century: Personality and behavior among American leaders* (pp. 3–8). Westport, CT: Praeger.

Greenstein, F. I. (2009). *The presidential difference: Leadership style from FDR to Barack Obama*. Princeton, NJ: Princeton University Press.

Grint, K. (2005). *Leadership: Limits and possibilities*. New York, NY: Palgrave Macmillan.

Guimond, S., & Dubé-Simard, L. (1983). Relative deprivation theory and the Quebec nationalist movement: The cognition–emotion distinction and the person–group deprivation issue. *Journal of Personality and Social Psychology, 44*, 526–535. doi:10.1037/0022-3514.44.3.526

Guinote, A., Weick, M., & Cai, A. (2012). Does power magnify the expression of disposition? *Psychological Science, 23*, 475–482. doi:10.1177/0956797611428472

Hadenius, A., & Teorell, J. (2007). Pathways from authoritarianism. *Journal of Democracy, 18*, 143–157. doi:10.1353/jod.2007.0009

Haggerty, K. D., & Samatas, M. (2010). *Surveillance and democracy*. Abingdon, England: Routledge-Cavendish.

Harden, B. (2012). *Escape from Camp 14*. New York, NY: Viking.

Harlan, C. (2011, December 26). In N. Korea, signs of smooth transfer of power. *The Washington Post*, p. A17.

Harré, R., & Moghaddam, F. M. (Eds.). (2012). *Psychology for the third millennium: Integrating cultural and neuroscience perspectives*. Thousand Oaks, CA: Sage.

Hauser, M. D. (2006). *Moral minds*. New York, NY: HarperCollins.

Heidegger, M. (1996). Being and time (J. Stambaugh, Trans.). Albany: State University of New York Press.

Heider, F. (1946). Attitudes and cognitive organization. *Journal of Psychology: Interdisciplinary and Applied, 21*, 107–112. doi:10.1080/00223980.1946.9917275

Heider, F. (1958). *The psychology of interpersonal relations*. New York, NY: Wiley. doi:10.1037/10628-000

Hetherington, E., & Suhay, E. (2011). Authoritarianism, threat, and Americans' support for the war on terror. *American Journal of Political Science, 55*, 546–560. doi:10.1111/j.1540-5907.2011.00514.x

Hill, L. (2006). Low voter turnout in the United States: Is compulsory voting a viable solution? *Journal of Theoretical Politics, 18*, 207–232. doi:10.1177/0951629806061868

Hindman, M. (2008). *The myth of digital democracy*. Princeton, NJ: Princeton University Press.

Hogg, M. A. (2001). The social identity theory of leadership. *Personality and Social Psychology Review, 5*, 184–200. doi:10.1207/S15327957PSPR0503_1

Hogg, M. A. (2007). Uncertainty-identity theory. In M. P. Zanna (Ed.), *Advances in experimental social psychology* (Vol. 39, pp. 69–126). San Diego, CA: Academic Press.

Hogg, M. A. (2009). Managing self-uncertainty through group identification. *Psychological Inquiry, 20,* 221–224. doi:10.1080/10478400903333452

Hogg, M. A. (2010). Influence and leadership. In S. T. Fiske, D. T. Gilbert, & G. Lindzey (Eds.), *Handbook of social psychology* (5th ed., Vol. 2, pp. 1166–1207). New York, NY: Wiley.

Hogg, M. A. (2012). Self-uncertainty, social identity, and the solace of extremism. In M. A. Hogg & D. L. Blaylock (Eds.), *Extremism and the psychology of uncertainty* (pp. 19–35). Oxford, England: Wiley-Blackwell.

Hogg, M. A., & Blaylock, D. L. (Eds.). (2012). *Extremism and the psychology of uncertainty.* Oxford, England: Wiley-Blackwell.

Horwitz, S., Asokan, S., & Tate, J. (2011, December 2). High-tech help for repressive regimes? *The Washington Post,* pp. A1, A6.

House, R. J., & Mitchell, T. R. (1974). Path-goal theory of leadership. *Journal of Contemporary Business, 3,* 81–97.

Human Rights Watch. (2005). *Black hole: The fate of Islamists rendered to Egypt.* Retrieved from http://www.hrw.org/reports/2005/egypt0505

Hummon, N. P., & Doreian, P. (2003). Some dynamics of social balance processes: Bringing Heider back into balance theory. *Social Networks, 25,* 17–49. doi:10.1016/S0378-8733(02)00019-9

Hunt, I. A. (2005). *On Hitler's mountain: Overcoming the legacy of a Nazi childhood.* New York, NY: Harper Perennial.

Huntington, S. (1991). *The third wave: Democratization in the late 20th century.* Norman: University of Oklahoma Press.

Inzlicht, M., & Schmader, T. (Eds.). (2012). *Stereotype threat: Theory, process, and application.* New York, NY: Oxford University Press.

Jacobs, R. C., & Campbell, D. T. (1961). The perpetuation of an arbitrary tradition through several generations of a laboratory microculture. *The Journal of Abnormal and Social Psychology, 62,* 649–658. doi:10.1037/h0044182

Janis, I. I. (1971, November). Groupthink. *Psychology Today, 5,* 43–46, 74–76.

Janis, I. I. (1972). *Victims of groupthink: A psychological study of foreign policy decisions and fiascoes.* Boston, MA: Houghton Mifflin.

Janis, I. I. (1982). *Groupthink* (2nd. ed.). Boston, MA: Houghton Mifflin.

Jetten, J., & Iyer, A. (2010). Different meanings of the social dominance orientation concept: Predicting political attitudes over time. *British Journal of Social Psychology, 49,* 385–404. doi:10.1348/014466609X435723

Johansson, P. M., Eriksson, L. S., Sadigh, S., Rehnberg, C., & Tillgren, P. E. (2009). Participation, resource mobilization and financial incentives in community-based health promotion: An economic evaluation perspective from Sweden. *Health Promotion International, 24,* 177–184. doi:10.1093/heapro/dap008

Johnson, A. M., Vernon, P. A., Harris, J. A., & Jang, K. L. (2004). A behavioral investigation of the relationship between leadership and personality. *Twin Research, 7,* 27–32.

Johnson, A. M., Vernon, P. A., McCarthy, J. M., Molson, M., Harris, J. A., & Jang, K. J. (1998). Nature vs. nurture: Are leaders born or made? A behavior genetic investigation of leadership style. *Twin Research, 1*, 216–223.

Jost, J. T., Banaji, M. R., & Nosek, B. A. (2004). A decade of system justification theory: Accumulated evidence for conscious and unconscious bolstering of the status quo. *Political Psychology, 25*, 881–919. doi:10.1111/j.1467-9221.2004.00402.x

Jost, J. T., Napier, J. L., Thorisdottir, H., Gosling, S. D., Palfai, T. P., & Ostafin, B. (2007). Are needs to manage uncertainty and threat associated with political conservativism or ideological extremity? *Personality and Social Psychology Bulletin, 33*, 989–1007. doi:10.1177/0146167207301028

Jost, J. T., & van der Toorn, J. (2012). System justification theory. In P. A. M. Van Lange, A. W. Kruglanski, & E. T. Higgins (Eds.), *Handbook of theories of social psychology* (Vol. 2, pp. 313–343). London, England: Sage.

Judge, T. A., Bono, J. E., Ilies, R., & Gerhart, M. W. (2002). Personality and leadership: A qualitative and quantitative review. *Journal of Applied Psychology, 87*, 765–780. doi:10.1037/0021-9010.87.4.765

Kahneman, D. (2011). *Thinking, fast and slow*. New York, NY: Farrar, Straus & Giroux.

Kaiser, S. (2002). Escraches: Demonstrations, communication, and political memory in post-dictatorial Argentina. *Media Culture & Society, 24*, 499–516. doi:10.1177/016344370202400403

Kamalipour, Y. R. (2010). *Media, power, and politics in the digital age: The 2009 presidential election uprising in Iran*. Lanham, MD: Rowman & Littlefield.

Kantola, S. J., Syme, G. J., & Campbell, N. A. (1984). Cognitive dissonance and energy conservation. *Journal of Applied Psychology, 69*, 416–421. doi:10.1037/0021-9010.69.3.416

Karau, S. J., & Williams, K. D. (1993). Social loafing: A meta-analytic review and theoretical integration. *Journal of Personality and Social Psychology, 65*, 681–706. doi:10.1037/0022-3514.65.4.681

Kellerman, B. (2004). *Bad leadership: What is it, how it happens, why it matters*. Boston, MA: Harvard Business School Press.

Kelman, H., & Hamilton, V. L. (1989). *Crimes of obedience: Toward a social psychology of authority and responsibility*. New Haven, CT: Yale University Press.

Kershaw, I. (1993). "Working towards the Führer": Reflections on the nature of the Hitler dictatorship. *Contemporary European History, 2*, 103–118. doi:10.1017/S0960777300000382

Khomeini, R. (1979). Islamic government. *Joint Publications Research Service*. New York, NY: Manor Books.

Kiernan, V. G. (1996). *The lords of humankind: European attitudes toward the outside world in the Imperial Age*. Harmondsworth, England: Penguin Books. (Original work published 1972)

Kilham, W., & Mann, L. (1974). Level of destructive obedience as a function of transmitter and executants roles in the Milgram obedience paradigm. *Journal of Personality and Social Psychology, 29*, 696–702. doi:10.1037/h0036636

Kritz, B. A. (in press). Rule of law and conflict mainstreaming. In C. Zelizer (Ed.), *Integrated peacebuilding: Innovative approaches to transforming conflict.* Boulder, CO: Westview Press.

Kruglanski, A. W. (2004). *The psychology of closed mindedness.* New York, NY: Psychology Press.

Kruglanski, A. W., & Orehek, E. (2012). The need for certainty as a psychological nexus for individuals and society. In M. A. Hogg & D. L. Blaylock (Eds.), *Extremism and the psychology of uncertainty* (pp. 1–18). Oxford, England: Wiley-Blackwell.

Kruglanski, A. W., Pierro, A., Mannetti, L., & De Granda, E. (2006). Groups as epistemic providers: Need for closure and the unfolding of group centrism. *Psychological Review, 113*, 84–100. doi:10.1037/0033-295X.113.1.84

Kula, M. (2009). Poland: The silence of those deprived of voice. In P. Corner (Ed.), *Popular opinion in totalitarian regimes* (pp. 149–167). New York, NY: Oxford University Press.

Lamiell, J. T. (2003). *Beyond individual and group differences: Human individuality, scientific psychology, and William Stern.* Thousand Oaks, CA: Sage.

Langer, W. C. (1972). *The mind of Adolf Hitler: The secret wartime report.* New York, NY: Basic Books.

Lansing, C. B. (2010). *From Nazism to communism: German schoolteachers under two dictatorships.* Cambridge, MA: Harvard University Press.

Lasswell, H., Horowitz, I. L., & Stanley, J. (1997). *Essays on the garrison state.* New Brunswick, NJ: Transaction.

Leadership. (2007). [Special issue]. *American Psychologist, 62*(1).

Leana, C. R. (1985). A partial test of Janis' groupthink model: Effects of group cohesiveness and leader behavior on defective decision making. *Journal of Management, 11*, 5–18. doi:10.1177/014920638501100102

Leder, M. M. (2001). *My life in Stalinist Russia: An American woman looks back.* Bloomington: Indiana University Press.

Leese, D. (2011). *Mao cult: Rhetoric and ritual in China's cultural revolution.* New York, NY: Cambridge University Press. doi:10.1017/CBO9780511984754

Lehoucq, F. (2003). Electoral fraud: Causes, types, and consequences. *Annual Review of Political Science, 6*, 233–256. doi:10.1146/annurev.polisci.6.121901.085655

Leighley, J. E. (Ed.). (2010). *The Oxford handbook of American elections and political behavior.* New York, NY: Oxford University Press. doi:10.1093/oxfordhb/9780199235476.001.0001

Lemos, G. (2012). *The end of the Chinese dream: Why Chinese people fear the future.* New Haven, CT: Yale University Press.

Lenin, V. I. (1989). *What is to be done?* (J. Fineberg & G. Hanna, Trans.). London, England & New York, NY: Penguin Books. (Original work published 1902)

Leung, J. K., & Kau, M. Y. M. (1992). *The writings of Mao Zedong, 1949–1976: Vol. 2. January 1956–December 1957.* New York, NY: M. E. Sharpe.

LeVert, S. (1995). *Huey Long: The kingfish of Louisiana.* New York, NY: Facts on File.

Levintova, E. (2011). Official ideological discourse in pre-transition and post-communist Russia: What has really changed since the communist period? In E. Andrews (Ed.), *Legacies of totalitarian language in the discourse culture of the post-totalitarian era* (pp. 155–182). New York, NY: Lexington Books.

Levy, J. (1989). The diversionary theory of war: A critique. In M. Midlarsky (Ed.), *Handbook of war studies* (pp. 259–288). Boston, MA: Unwin Hyman.

Lewin, K. (1951). *Field theory in social science.* New York, NY: Harper.

Lewin, K., & Lippitt, R. (1938). An experimental approach to the study of autocracy and democracy: A preliminary note. *Sociometry, 1,* 292–300. doi:10.2307/2785585

Lewin, K., Lippitt, R., & White, R. K. (1939). Patterns of aggressive behavior in experimentally created "social climates." *The Journal of Social Psychology, 10,* 269–299. doi:10.1080/00224545.1939.9713366

Lincoln, A. (1984). *Right principles: Conservative philosophy of politics.* New York, NY: Blackwell.

Lintott, A. W. (1999). *The constitution of the Roman Republic.* Oxford, England: Clarendon.

Lipman-Blumen, J. (2006). *The allure of toxic leaders: Why we follow destructive bosses and corrupt politicians—and how we can survive them.* New York, NY: Oxford University Press.

Lippitt, R. (1940). An experimental study of the effect of democratic and authoritarian group atmospheres. *University of Iowa Studies in Child Welfare, 16,* 43–195.

Locke, E. A., & Schweiger, D. M. (1979). Participation in decision-making: One more look. *Research in Organizational Behavior, 1,* 265–339.

Lofland, J. (1996). *Social movement organizations: Guide to research on insurgent realities.* Edison, NJ: Aldine Transaction.

Malici, A. (2005). Discord and collaboration between allies: Managing external threats and internal cohesion in Franco-British relations during the 9/11 era. *Journal of Conflict Resolution, 49,* 90–119. doi:10.1177/0022002704269356

Mampe, B., Friederici, A. D., & Wermke, K. (2009). Newborns' cry melody is shaped by their native language. *Current Biology, 19,* 1994–1997. doi:10.1016/j.cub.2009.09.064

Mann, T. E., & Ornstein, N. J. (2012). *It's even worse than it looks: How the American constitutional system collided with the new politics of extremism.* New York, NY: Basic Books.

Mantell, D. M. (1971). The potential for violence in Germany. *Journal of Social Issues, 27,* 101–112. doi:10.1111/j.1540-4560.1971.tb00680.x

Marmot, M. G. (2004). *The status syndrome: How social standing affects our health and longevity.* New York, NY: Times Books With Holt.

Marsella, A. J., Dubanoski, J., Hamada, W. C., & Morse, H. (2000). The measurement of personality across cultures: Historical, conceptual, and methodological issues and considerations. *American Behavioral Scientist, 44,* 41–62. doi:10.1177/00027640021956080

Marx, K. (1979). The eighteenth brumaire of Louis Bonaparte. In *Collected works of Karl Marx and Frederick Engels* (Vol. 11, pp. 99–197). London, England: Lawrence & Wishart. (Original work published 1852)

Marx, K., & Engels, F. (1967). *The Communist manifesto.* New York, NY: Pantheon. (Original work published 1848)

Massie, R. K. (1980). *Peter the Great: His life and world.* New York, NY: Knopf.

Matz, D. C., & Wood, W. (2005). Cognitive dissonance in groups: The consequences of disagreement. *Journal of Personality and Social Psychology, 88,* 22–37. doi:10.1037/0022-3514.88.1.22

McBride, C. M., Emmons, K. M., & Lipkus, I. M. (2003). Understanding the potential of teachable moments: The case of smoking cessation. *Health Education Research, 18,* 156–170. doi:10.1093/her/18.2.156

McCarthy, T. D., & Zald, M. N. (1977). Resource mobilization and social movements: A partial theory. *American Journal of Sociology, 82,* 1212–1241. doi:10.1086/226464

McCormick, J. P. (1997). The dilemmas of dictatorship: Carl Schmitt and constitutional emergency powers. *Canadian Journal of Law and Jurisprudence, 10,* 163–187.

McCormick, J. P. (2006). Contain the wealthy and patrol the magistrates: Restoring elite accountability to popular government. *The American Political Science Review, 100,* 147–163. doi:10.1017/S0003055406062071

McCormick, J. P. (2011). *Machiavellian democracy.* Cambridge, England: Cambridge University Press. doi:10.1017/CBO9780511975325

McGregor, I., Haji, R., Nash, K. A., & Teper, R. (2008). Religious zeal and the uncertain self. *Basic and Applied Social Psychology, 30,* 183–188. doi:10.1080/01973530802209251

McGregor, I., Prentice, M., & Nash, K. A. (2009). Personal uncertainty management by reactive approach motivation. *Psychological Inquiry, 20,* 225–229. doi:10.1080/10478400903333460

Meade, R. (1967). An experimental study of leadership in India. *The Journal of Social Psychology, 72,* 35–43. doi:10.1080/00224545.1967.9922297

Meade, R. (1970). Leadership studies of Chinese and Chinese Americans. *Journal of Cross-Cultural Psychology, 1,* 325–332. doi:10.1177/135910457000100404

Meade, R. (1985). Experimental studies of authoritarian and democratic leadership in four cultures: American, Indian, Chinese, and Chinese-American. *The High School Journal, 68,* 293–295.

Meeus, H. J. W., & Raaijmakers, A. W. (1986). Obedience in modern society: The Utrecht studies. *Journal of Social Issues, 5,* 155–176.

Merolla, J. L., Ramos, J. M., & Zechmeister, E. J. (2012). Authoritarianism, need for closure, and conditions of threat. In M. A. Hogg & D. L. Blaylock (Eds.), *Extremism and the psychology of uncertainty* (pp. 212–227). Oxford, England: Wiley-Blackwell.

Middlebrook, K. J. (1995). *The paradox of revolution: Labor, state, and authoritarianism in Mexico.* Baltimore, MD: Johns Hopkins University Press.

Mignone, E. F. (1988). *Witness to the truth: The complicity of church and dictatorship in Argentina, 1976–1983.* Maryknoll, NY: Orbis Books.

Milgram, S. (1974). *Obedience to authority: An experimental view.* New York, NY: Harper & Row.

Miller, K., & Monge, P. R. (1986). Participation, satisfaction, and productivity: A meta-analytic review. *Academy of Management Journal, 29,* 727–753. doi:10.2307/255942

Miller, N., Pederson, W. C., Earlywine, M., & Pollock, V. E. (2003). A theoretical model of triggered displaced aggression. *Personality and Social Psychology Review, 7,* 57–97. doi:10.1207/S15327957PSPR0701_5

Moghaddam, F. M. (1987). Psychology in the three worlds: As reflected by the crisis in social psychology and the move toward indigenous third world psychology. *American Psychologist, 42,* 912–920. doi:10.1037/0003-066X.42.10.912

Moghaddam, F. M. (1990). Modulative and generative orientations in psychology: Implications for psychology in the three worlds. *Journal of Social Issues, 46,* 21–41. doi:10.1111/j.1540-4560.1990.tb01932.x

Moghaddam, F. M. (1996). Training for developing world psychologists: Can the training be better than the psychology? In S. C. Carr & J. F. Schumaker (Eds.), *Psychology and the developing world* (pp. 49–59). New York, NY: Praeger.

Moghaddam, F. M. (1997). *The specialized society: The plight of the individual in an age of individualism.* Westport, CT: Praeger.

Moghaddam, F. M. (1998). *Social psychology: Exploring universals across cultures.* New York, NY: Freeman.

Moghaddam, F. M. (2002). *The individual and society: A cultural integration.* New York, NY: Worth.

Moghaddam, F. M. (2004). The cycle of rights and duties in intergroup relations in interobjectivity and perceived justice re-assessed. *New Review of Social Psychology, 3,* 125–130.

Moghaddam, F. M. (2005). *Great ideas in psychology.* Oxford, England: Oneworld.

Moghaddam, F. M. (2006). Catastrophic evolution, culture, and diversity management policy. *Culture & Psychology, 12,* 415–434. doi:10.1177/1354067X06067145

Moghaddam, F. M. (2008a). *How globalization spurs terrorism.* Westport, CT: Praeger.

Moghaddam, F. M. (2008b). *Multiculturalism and intergroup relations: Implications for democracy in global context.* Washington, DC: American Psychological Association. doi:10.1037/11682-000

Moghaddam, F. M. (2008c). The psychological citizen and the two concepts of the social contract: A preliminary analysis. *Political Psychology, 29*, 881–901. doi:10.1111/j.1467-9221.2008.00671.x

Moghaddam, F. M. (2010). Intersubjectivity, interobjectivity, and the embryonic fallacy in developmental science. *Culture & Psychology, 16*, 465–475. doi:10.1177/1354067X10380160

Moghaddam, F. M., & Breckenridge, J. (2011). The post-tragedy "opportunity-bubble" and the prospect of citizen engagement. *Homeland Security Affairs, 7*, 1–4.

Moghaddam, F. M., & Lee, N. (2006). Double reification: The process of universalizing psychology in the three worlds. In A. Brock (Ed.), *Internationalizing the history of psychology* (pp. 163–182). New York: New York University Press.

Moghaddam, F. M., & Riley, C. J. (2005). Toward a cultural theory of human rights and duties in human development. In N. J. Finkel & F. M. Moghaddam (Eds.), *The psychology of human rights and duties: Empirical contributions and normative commentaries* (pp. 75–104). Washington, DC: American Psychologial Association. doi:10.1037/10872-004

Moghaddam, F. M., & Taylor, D. M. (1985). Psychology in the developing world: An evaluation through the concepts of "dual perception" and "parallel growth." *American Psychologist, 40*, 1144–1146. doi:10.1037/0003-066X.40.10.1144

Moghaddam, F. M., & Taylor, D. M. (1986). What constitutes an "appropriate psychology" for the developing world? *International Journal of Psychology, 21*, 253–267. doi:10.1080/00207598608247589

Mok, A., & Morris, M. W. (2010). An upside to bicultural identity conflict: Resisting groupthink in cultural ingroups. *Journal of Experimental Social Psychology, 46*, 1114–1117. doi:10.1016/j.jesp.2010.05.020

Montefiore, S. S. (2003). *Stalin: The court of the red tsar*. London, England: Weidenfeld & Nicholson.

Moore, B. (1966). *Social origins of dictatorship and democracy: Lord and peasant in the making of the modern world*. Boston, MA: Beacon Press.

Morozov, E. (2011). *The net delusion: The dark side of Internet freedom*. New York, NY: PublicAffairs.

Moscovici, S., & Duveen, G. (Eds.). (2001). *Social representations: Explorations in social psychology*. New York: New York University Press.

Moscovici, S., Mucchi-Faina, A., & Maas, A. (Eds.). (1994). *Minority influence*. Chicago, IL: Nelson Hall.

Munroe, R. L., Munroe, R. H., & Whiting, B. B. (Eds.). (1981). *Handbook of cross-cultural development*. Monterey, CA: Brooks/Cole.

Nemat, M. (2008). *Prisoner of Tehran: A memoir*. New York, NY: Free Press.

Newcomb, T. M. (1961). *The acquaintance process*. New York, NY: Holt, Rinehart & Winston. doi:10.1037/13156-000

Nicholls, A. J. (1997). The final step to power. In A. Mitchell (Ed.), *The Nazi revolution* (pp. 42–47). Boston, MA: Houghton Mifflin.

Nicholls, N. H., Huth, P. K., & Appel, B. (2010). When is domestic political unrest related to international conflict? Diversionary theory and Japanese foreign policy, 1890–1941. *International Studies Quarterly, 54,* 915–937. doi:10.1111/j.1468-2478.2010.00620.x

Nicholson, N., Cole, S. G., & Rocklin, T. (1985). Conformity in the Asch situation: A comparison between contemporary British and US university students. *British Journal of Social Psychology, 24,* 59–63. doi:10.1111/j.2044-8309.1985.tb00660.x

Noah, T. (2012). *The great divergence.* New York, NY: Bloomsbury Press.

Noriyuki, M. (1985). Strong, quasi-, and weak conformity among Japanese in the modified Asch procedure. *Journal of Cross-Cultural Psychology, 16,* 83–97. doi:10.1177/0022002185016001007

Norton, M. I., Monin, B., Cooper, J., & Hogg, M. A. (2003). Vicarious dissonance: Attitude change from the inconsistency of others. *Journal of Personality and Social Psychology, 85,* 47–62. doi:10.1037/0022-3514.85.1.47

Orr, H. A. (2009). Darwin and Darwinism: The (alleged) social implications of *The Origin of Species. Genetics, 183,* 767–772. doi:10.1534/genetics.109.110445

Orwell, G. (1960). *1984.* New York, NY: Signet. (Original work published 1949)

Osbeck, L., Moghaddam, F. M., & Perreault, S. (1997). Similarity and intergroup relations. *International Journal of Intercultural Relations, 21,* 113–123. doi:10.1016/S0147-1767(96)00016-8

Overy, R. J. (2004). *The dictators: Hitler's Germany and Stalin's Russia.* New York, NY: Norton.

Packer, D. J., & Chasteen, A. L. (2010). Loyal deviance: Testing the normative conflict model of dissent in social groups. *Personality and Social Psychology Bulletin, 36,* 5–18. doi:10.1177/0146167209350628

Page, J., & Spegele, B. (2011, December 16). Beijing set to "strike hard" at revolt. *The Wall Street Journal,* p. A10.

Pareto, V. (1935). *The mind and society: A treatise on general sociology* (Vols. 1–4). New York, NY: Dover.

Penchaszadeh, V. B. (1992). Abduction of children of political dissidents in Argentina and the role of human genetics in their restitution. *Journal of Public Health Policy, 13,* 291–305. doi:10.2307/3342729

Perry, R., & Sibley, C. G. (2011). Social dominance orientation: Mapping a baseline individual difference component across self-categorizations. *Journal of Individual Differences, 32,* 110–116. doi:10.1027/1614-0001/a000042

Pickering, J., & Kisangarri, E. F. (2010). Diversionary despots? Comparing autocracies' propensities to use and to benefit from military force. *American Journal of Political Science, 54,* 477–493. doi:10.1111/j.1540-5907.2010.00442.x

Pierro, A., Kruglanski, A. W., & Raven, B. H. (2012). Motivated underpinnings of social influence in work settings: Bases of social power and the need for cognitive closure. *European Journal of Social Psychology, 42,* 41–52. doi:10.1002/ejsp.836

Pinter, H. (1998). The new world order. In *Harold Pinter: Plays 4* (pp. 270–278). London, England: Faber & Faber.

Pipes, R. (1990). *The Russian revolution.* New York, NY: Knopf.

Plamper, J. (2009). Beyond binaries: Popular opinion in Stalinism. In P. Corner (Ed.), *Popular opinion in totalitarian regimes: Fascism, Nazism, communism* (pp. 64–80). New York, NY: Oxford University Press.

Plato. (1987). *Republic* (D. Lee, Trans.). Harmondsworth, England: Penguin Books.

Ployhart, R. E., & Bliese, P. D. (2006). Individual ADAPTability (I-ADAPT) theory: Conceptualizing the antecedents, consequences, and measurement of individual differences in adaptability. In S. Burke, L. Pierce, & E. Salas (Eds.), *Understanding adaptability: A prerequisite for effective performance within complex environments* (pp. 3–39). St. Louis, MO: Elsevier Science. doi:10.1016/S1479-3601(05)06001-7

Point of view. (2010, October). *Vogue,* 265.

Pollock, E. (2006). *Stalin and the Soviet science wars.* Princeton, NJ: Princeton University Press.

Pool, J., & Pool, S. (1979). *Who financed Hitler: The secret funding of Hitler's rise to power 1919–1933.* New York, NY: The Dial Press.

Postmes, T., & Jetten, J. (Eds.). (2006). *Individuality and the group: Advances in social identity.* London, England: Sage.

Pratto, F., Sidanius, J., Stallworth, L. M., & Malle, B. F. (1994). Social dominance orientation: A personality variable predicting social and political attitudes. *Journal of Personality and Social Psychology, 67,* 741–763. doi:10.1037/0022-3514.67.4.741

Pratto, F., & Stewart, A. L. (2012). Group dominance and the half-blindness of privilege. *Journal of Social Issues, 68,* 28–45. doi:10.1111/j.1540-4560.2011.01734.x

Prentice, D. A., & Eberhardt, J. L. (2008). The neural underpinnings of group life. *Group Processes & Intergroup Relations, 11,* 139–142.

Pringle, P. (2008). *The murder of Nikolai Vavilov.* New York, NY: Simon & Schuster.

Prochaska, J. O., DiClemente, C. C., & Norcross, J. C. (1992). In search of how people change: Applications to addictive behaviors. *American Psychologist, 47,* 1102–1114.

Proulx, T., & Heine, S. J. (2006). Death and black diamonds: Meaning, mortality, and the meaning maintenance model. *Psychological Inquiry, 17,* 309–318.

Putin, V. (2000). *First person: An astonishingly frank self-portrait of Russia's president* (C. A. Fitzpatrick, Trans.). New York, NY: PublicAffairs.

Pyszczynski, T., Solomon, S., & Greenberg, J. (2004). *In the wake of 9/11: The psychology of terror.* Washington, DC: American Psychological Association.

Quintelier, E., Hooghe, M., & Marien, S. (2011). The effect of compulsory voting on turnout stratification patterns: A cross-national analysis. *International Political Science Review, 32,* 396–416. doi:10.1177/0192512110382016

Ra'anan, U. (2006). Sic transit: Stalin's heirs. In U. Ra'anan (Ed.), *Flawed succession: Russia's power transfer crises* (pp. 1–55). New York, NY: Lexington Books.

Rand, A. (1971). *The fountainhead*. New York, NY: Signet Classic. (Original work published 1943)

Reich, W. (1970). *The mass psychology of fascism*. New York, NY: Farrar, Straus & Giroux.

Reicher, S., & Haslam, S. A. (2006). Rethinking the psychology of tyranny: The BBC prison study. *British Journal of Social Psychology, 45*, 1–40. doi:10.1348/014466605X48998

Rejali, D. M. (1994). *Torture and modernity*. Boulder, CO: Westview Press.

Rejali, D. M. (2007). *Torture and democracy*. Princeton, NJ: Princeton University Press.

Rennie, D. (1999). Editorial peer review: Its development and rational. In F. Godlee & T. Jefferson (Eds.), *Peer review in health sciences* (pp. 1–13). London, England: British Medical Journal Books.

Richburg, K. B. (2012, May 2). Chen, Bo cases highlight abusive behavior by China's local officials. *The Washington Post*, p. A10.

Roiser, M., & Willig, C. (2002). The strange death of the authoritarian personality: 50 years of psychological political debate. *History of the Human Sciences, 15*, 71–96.

Rose-Ackerman, S. (1999). *Corruption and government: Causes, consequences, and reform*. Cambridge, England: Cambridge University Press. doi:10.1017/CBO9781139175098

Rosnow, R. L. (2001). Rumor and gossip in interpersonal interaction and beyond: A social exchange perspective. In R. M. Kowalski (Ed.), *Behaving badly: Aversive behaviors in interpersonal relations* (pp. 203–232). Washington, DC: American Psychological Association. doi:10.1037/10365-008

Rothbart, D., & Korostelina, K. V. (Eds.). (2006). *Identity, morality, and threat: Studies in violent conflict*. Lanham, MD: Lexington Books.

Rothbart, M. K., & Bates, J. E. (2006). Temperament. In N. Eisenberg (Vol. Ed.) & W. Damon & R. M Lerner (Series Eds.), *Handbook of child psychology: Vol. 3. Social, emotional, and personality development* (6th ed., pp. 99–166). New York, NY: Wiley.

Rowe, M. (2009). Napoleon's France: A forerunner of Europe's twentieth-century dictatorships? In C. C. W. Szejnmann (Ed.), *Rethinking history, dictatorship and war* (pp. 87–106). London, England: Continuum.

Rueschemeyer, D., Stephens, E. H., & Stephens, J. D. (1992). *Capitalist development and democracy*. Chicago, IL: University of Chicago Press.

Runciman, W. G. (1966). *Relative deprivation and social justice*. Harmondsworth, England: Penguin Books.

Russell, P. H., & O'Brien, D. M. (Eds.). (2001). *Judicial independence in the age of democracy: Critical perspectives from around the world*. Charlottesville: University of Virginia Press.

Ryan, P. B. (1985). *The Iranian rescue mission: Why it failed*. Annapolis, MD: Naval Institute Press.

Ryavec, K. W. (2003). *Russian bureaucracy: Power and pathology*. Boulder, CO: Rowman & Littlefield.

Sales, S. M. (1972). Threat as a factor in authoritarianism. *Journal of Personality and Social Psychology, 23*, 420–428. doi:10.1037/h0033157

Sales, S. M. (1973). Success and failure as determinants of level of authoritarianism. *Journal of Personality and Social Psychology, 28*, 44–57. doi:10.1037/h0035588

Sales, S. M., & Friend, D. E. (2007). Success and failure as determinants of level of authoritarianism. *Behavioral Science, 18*, 163–172.

Salisbury, H. E. (1992). *The new emperors: China in the era of Mao and Deng*. New York, NY: Avon.

Sampson, E. E. (1977). Psychology and the American ideal. *Journal of Personality and Social Psychology, 35*, 767–782. doi:10.1037/0022-3514.35.11.767

Sampson, E. E. (1981). Cognitive psychology as ideology. *American Psychologist, 36*, 730–743. doi:10.1037/0003-066X.36.7.730

Schaffer, F. C. (Ed.). (2007). *Elections for sale: The causes and consequences of vote buying*. Boulder, CO: Lynne Rienner.

Schama, S. (1989). *Citizens: A chronicle of the French Revolution*. New York, NY: Vintage.

Schedler, A. (2006). *Electoral authoritarianism: The dynamics of unfree competition*. Boulder, CO: Lynne Rienner.

Schmader, T. (2010). Stereotype threat deconstructed. *Current Directions in Psychological Science, 19*, 14–18. doi:10.1177/0963721409359292

Schock, K. (2005). *Unarmed insurrections: People power movements in nondemocracies*. Minneapolis: University of Minnesota Press.

Secor, L. (2012, May 7). Election, monitored: The tragic farce of voting in Iran. *The New Yorker*, pp. 48–59.

Seib, P. M. (2008). *The Al Jazeera effect: How the new global media is reshaping world politics*. Washington, DC: Potomac Books.

Selden, S. (1999). *Inheriting shame: The story of eugenics and racism in America*. New York, NY: Teachers College Press.

Shah, I. (1993). *The pleasantries of the incredible Mulla Nasrudin*. New York, NY: Penguin Books.

Shamir, M., & Sagiv-Schifter, T. (2006). Conflict, identity, and tolerance: Israel in the Al-Aqsa intifada. *Political Psychology, 27*, 569–595. doi:10.1111/j.1467-9221.2006.00523.x

Shanab, M. E., & Yahya, K. A. (1977). A behavioral study of obedience in children. *Journal of Personality and Social Psychology, 35*, 530–536. doi:10.1037/0022-3514.35.7.530

Sharansky, A., & Dermer, R. (2004). *The case for democracy: The power of freedom to overcome tyranny and terror*. New York, NY: PublicAffairs.

Sharp, G. (2010). *From dictatorship to democracy: A conceptual framework for liberation* (4th ed.). East Boston, MA: The Albert Einstein Institute.

Sherif, M. (1935). A study of some special factors in perception. *Archives of Psychology, 27*(187), 1–60.

Sherif, M. (1936). *The psychology of social norms*. New York, NY: Harpers.

Sherif, M. (1973). *Groups in harmony and tension: An integration of studies on intergroup relations*. New York, NY: Octagon Books.

Sherif, M., Harvey, O. J., White, B. J., Hood, W. R., & Sherif, C. W. (1961). *Intergroup group conflict and cooperation: The robber's cave experiment*. Norman: University of Oklahoma.

Shipler, D. K. (2011). *The rights of the people: How our search for safety invades our liberties*. New York, NY: Knopf.

Sibley, C. G., & Liu, J. H. (2010). Social dominance orientation: Testing a global individual difference perspective. *Political Psychology, 31*, 175–207. doi:10.1111/j.1467-9221.2009.00748.x

Sidanius, J., & Pratto, F. (1999). *Social dominance: An intergroup theory of social dominance and oppression*. New York, NY: Cambridge University Press. doi:10.1017/CBO9781139175043

Sitsky, L. (1994). *Music of the repressed Russian avant-garde, 1900–1929*. Westport, CT: Greenwood.

Smith, H. J., Pettigrew, T. F., Pippin, G. M., & Bialosiewicz, S. (2012). Relative deprivation: A theoretical meta-analytic review. *Personality and Social Psychology Review, 16*, 203–232. doi:10.1177/1088868311430825

Smith, J. L., & White, P. H. (2002). An examination of implicitly activated, explicitly activated, and nullified stereotypes on mathematical performance: It's not just a women's issue. *Sex Roles, 47*, 179–191. doi:10.1023/A:1021051223441

Smrt, D. C., & Karau, S. J. (2011). Protestant work ethic moderates social loafing. *Group Dynamics: Theory, Research, and Practice, 15*, 267–274. doi:10.1037/a0024484

Son Hing, L. S., Li, W., & Zanna, M. P. (2002). Inducing hypocrisy to reduce prejudicial responses among aversive racists. *Journal of Experimental Social Psychology, 38*, 71–78. doi:10.1006/jesp.2001.1484

South Africa Truth and Reconciliation Commission. (1999). *Truth and Reconciliation Commission of South Africa Report* (Vols. 1–5). Cape Town, South Africa: Author.

Soyfer, V. N. (1994). *Lysenko and the tragedy of Soviet science*. New Brunswick, NJ: Rutgers University Press.

Speer, A. (1970). *Inside the Third Reich: Memoirs* (R. Winston & C. Winston, Trans.). New York, NY: Macmillan.

Stadler, J. (2003). Gossip and blame: Implications for HIV/AIDS prevention in South African Lowveld. *AIDS Education and Prevention, 15*, 357–368. doi:10.1521/aeap.15.5.357.23823

Stagner, R. (1936). Fascist attitudes: An exploratory study. *The Journal of Social Psychology, 7*, 309–319. doi:10.1080/00224545.1936.9919882

Staub, E. (1997). Blind versus constructive patriotism: Moving from embeddedness in the group to critical loyalty and action. In D. Bar-Tal & E. Staub (Eds.), *Patriotism: In the lives of individuals and nations* (pp. 213–228). Chicago, IL: Nelson Hall.

Staub, E. (2011). *Overcoming evil: Genocide, violent conflict, and terrorism*. New York, NY: Oxford University Press.

Steele, C. (2010). *Whistling Vivaldi: And other clues to how stereotypes affect us*. New York, NY: Norton.

Stein, A. (1976). Conflict and cohesion. *The Journal of Conflict Resolution, 20*, 143–172. doi:10.1177/002200277602000106

Stephanopolous, G. (Interviewer) & Obama, B. (Interviewee). (2010). *President Obama to Pastor Jones: "Stunt" endangers troops*. George's Bottom Line, ABC News. Retrieved from http://blogs.abcnews.com/george/2010/09/president-obama-to-pastor-jones-stunt-endangers-troops-full-transcript-of-exclusive-interview.html

Stigler, J. W., Shweder, R. A., & Herdt, G. H. (Eds.). (1990). *Cultural psychology: Essays on human comparative development*. New York, NY: Cambridge University Press. doi:10.1017/CBO9781139173728

Stone, J., & Fernandez, N. C. (2008). To practice what we preach: The use of hypocrisy and cognitive dissonance to motivate behavior change. *Social and Personality Psychology Compass, 2*, 1024–1051. doi:10.1111/j.1751-9004.2008.00088.x

Stone, W. F., & Smith, L. D. (1993). Authoritarianism: Left and right. In W. F. Stone, G. Lederer, & R. Christie (Eds.), *Strengths and weaknesses: The authoritarian personality today* (pp. 144–156). New York, NY: Springer.

Stouffer, S. A. (1955). *Communism, conformity, and civil liberties*. New York, NY: Doubleday.

Stouffer, S. A., Suchman, E. A., De Vinney, L. C., Star, S. A., & Williams, R. M. (1949). *The American soldier: Adjustments during army life* (Vol. 1). Princeton, NJ: Princeton University Press.

Subramanyam, M., Kawachi, I., Berkman, L., & Subramanian, S. V. (2009). Relative deprivation in income and self-rated health in the United States. *Social Science & Medicine, 69*, 327–334. doi:10.1016/j.socscimed.2009.06.008

Sullivan, K. M. (2010). Two concepts of freedom of speech. *Harvard Law Review, 124*, 143–177.

Sumner, W. G. (1906). *Folkways*. Boston, MA: Ginn Press.

Sunstein, C. R. (2009). *Republic.com 2.0*. Princeton, NJ: Princeton University Press.

Svolik, M. W. (2009). Power sharing and leadership dynamics in authoritarian regimes. *American Journal of Political Science, 53*, 477–494. doi:10.1111/j.1540-5907.2009.00382.x

Taheri, A. (1988). *Nest of spies: America's journey to disaster in Iran*. London, England: Hutchinson.

Tajfel, H. (1974). *Intergroup behavior, social identity, and social change*. Unpublished manuscript, Katz-Newcomb Lectures, University of Michigan, Ann Arbor.

Tajfel, H., Flament, C., Billig, M. G., & Bundy, R. F. (1971). Social categorization and intergroup behaviour. *European Journal of Social Psychology, 1*, 149–178. doi:10.1002/ejsp.2420010202

Tajfel, H., & Turner, J. C. (1979). An integrative theory of intergroup conflict. In W. G. Austin & S. Worchel (Eds.), *The social psychology of intergroup relations* (pp. 33–47). Monterey, CA: Brooks/Cole.

Takaku, S. (2006). Reducing road rage: An application of the dissonance-attribution model of interpersonal forgiveness. *Journal of Applied Social Psychology, 36*, 2362–2378. doi:10.1111/j.0021-9029.2006.00107.x

Talmon, J. L. (1952). *The origins of totalitarian democracy*. London, England: Secker & Warburg.

Taylor, D. M. (2002). *The quest for identity*. Westport, CT: Praeger.

Taylor, D. M., & McKirnan, D. J. (1984). A five-stage model of intergroup relations. *British Journal of Social Psychology, 23*, 291–300. doi:10.1111/j.2044-8309.1984.tb00644.x

Taylor, D. M., & Moghaddam, F. M. (1987). *Theories of intergroup relations: International social psychological perspectives*. Westport, CT: Praeger.

Taylor, D. M., Moghaddam, F. M., & Bellerose, J. (1989). Social comparison in an intergroup context. *The Journal of Social Psychology, 129*, 499–515. doi:10.1080/00224545.1989.9712068

Taylor, D. M., Moghaddam, F. M., Gamble, I., & Zellerer, E. (1987). Disadvantaged group responses to perceived inequality: From passive acceptance to collective action. *The Journal of Social Psychology, 127*, 259–272. doi:10.1080/00224545.1987.9713692

Tetlock, P. E., Peterson, R. S., McGuire, C., Chang, S., & Feld, P. (1992). Assessing political group dynamics: A test of the groupthink model. *Journal of Personality and Social Psychology, 63*, 403–425. doi:10.1037/0022-3514.63.3.403

Tilly, C. (2007). *Democracy*. New York, NY: Cambridge University Press.

Tir, J. (2010). Territorial diversion: Diversionary theory of war and territorial conflict. *The Journal of Politics, 72*, 413–425. doi:10.1017/S0022381609990879

Tir, J., & Jasinski, M. (2008). Domestic-level diversionary theory of war: Targeting ethnic minorities. *Journal of Conflict Resolution, 52*, 641–664. doi:10.1177/0022002708318565

Tooze, A. (2006). *The wages of destruction: The making and breaking of the Nazi economy*. London, England: Penguin Books.

Tucker, J. (2007). Enough! Electoral fraud, collective action problems, and post-Communist democratic revolutions. *Perspectives on Politics, 5*, 535–551. doi:10.1017/S1537592707071538

Tucker, R. C. (1979). The rise of Stalin's personality cult. *The American Historical Review, 84*, 347–366.

Turley, J. (2012, January 15). Ten reasons why we are no longer the land of the free. *The Washington Post*, pp. B1, B4.

Turner, J. C., & Reynolds, K. J. (2003). Why social dominance theory has been falsified. *British Journal of Social Psychology, 42*, 199–206. doi:10.1348/014466603322127184

Turner, J. C., & Reynolds, K. J. (2012). Self-categorization theory. In P. A. M. Van Lange & A. Kruglanski (Eds.), *Handbook of theories of social psychology* (pp. 399–417). London, England: Sage.

Turner, P. A. (1993). *I heard it through the grapevine: Rumor in African American culture*. Berkley: University of California Press.

Tyler, T. R. (2012). Justice theory. In P. A. M. Van Lange, A. W. Kruglanski, & E. T. Higgins (Eds.), *Handbook of theories of social psychology* (pp. 344–361). London, England: Sage.

Ung, L. (2000). *First they killed my father: A daughter of Cambodia remembers*. New York, NY: HarperCollins.

Unger, D. C. (2012). *The emergency state: America's pursuit of absolute emergency at all costs*. New York, NY: Penguin Books.

United Nations (1948). *The universal declaration of human rights*. Retrieved from http://www.un.org/en/documents/udhr/

Valsiner, J. (2000). *Culture and human development*. Santa Barbara, CA: Sage.

Valsiner, J., & Rosa, A. (Eds.). (2007). *The Cambridge handbook of sociocultural psychology*. New York, NY: Cambridge University Press. doi:10.1017/CBO9780511611162

van den Bos, K. (2009). Making sense of life: The existential self trying to deal with personal uncertainty. *Psychological Inquiry, 20*, 197–217. doi:10.1080/10478400903333411

Vargas Llosa, M. (2000). The feast of the goat (E. Grossman, Trans.). New York, NY: Farrar, Straus & Giroux.

Vasquez, E. A., Lickel, B., & Hennigan, K. (2010). Gangs, displaced and group-based aggression. *Aggression and Violent Behavior, 15*, 130–140. doi:10.1016/j.avb.2009.08.001

Verbitsky, H. (1996). *The flight: Confessions of an Argentinian dirty warrior* (E. Allen, Trans.). New York, NY: The New Press.

Vohs, K. D. (2006, November 17). The psychological consequences of money. *Science, 314*, 1154–1156. doi:10.1126/science.1132491

Vroom, V. H. (2000). Leadership and the decision-making process. *Organizational Dynamics, 28*, 82–94. doi:10.1016/S0090-2616(00)00003-6

Vroom, V. H., & Jago, A. G. (2007). The role of the situation in leadership. *American Psychologist, 62*, 17–24. doi:10.1037/0003-066X.62.1.17

Wagner, J. A. (1994). Participation's effects on performance and satisfaction: A reconsideration of research evidence. *The Academy of Management Review, 19*, 312–330.

Warf, B. (2007). Oligopolization of global media and telecommunications and its implications for democracy. *Ethics Place and Environment, 10,* 89–105. doi:10.1080/13668790601153465

Watzlawick, P., Weakland, J. H., & Fisch, R. (1974). *Change: Principles of problem formation and problem resolution.* New York, NY: Norton.

Webster, D. M., & Kruglanski, A. W. (1994). Individual differences and the need for cognitive closure. *Journal of Personality and Social Psychology, 67,* 1049–1062. doi:10.1037/0022-3514.67.6.1049

Wegner, D. M. (2002). *The illusion of conscious will.* Cambridge, MA: MIT Press.

Wilson, G. (1973). *The psychology of conservatism.* New York, NY: Academic Press.

Wittgenstein, L. (1953). *Philosophical investigations* (G. E. M. Anscombe & G. H. Von Wright, Trans.). Oxford, England: Blackwell.

Wong, G. (2011, December 15). Chinese police blockade village amid uprising over land, detainee's death. *The Washington Post,* p. A21.

Worthington, P. (2012, October 11). Libyan déjà vu: When volunteer doctors flee the country, it's not a good sign. *Toronto Sun.* Retrieved from http://www.torontosun.com/2012/02/03/libyan-deja-vu-when-volunteer-doctors-flee-the-country-its-not-a-good-sign?%20it%E2%80%99s%20not%20a%20good%20sign

Wright, S. C., Taylor, D. M., & Moghaddam, F. M. (1990). Responding to membership in a disadvantaged group: From acceptance to collective protest. *Journal of Personality and Social Psychology, 58,* 994–1003. doi:10.1037/0022-3514.58.6.994

Yeats, W. B. (1962). *W. B. Yeats selected poetry* (A. N. Jeffares, Ed.). London, England: Macmillan. (Original work published 1921)

Zaccaro, S. J. (2007). Trait-based perspectives of leadership. *American Psychologist, 62,* 6–16. doi:10.1037/0003-066X.62.1.6

Zimbardo, P. (1972). Pathology of imprisonment. *Society, 9,* 4–8.

Zimbardo, P. (2008). *The Lucifer effect: Understanding how good people turn evil.* New York, NY: Random House.

INDEX

Buck, J. J., 123
Bulgaria, 5
Bullock, A., 63, 81, 170
Bureaucracies, 78–79
Burma, 22
Burns, J. M., 162
Bush, George W., 23, 67–68, 128

Cambodia, 38, 80
Canada, 16
Canovan, M., 169
Capitalism, 206
Carlyle, T., 163
Carter, Jimmy, 69, 116
Cartwright, D., 155
Castro, Fidel, 33, 63, 144
Castro, Raúl, 63
Catastrophic evolution, 62, 208–209
Categorization, as cognitive process, 48
Catholic Church, 38
Causality, 15, 49–50
Cawelti, J. G., 206
Ceausescu, Nicolae, 161
Central Intelligence Agency (CIA),
    115, 127–128
Certainty, need for, 188
Chamberlain, Neville, 128
Charisma, 60–61, 81
Chavez, Hugo, 49
Chen, Guangcheng, 77
Cheung, F. M., 166
Chidester, D., 145
Children, 82–83
China
    communist ideal in, 33
    continuity of leadership in, 88–90
    economic boom in, 87–89, 169
    elites in, 199
    external threats to, 70
    global supremacy of, 30–31
    little dictators in, 77
    social loafing in, 192
    state ideology in, 22
    type of dictatorship in, 18, 19
    uncertainty in, 80
Chinese Communist Party, 88
Chirwa, W. C., 180
Chomsky, Noam, 40
Churchill, Winston, 95, 205

CIA (Central Intelligence Agency),
    115, 127–128
Clinton, Hillary Rodham, 92
Closed societies, 10, 150–152
Closedmindedness, 10, 81, 152
Closure, 188, 190
"Coerced democracy," 31
Coercion, 141–158
    and cognitive dissonance, 153–157
    and reality construction, 150–152
    repression and, 146–149
    role of supreme dictator and, 143–146
Cognitive alternatives, to dictatorship,
    191–195
Cognitive closure, 190
Cognitive dissonance, 142
    coercion and, 153–157
    in culture, 154–155
    in dictatorships, 155–157
Cohesion
    of elites, 26–27, 82, 98, 101, 199, 200
    and groupthink, 129
    internal, 67–70, 109–119
Collective identity, loss of, 72–73
Communism, 33, 88, 193
Compensatory conviction model, 61, 62
Conformity, 48–49, 101, 147
    and autokinetic effect, 127
    and behavior regulation, 125–126,
        131–132
    defined, 8–9
    mass, 199
    by minorities, 131–132
    and norms, 129–131
    in scholars, 125–126
    use of, by dictators, 135–139
Consciousness, false, 4
Conservative Party (United Kingdom),
    24
Contextual aspects, of leadership,
    167–168
Continuity, 56–58, 87–103
    in China, 88–90
    and culture of silence, 99–101
    and everyday social life, 96–98
    in Iran, 93–94
    and paradox of revolution, 93–95
    and rules/norms, 90–91
    and sacred carriers, 95–98

and system justification, 101–102
and terror, 98–99
Control, 4, 136–137
Corner, P., 95, 96
Corruption, and displaced aggression,
    119–121
Cotton, J. L., 171
Council of Guardians, 125
Counterelites, 74–75
Crisis incidents, situational factors in,
    79–80
Cuba, 33, 63, 68, 127–128
Cultural continuity, 92
Cultural Revolution, 64, 80, 94, 159, 176
Cultural revolutions, 82
Cultural traditions, 77–78
Culture, 185
"Culture of gender," 166
Culture of silence, 99–101

"Dancing Toward Dictatorship"
    (Chirwa), 180
Darwin, C., 6, 163
DDR Museum, 101
De Klerk, F. W., 12
Democracies, 204–214
    apathy vs. engagement in, 213–214
    and catastrophic evolution, 208–209
    dictatorship–democracy continuum,
        7, 19, 28, 143
    dictatorships vs., 16–18
    fear vs. trust in, 213–214
    and globalization, 204–208
    minimal conditions for, 19–21
    resource inequality in, 210–212
    satisfaction in, 171
    transitions of dictatorships and,
        171–172, 209–210
    voting in, 211–212
Democracy and Dictatorships (Barbu), 5
Democratic dictatorship, 28
Democratic Party (United States), 23,
    24, 33
Deprivation
    egoistic, 65
    fraternal, 65–66
Dictatorial leadership, 169–181
    and the arts, 180–181
    efficiency of, 170–175

and gender relations, 177–179
    in Iran, 174–175
    mistakes from, 175–177
    in Nazi Germany, 172–173
    in Soviet Union, 173–174
Dictators
    deaths of, 176–177
    personalities of, 13
    religion and, 96
    women as, 6–7
Dictator's fallacy, 147–149
Dictatorship(s)
    challenges after fall of, 201–204
    cohesion of ruling elite in, 26–27,
        82, 98, 101, 199, 200
    and contemporary society, 22
    defined, 16, 18–19
    democracy vs., 16–18
    elections in, 31–32
    ending, 198–201
    hierarchies of, 77–78
    meaning making in, 42–44
    psychological explanations of,
        14–15
    psychology of, 44–45
    reasons for studying, 27–33
    transformational, 32–33, 209–210
Dictatorship–democracy continuum, 7,
    19, 28, 143
Diouf, Abdou, 49
Discipline and Punish (Foucault), 4
Disobedience, in dictatorships, 96, 97
Displaced aggression, 105–121
    and corruption, 119–121
    Freud's view of, 107–108
    and internal cohesion, 109–119
    in Mugabe's Zimbabwe, 105–107
Dissidents, 120
Dissonance. See Cognitive dissonance
Distress, 61, 62
Diversionary theory of war, 110–111
Doctors Without Borders, 75
Dominant ideology thesis, 101–102
Dominant–subordinate relations,
    135–136
Dominican Republic, 76
Dress codes, 94
Duvalier, Jean-Claude, 75
Dzeliwe, queen of Swaziland, 7

Gender, 177–179, 194
Genetics, and leadership, 163–166
Germany, 16, 32. *See also* Nazi Germany
  East, 51, 101, 179
  post-WWI era, 53–54, 71
Gilbert, G. M., 5, 81
Glasnost, 200
Globalization, 197, 204–208
Goal-regulation processes, 61
Godwin, P., 98
Goffman, E., 53
Golding, W., 32
Gorbachev, Mikhail, 200
Grafton, R. Q., 75
Great Britain, 16
Great Depression, 207
Great Leap Forward, 80, 88–89
Grint, K., 159
Group functioning, 132
Groupthink, 43, 127–129

Haiti, 7, 75
Halpern, D. F., 166
Harary, F., 155
Harvey, O. J., 61
Heider, F., 155
Hejab, 112, 179, 202
Henry IV (Shakespeare), 67
Hereditary Genius (Galton), 163
Hero worship, 151–152
Hierarchies, 189
Hierarchies of dictatorship, 77–78
Higher education, in Iran, 176–177, 179
Hindman, M., 29–30
Hitler, Adolf
  absolute power of, 173
  control of the arts by, 181
  dedication to, 160
  and economic efficiency, 170
  emergency powers of, 16
  external threats to, 70
  and groupthink, 128
  and ideal Nazi citizen, 32, 33
  leadership by, 162
  in post-WWI era, 53
  purges by, 119, 149
  and Reichstag incident, 80
  as sacred carrier, 145
Hogg, M. A., 61, 62

Holocaust, 132
Hood, W. R., 61
Hooke, Robert, 6
Hoover, J. Edgar, 78
Horwitz, S., 27
Hostage crisis, Iranian, 64, 69, 80,
  111–112, 114–117
House, R. J., 158
Hungary, 27
Hunt, I. A., 145
Hussein, Saddam, 13, 117–119
Hypocrisy paradigm, 154

Identity, 72–73, 129
Ideologies, 3–4, 98–99, 199–200
Illusions of permanence, 30–31
Independent judiciaries, 21
India, 27
Individual difference measures, in psy-
  chological processes, 186–190
Indonesia, 27
Inequality, resource, 210–212
Ingroup language, 47–48
Institutions, situational factors and, 75–76
Internal cohesion
  displaced aggression and, 109–119
  and external threat, 67–70
Internal enemies, as perceived threats,
  70–71
International Fascism movement, 188
Internet, 29
Intifadas, 63
Iran, 6
  absolute power in, 174–175
  anti-Shah revolution in, 12–13, 58, 76
  and Carter administration, 69
  continuity of dictatorship in, 8,
    93–94, 199
  criticism of Supreme Leader in, 20
  Cultural Revolution in, 64
  democracy in, 31, 54
  dictator as sacred carrier in, 97–98
  dictatorial leadership in, 174–175
  higher education in, 176–177, 179
  hostage-taking crisis in, 64, 69, 80,
    111–112, 114–117
  influence of, in Mideast, 128
  intolerance towards science in,
    188–189

Newton, Isaac, 6
The New World Order (Pinter), 141
New York City, 62
Nicholls, A. J., 79
Night of the Long Knives, 149
1984 (Orwell), 150
Nixon, Richard, 43
Nonconformity, 131–132
Nonelites, 199–201
Normative psychology, 49–52, 168
Norms, 155
 arbitrary, 129–131
 continuity and, 90–91
 manipulated, 127
 power of, 129–131
North Korea
 as closed society, 150
 elites in, 199
 external enemies of, 68
 military in, 150–151
 nonconformity in, 131
 state ideology of, 22
 transitions of power in, 27
Norway, 209
Ntombi, queen of Swaziland, 7
Nuremberg Trials, 81, 172

Obama, Barack, 33, 91, 169, 194, 206
Obedience
 absolute, 177
 and conformity, 126
 defined, 8
 dictators' use of, 136–139, 147
 as human tendency, 48–49
 institutions and, 135–136
 Milgram experiments on, 132–134
 in religious-based dictatorships, 131
Occupy Wall Street, 48, 49
Office of Strategic Services (OSS), 13
On Heroes, Hero Worship, and the Heroic
 in History (Carlyle), 163
Opposition oppression, in Iran, 137–138
The Origin of Species (Darwin), 163
Orwell, G., 150, 183
OSS (Office of Strategic Services), 13
Overy, R. J., 144

Pahlavi dynasty, 111
Pakistan, 92

Palestine, 63
Palo Alto group, 91
Paradox of revolution, 55–56, 93–95
Pareto, V., 25, 26, 74, 75, 102, 189, 200
Pascal-Trouillot, Ertha, 7
Penchaszadeh, V. B., 37, 38
Perceived threats, 61–73
 external enemies as, 67–70
 globalization as, 209
 internal enemies as, 70–71
 loss of collective identity as, 72–73
 in post-9/11 era, 210
 and relative deprivation, 63–67
 and social chaos, 71–72
 in springboard model, 60
 in terror management theory, 208
 uncertainty as, 62–63
Perceptual shifts, 184–185
Perestroika, 200
Performance capacity, 41–42
Performance content, 41–42
Permanence, illusions of, 30–31
Perot, Ross, 211
Perry, Ruth, 7
Personality(-ies)
 authoritarian, 186–187
 of dictators, 13
 in springboard model, 59–61
Personality traits, 44, 166–167
Person grammar (P-grammar), 50
Peru, 16
Peter the Great, 55
Petraeus, General David, 92
P-grammar (person grammar), 50
Pinochet, Augosto, 144
Pinter, H., 141
Pipes, R., 161
Plamper, J., 143, 145
Plato, 163, 189
Plaza de Mayo, 38
Police, morality, 179, 199
Political change, perceived threats and,
 62–63
Political parties, 135. *See also specific*
 parties
Pollock, E., 173–174
Pol Pot, 38, 80
Pope, A., 6
Pratto, F., 189

and ideal communist citizen, 32
  influence of, on scientific research,
      173–174
  inner circle of, 33
  purges of, 82, 119, 149, 160–161
  as sacred carrier, 97, 144, 145
  and springboard model of dictator-
      ship, 54, 65
Stanford University, 135
Stasi, 101
Staub, E., 187
Steele, C., 193, 194
Stereotype threat, 194–195
Stouffer, S. A., 61
Strategically open democracies, 22, 142
Subordinate–dominant relations,
    135–136
Substantivist rule of law, 17
Sumner, W. G., 109, 110
Supreme dictator, coercion by,
    143–146
Surplus, control of, 59
Svolik, M. W., 25
Swaziland, 7
Sweden, 210
Symbolic carriers. *See* Sacred carriers
Symbols, 95
Syria, 4, 22, 80, 184
System justification, continuity and,
    101–102

Taiwan, 88
Tajfel, H., 62, 73, 191, 193
Tate, J., 27
Teachers, 179
Technology, 28–30
Temperament, 163
Tension, in democracies, 74
Terror, 157
  behavior regulation and, 138–139
  continuity and, 98–99
Thatcher, Margaret, 67
Third-order system, 90–91
Third Reich, 160, 179
Threats. *See* External threat(s);
    Perceived threats
Tiananmen Square protest, 89
Titchener, Edward, 39
Tooze, A., 71, 172–173

Torture, 127, 142, 157
Totalitarian democracy, 28
Town square test, 19–20
Traditions, cultural, 77–78
Trait-based approach, 166–167
Transactional leadership, 162
Transformational dictatorship, 32–33,
    209–210
Transformational leadership, 9
Transformative leadership, 162
Trotsky, Leon, 33
Trujillo, Rafael, 76
Tsvangirai, Morgan, 98
Tunisia, 26, 75, 90, 183, 184, 191, 193
Turley, J., 209, 210
Turner, B. S., 101–102
Turner, J. C., 62, 73, 191, 193
Twins studies, 165–166
Tyler, T. R., 136

Uganda, 161
Ukraine, 27, 90
Uncertainty, 61, 62
Uncertainty-identity theory, 61
Uncertainty management model, 61
Unger, D. C., 210
Unidirectional change, 56–58
United Nations, 15, 17, 22
United States
  economic decline of, 31, 169
  eugenics in, 164
  as external threat, 68, 69, 114–117,
      151
  external threats to, 70, 209–210
  flag as sacred carrier in, 96
  illusions of permanence for, 30–31
  invasion of Iraq, 128
  presidential elections (2012), 32–33
  Prohibition in, 47
  slavery in, 95
  social loafing in, 192
  social mobility in, 206
  as strategically open democracy, 22,
      142
  support of dictators by, 80
  tolerance of science in, 188–189
  whistle-blowers in, 20
Universal Declaration of Human Rights
    (United Nations), 17, 22

Uruguay, 16
U.S. Supreme Court, 211
USSR. *See* Soviet Union

Van de Walle, N., 55
Vavilov, Nikolai, 174
Velayat-e-faghih, Ruhollah Khomeini
    as, 114
Venezuela, 49
Verbitsky, Horacio, 37
Versailles, Treaty of, 53
Vietnam War, 128
Vogue (magazine), 124–125
Voice, lack of, 18
Vollrath, D. A., 171
Vose, E., 173
Vote-them-out test, 20
Vroom, V. H., 158, 167

Wade, Abdoulaye, 49
Wagner, J. A., 171
Walumbwa, F. O., 163
Wang, Lijun, 77
War, diversionary theory of, 110–111
Washington, George, 12
Washington Post, 28–29
Watergate scandal, 43
Watson, John, 39
Webster, D. M., 190
Weimar Republic, 71
Wermke, K., 47
What is to Be Done? (Lenin), 25
What's the Matter With Kansas?
    (Frank), 23
White, B. J., 61
White, R. K., 170

White minority, in Zimbabwe,
    106–107
Wilson, G., 207
Within-system change, 91
Wittgenstein, L., 40
Women, 187
    behavior regulation of, 138
    as dictators, 6–7
    in Fascist Italy, 178
    in Iran, 109–110, 112
    leadership roles of, 166–167
    morality policing of, 136, 139
    role of, in dictatorships, 177–179
    and Sharia law, 187
    social freedoms of, 147
    and stereotype threat, 194
Wong, G., 87
Working classes, 101
Wundt, Wilhelm, 39

Yale University, 133
Yeats, W. B., 197
Yemen, 184
Youth, socialization of, 145–146
Youth bulges, 199
Yugoslavia, 79

Zanu-PF party (Zimbabwe), 98
Zardari, Asif Ali, 92
Zhang, Z., 165–166
Zhdanov, Andrei, 180
Zimbabwe
    displaced aggression in, 105–107
    Mugabe's rule of, 106–107
    political parties in, 98
Zimbardo, P., 62, 135

ABOUT THE AUTHOR

Fathali M. Moghaddam, PhD, is a professor in the Department of Psychology and the director of the Conflict Resolution Program, Department of Government at Georgetown University. Dr. Moghaddam was born in Iran, educated from an early age in England, and worked for the United Nations and for McGill University before joining Georgetown University in 1990. He returned to Iran in the spring of revolution in 1979 and was researching there during the hostage-taking crisis and the early years of the Iran–Iraq War. He has conducted experimental and field research in numerous cultural contexts and published extensively on radicalization, intergroup conflict, human rights and duties, and the psychology of globalization. His most recent books include *Multiculturalism and Intergroup Relations* (2008); *How Globalization Spurs Terrorism* (2008); *The New Global Insecurity* (2010); *Words of Conflict, Words of War* (2010, with Rom Harré); and *Psychology for the Third Millennium* (2012, with Rom Harré). Dr. Moghaddam is the next editor of *Peace and Conflict: Journal of Peace Psychology,* and he has received a number of recognitions for his scholarly contributions, the most recent being the Outstanding International Psychologist Award for 2012 from the American Psychological Association's Division of International Psychology. More about his research can be found on his website: www.fathalimoghaddam.com.